Barnes & Noble Shakespeare

David Scott Kastan
Series Editor

BARNES & NOBLE SHAKESPEARE features newly edited texts of the plays prepared by the world's premiere Shakespeare scholars. Each edition provides new scholarship with an introduction, commentary, unusually full and informative notes, an account of the play as it would have been performed in Shakespeare's theaters, and an essay on how to read Shakespeare's language.

DAVID SCOTT KASTAN is the Old Dominion Foundation Professor in the Humanities at Columbia University and one of the world's leading authorities on Shakespeare.

Barnes & Noble Shakespeare
Published by Barnes & Noble
122 Fifth Avenue
New York, NY 10011
www.barnesandnoble.com/shakespeare

© 2007 Barnes & Noble, Inc.

Image on p. 332:
Shakespeare, William. *Romeo and Juliet.* London, 1599 [A3r]. This item is reproduced by permission of *The Huntington Library, San Marino, California,* RB 69362.

Barnes & Noble Shakespeare and the Barnes & Noble Shakespeare colophon are trademarks of Barnes & Noble, Inc.

Library of Congress Cataloging-in-Publication Data

Shakespeare, William, 1564–1616.
  Romeo and Juliet / [William Shakespeare].
    p. cm. — (Barnes and Noble Shakespeare)
  Includes bibliographical references.
  ISBN-13: 978-1-4114-0036-8 (alk. paper)
  ISBN-10: 1-4114-0036-4 (alk. paper)
  1. Romeo (Fictitious character)—Drama. 2. Juliet (Fictitious character)—Drama.
3. Conflict of generations—Drama. 4. Verona (Italy)—Drama. 5. Vendetta—Drama.
6. Youth—Drama. I. Title. II. Series: Shakespeare, William, 1564–1616. Works. 2006.

PR2831.A1 2006
822.3'3—dc22   2006009007

Printed and bound in the United States.
40 39 38 37 36 35 34 33 32 31

ROMEO AND JULIET

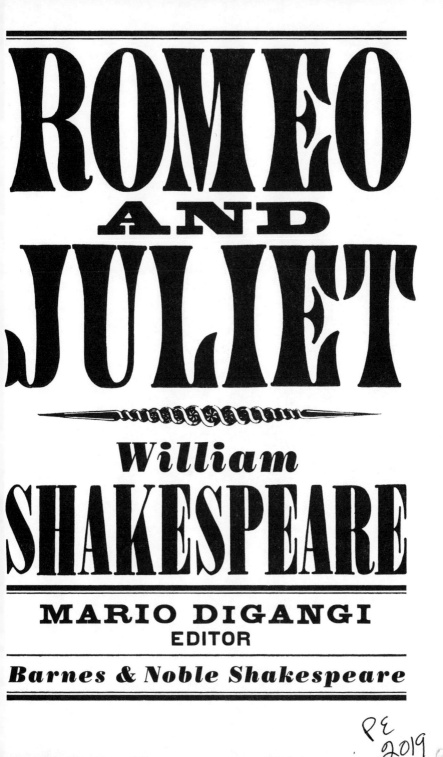

William
SHAKESPEARE

MARIO DiGANGI
EDITOR

Barnes & Noble Shakespeare

Contents

Introduction to *Romeo and Juliet*
by Mario DiGangi

omeo, Romeo! Wherefore art thou Romeo?"
So familiar is *Romeo and Juliet* to us that it takes
an act of conscious will to imagine a time when
Juliet's question was not a cliché. In its immediate
dramatic context, Juliet's question is the spontane-
ous, tentative, and private expression of a young
woman's burgeoning erotic desire. It also serves to confirm Juliet's true
feelings for Romeo, who overhears her confession from beneath her
window. Yet in our own time, Juliet's anguished question is repeated
again and again in the classroom, on the stage, and in popular culture
as part of an enduring myth of romantic love associated with Shakespeare's play. As a result, we are perhaps far more likely to regard "Romeo,
Romeo! Wherefore art thou Romeo?" as something that Shakespeare,
rather than Juliet, said. Detached from its dramatic context, Juliet's
question can be taken as a prime example of the Bard's romantic lyricism, or, less reverently, as a piece of romantic sentiment irresist-
ibly ripe for burlesque—perhaps most memorably in Bugs Bunny's
absurdly exaggerated, cross-dressed performance of Juliet's passion.

The modern understanding of Romeo and Juliet as archetypi-
cal tragic lovers has been shaped by centuries of performance history and
critical commentary, and, more recently, by popular movies and secondary

school curricula. Yet Elizabethan audiences might have been surprised to find that they were being asked to regard this pair of contemporary Italian adolescents as serious tragic protagonists. The most elevated dramatic genre, tragedy traditionally dealt with the fall of great men— "great" because both aristocratic and historically important. Romeo and Juliet are neither. Thus part of the Chorus's job is to persuade his audience to bring "patient ears" to this unconventional, but nonetheless "piteous" and "fearful," tragedy featuring "star-crossed lovers" rather than great historical figures (Prologue 13, 7, 9, 6). By defining Romeo and Juliet as "star-crossed lovers" instead of as son and daughter, boy and girl, Montague and Capulet, or husband and wife, the Prologue places the protagonists in a lofty tradition of legendary and historical tragic couples such as Dido and Aeneas and Antony and Cleopatra. Romeo and Juliet, however, are non-noble, nonlegendary lovers whose story originated not in ancient epic or historical narratives but in modern romances. As such, an Elizabethan audience might well have felt skeptical about the value of a tragedy centered on their lives and loves. Shakespeare's unconventional protagonists might have further alienated the sympathies of many London playgoers through their association with Catholicism, the extremely young age at which they enter into a clandestine marriage, and their sacrilegious acts of suicide.

In order to find Romeo and Juliet figures worthy of tragic treatment, then, Shakespeare's audience would have to find value in their love. The Prologue's reference to the protagonists as "star-crossed" begins to establish this value by attributing cosmic significance to their story. But the value of Romeo and Juliet's experience emerges most forcefully from the way that Shakespeare invests their love with depth and dimension as a force of personal and social change. Whereas the mature protagonists of Shakespeare's later love tragedies *Othello* and *Antony and Cleopatra* discover that their personal histories and social identities thwart their ability to sustain romantic intimacy, the young lovers of *Romeo and Juliet* discover that romantic intimacy provides an opportunity to challenge and transform their inherited social identities as enemies. Romeo and Juliet believe that they can shape a future that will reward their own standards of value. In one of the play's most poignant moments, Romeo assures Juliet that "these woes shall serve / For sweet discourses in our times to come" (3.5.51–52). (The more experienced Friar regards the future with greater apprehension: "So smile the heavens upon this holy act / That after-hours with sorrow chide us not" [2.6.1–2]). Like the protagonists of Shakespeare's later tragedies, however, Romeo and Juliet are not simply "star-crossed" victims of fate: they actively participate in bringing about the woes that will prevent a sweeter future from being realized. Evading public recognition of the transformations wrought by their love, Romeo and Juliet disastrously underestimate the power exerted over their lives by the very familial and social forces whose standards of value they have attempted to circumvent.

Despite all the misgivings an Elizabethan or modern audience might feel about the prudence of the young lovers' actions, Shakespeare enlists our sympathies by depicting their love as a potential force of change in a society paralyzed by self-consuming passions. In the first part of the play, both Romeo's infatuation with Rosaline and the recursive violence of the feud are driven by passions that are paradoxically self-sustaining and self-defeating. The opening scene encapsulates the ethos of the feud through the aimless banter of two idle servants, whose bawdy puns on "stand," "tool," and "naked weapon" sexualize the violent encounters between Verona's young men (1.1.10, 29, 31). Charged by the erotic energy of aggressive masculinity, the feud continues to run on its own juices, detached from any evident origin or goal.

Although Romeo has removed himself from the feud's sterile cycle of violence, he is stuck in a no less sterile identity as a Petrarchan lover. In the literary tradition derived from the fourteenth-century Italian poet Petrarch, the lover uses antithetical phrases such as "bright smoke," "cold fire," and "sick health" to express the paradoxical mixture of joy and sorrow he feels in devoting himself to a woman who does not return his affection (1.1.174). Caught in a highly stylized representation of love that prevents him from experiencing desire as an immediate, deeply felt emotion, Romeo languishes in melancholy solitude. Montague worries that his sole heir will fail to blossom into a healthy and prosperous young man, that he will wither like "the bud bit with an envious worm / Ere he can spread his sweet leaves to the air / Or dedicate his beauty to the same" (1.1.145–147). This image of thwarted love as a withering bud will later be replaced by Juliet's hopeful image of love's flourishing: "This bud of love, by summer's ripening breath, / May prove a beauteous flower when next we meet" (2.2.121–122). Rosaline, impervious to love's "ripening" powers, will remain an unopened bud frozen in time; in dedicating his life to her service, Romeo must therefore "live dead" (1.1.218).

Encouraging Romeo to regard Rosaline as an object of sexual desire, not a subject of poetic adoration, Mercutio attempts to return his lovesick friend to the social world of aggressive masculinity from which he has strayed. In Shakespeare's primary source for *Romeo and Juliet*, Arthur Brooke's narrative poem *The Tragical History of Romeus and Juliet* (1562), Mercutio appears in a single passage as a courtier who competes with Romeus for Juliet's love. In *Romeo and Juliet*, Mercutio competes with women for Romeo's love, trying to cure his friend of the romantic infatuations that keep him from male society. Echoing Sampson and Gregory's punning associations between sex and violence in the play's first scene, Mercutio claims that Romeo can only be "move[d]" or "stirre[d]" out of his amorous lethargy by taking sexual possession of his mistress (2.1.16). Whereas Petrarchan poetry bestows a unique value on the chaste mistress, Mercutio believes that Romeo should understand Rosaline as a collection of body parts—"bright eyes," "scarlet lip," "fine foot, straight leg, and quivering thigh"—that are conveniently available "to raise [him] up," or stimulate him into an erection (2.1.18–20, 30).

Romeo's idealistic Petrarchanism and Mercutio's coarse anti-Petrarchanism seem to represent antithetical positions on love. Yet both attitudes devalue the mutuality of love, and hence love's transformative capacities, by erasing the woman's role as an actively desiring partner. For Romeo, Rosaline is to be praised from afar; for Mercutio, Rosaline is to be enjoyed in the flesh. That Rosaline apparently desires only to protect herself from the "siege of loving terms" and the lover's "assailing eyes" seems not to matter much to either man (1.1.206–207).

Living up to the "good will" of his name, Benvolio offers Romeo an escape from the narcissistic sterility of Petrarchan love. He does so, surprisingly, by introducing an analogy between love and commerce. Earlier, Romeo had drawn a different analogy between sexuality and economics in describing Rosaline's preservation of her virginity as a hoarding of riches. By preserving her virginity, Rosaline paradoxically "makes huge waste" of her beauty, because she will not have any children that might inherit and preserve that beauty (1.1.212). This language of hoarding associates Rosaline with the repellent figure of the miser or usurer, later described by Friar Laurence as one who "abound'st in all" and fails to make "true use" of his riches (3.3.123–124). Significantly, Benvolio evokes a very different model of financial exchange when he promises to help Romeo to forget Rosaline: "I'll pay that doctrine or else die in debt" (1.1.232). By playfully "indebting" his life to Romeo, Benvolio challenges himself to fulfill his promise to teach Romeo a new "doctrine" of love. Benvolio's view of economics as a risky venture that can produce profit ("pay") as well as loss ("debt") describes the quality of mutual exchange that will characterize the love between Romeo and Juliet. Shakespeare would develop this metaphor of love as economic exchange at greater length in *The Merchant of Venice*, but in *Romeo and Juliet* it serves to suggest the rewards and risks, and hence the value, of the "true use" of love.

Both the rewards and risks of love are apparent in Romeo and Juliet's first conversation. When they meet at the Capulet feast, Romeo and Juliet speak to each other in alternating lines of dialogue that combine to form a fourteen-line sonnet. While their dialogue produces a conventional poetic form, their mutual authorship of this poem significantly moves beyond Petrarchan convention in giving the woman an active voice of desire. By putting Petrarchan language to a less narcissistic use, Romeo reaches out across the borders that are everywhere constructed in Verona: significantly, the topic of the sonnet is a pilgrimage, a healing journey to a new land. Moreover, the sonnet's religious imagery of giving and taking sin echoes Benvolio's economic imagery of giving and taking payment. Romeo offers Juliet a kiss as amends for any offense done by his hand; when Juliet grants his prayer with a kiss, Romeo claims that his lips have purged or paid for the sin of his hand. Juliet, however, keeps the exchange going. She protests that Romeo's kiss has transferred his sin to her lips, tacitly inviting him to take back his sin through another kiss. Hence both have sinned, and both have pardoned each other's sin: as Romeo will later explain to the Friar, "one hath wounded [him] / That's by [him] wounded" (2.3.50–51). When Romeo and Juliet discover each other's true identity, they express their shock through a paradoxical language of simultaneous loss and gain. Romeo exclaims, "O dear account! My life is my foe's debt"; Juliet laments, "My only love sprung from my only hate" (1.5.116, 136). Although the imagery of death and hatred in these lines seems to foreshadow the lovers' demise, Romeo and Juliet must acknowledge the mutual risk and sacrifice involved in love before they can begin to fashion their new identities as lovers.

If Juliet appears to demonstrate greater emotional maturity about love and more courage in the face of adversity than Romeo, it might well be because she faces greater risks by engaging in a clandestine romance. In the Renaissance, much greater value was placed on female chastity than male chastity, since the orderly legal transmission of a man's name and property to his heirs was dependent on the secure knowledge that his children were really his own. Even for a woman to speak openly about her sexual desires could earn her a reputation as a whore. The play's famous balcony scene significantly focuses on the risks

Juliet takes in expressing her sexual desires to a young man she has just met. Since Romeo has overheard her confession of love, Juliet cannot take shelter in the conventional postures of female modesty. Thus, she rightly worries that Romeo might perceive her behavior as "light"—that is, whorish (2.2.99). Whereas Romeo rather insouciantly anticipates that Juliet will simply "cast . . . off" her virginity, it is left to Juliet to raise the issue of marriage in response to his complaint about being left "unsatisfied," a word with strong sexual connotations (2.2.125).

It is not that Romeo pressures Juliet into a sexual relationship. Juliet powerfully articulates her sexual desires in a soliloquy that calls upon night to veil the world in darkness so that she and Romeo might secretly perform their "amorous rites" (3.2.8). Juliet's gorgeously sensuous language of passion imparts great seriousness and depth to her feelings, a view of female sexuality not always found in Shakespeare. For instance, in the contemporary narrative poem *Venus and Adonis*, Venus, the goddess of love, demonstrates little of Juliet's solemn grace in her attempt to seduce the beautiful mortal boy Adonis. Like Juliet, Venus believes that acts of love are best performed in the dark, yet Venus's attitude toward sex is unabashedly "light": "Art thou ashamed to kiss? Then wink again, / And I will wink. So shall the day seem night. / Love keeps his revels where there are but twain. / Be bold to play—our sport is not in sight" (121–124). For the audience to find value in Juliet's passion, and in her willingness to die for that passion, she must neither speak nor act like the aggressively frolicsome Venus. Moreover, Juliet must acknowledge the importance of marriage as the social institution that legitimizes sexuality.

Marriage has been Juliet's destiny from the beginning of the play. The various episodes of consultation (1.2), persuasion (1.3), dispute (3.5), and courtship (4.1) that precede her arranged marriage to Paris reveal the collective effort spent on verbally negotiating the precise conditions under which that destiny will be fulfilled. Juliet accepts her destiny to become a wife. Nonetheless, she bypasses the judgment of the familial and social authorities that give marriage its public validity when she independently determines, from an argument that she conducts with herself, that Romeo is worthy to be her husband. Affirming that a rose "[b]y any other word would smell as sweet," Juliet concludes that Romeo's value derives from his inherent "perfection," not from the familial or social identity signified by his name (2.2.44, 46). As their secret relationship brings the lovers into open conflict with familial and social authorities, Juliet's belief that she and Romeo can simply refuse their inherited identities is revealed to be an untenable, if appealing, fantasy.

Through its focus on the power of language to shape experience, the play suggests that Romeo and Juliet cannot escape from conventional "names" (or social identities) because, as social beings, they cannot escape from conventional "words" (or names). Even the intensely personal and poetic language through which Romeo and Juliet fashion their secret romance depends on a common understanding of words such as "rose" and "sweet" (2.2.43, 72). Words and their meanings are determined by social convention, not by individuals; and though individuals have a certain freedom in how they use and interpret language, that freedom is also circumscribed by the particular contexts in which communication occurs. Thus the sweetness of the rose's smell to Juliet is not necessarily the same sweetness that she experiences in the "sweet sorrow" of parting from Romeo or that she attributes to the "sweet Nurse" who bears "sweet news" (2.2.187; 2.5.21, 23); or that Romeo mocks in the "sweet goose" Mercutio (2.4.76); or that Paris values in the "sweet water" that he sprinkles on the tomb of his "[s]weet flower" (5.3.14, 12). Just as Juliet cannot control the multiple meanings that the word "sweet" might acquire as it travels through the play, so she cannot control the meanings of Romeo's "name" or social identity as he travels through Verona in his multiple roles as son, friend, husband, subject, and enemy.

Juliet's insistence on determining for herself the value of Romeo's "perfection" suggests both the appeal and the danger of their love. Romeo and Juliet assume that they have the power to negotiate their love privately, to remove it from the realm of public knowledge and authorization. This assumption leads Juliet to conclude her meditation on naming with a fantasy in which Romeo gets everything for giving up nothing: "Romeo, doff thy name, / And for thy name, which is no part of thee, / Take all myself" (2.2.47–49). Juliet will later claim that her "bounty is as boundless" and her "love as deep" as the sea; consequently, "The more I give to thee, / The more I have, for both are infinite" (2.2.134–135). In this formulation, love no longer involves giving and taking, gaining and losing; instead, it has the miraculous power to produce infinite gain from infinite giving. It is this view of a constant, bountiful, and mutually transformative love that readers and playgoers have celebrated in *Romeo and Juliet*. Yet this view of love also involves a miscalculation about the relationship between the private and the public that sets in motion the lovers' demise.

The play's action overtly shifts to tragedy with Mercutio's death, for which Romeo must bear some responsibility. Having married Juliet, Romeo finds himself in a paradoxical position: he has altered his social status through an alliance with the Capulet family, but he cannot give that alteration in status a social meaning by naming his kinship to Tybalt. In response to Tybalt's challenge, Romeo's cryptic assurance that he "love[s]" Tybalt and "tender[s]" the name of Capulet as "dearly as [his] own" thus cannot help but be misunderstood (3.1.66, 68–69). Unaware of Romeo's new kinship with the Capulets, Mercutio regards Romeo's tranquil response to Tybalt's insults as a "dishonorable, vile submission" (3.1.70). Romeo's submission is "vile" because in failing to refute Tybalt's charge of "villainy" he dishonors his own name and, by association, Mercutio's name. The highly rhetorical, equivocal language that serves Romeo and Juliet so well in expressing the bittersweet emotions of love fails dismally in charged social situations. Romeo discovers that painful truth here, as Juliet will discover it when her father flatly rejects the "[c]hopped logic" she uses to reject his offer of Paris (3.5.148). Racked with guilt, grief, and anger over Mercutio's death, Romeo challenges Tybalt to a duel by returning to him the name of "villain" (3.1.122). With tragic consequences, Romeo finally acts in accordance with the violent code of masculine honor he has heretofore resisted.

Ironically, by dueling Tybalt, Romeo only confirms his dishonorable reputation as a "villain." Not only do Capulet's wife, Paris, and even Juliet identify Romeo as a "villain," but the Prince, whose words have the power to determine social identity, new baptizes and banishes him as a "vile" participant in "rude brawls" (3.1.138,186). Romeo's and Juliet's tormented reiterations of the word "banishèd," which Romeo calls "death mistermed" (3.3.21), point up the tragic irony that their private attempt to redefine their own identities has resulted in the highly public imposition of a stigmatized criminal identity. Less publicly, but with no less disastrous an impact on the choices Juliet will make, Capulet new baptizes his daughter as a "[d]isobedient wretch," "green sickness carrion," "young baggage," "wretched, puling fool," and so on (3.5.159, 155, 159, 183). Recalling the Prince's sentence upon Romeo, Capulet threatens forever to banish Juliet from his care should she refuse her new identity as Paris's bride.

As they make the decisions that rush them toward their violent deaths, Romeo and Juliet provide little indication that they have acquired any deeper insight into the causes of their tragic demise. In Shakespeare's later love tragedies, protagonists such as Othello and Cleopatra reveal an acute concern for how they will be remembered after their deaths. Through moving final speeches and highly theatrical suicides, they attempt to demonstrate to those who will report their deaths that they have achieved a complex understanding of their tragic circumstances and of the social and moral impact of their actions. Late in the play,

Romeo comes to refer to himself as a "man," as if to acknowledge the maturity that accompanies suffering (5.3.59). Yet neither Romeo nor Juliet overtly ponders the social or moral implications of the circumstances and choices that have brought about their shared tragedy.

Denying Romeo and Juliet the privacy that might encourage such self-reflection, the social world of Verona relentlessly impinges upon the isolation of the tomb in which they spend their last moments. Although Paris and Romeo each approach the Capulet tomb alone and in secret, their unfortunate encounter results in the second mortal duel that Romeo has unsuccessfully tried to avoid. Once in the tomb, Romeo addresses not only Juliet but also Paris, Tybalt, and Death, the male rivals and enemies who silently witness the act of fidelity he undertakes with the aid of the "true apothecary['s]" poison (5.3.119). Prior to ingesting the Friar's sleeping potion, Juliet, too, had imagined the tomb as a crowded place, packed with the bones of her ancestors and stalked by Tybalt's ghost. Juliet awakens to find herself in the cold company not of the silent dead, as she had initially feared, but of Friar Laurence, who hurriedly indicates Romeo's lifeless body slumped at her side and recommends that she spend the rest of her days in a convent. In the few moments of solitude between the Friar's furtive departure and the watch's clamorous arrival, Juliet has time only to reject the new identity that social authority would determine for her, choosing instead to share Romeo's fate.

Shakespearean tragedies typically close with a reconstitution of social order around the slain bodies of the protagonists. In the face of so much suffering and death, the survivors' attempts to draw a moral, to assert that justice (whether human or divine) has been served, or to affirm a brighter future are always vulnerable to the undercutting forces of irony and skepticism. The conclusion of each Shakespearean tragedy achieves a different tension between hope and despair, a different accounting of the price paid for the recognition of error and the resolution of conflict. The deaths of Romeo and Juliet end the feud, thus implying that a social value or "true use" might be made of even the most intensely antisocial romantic love. Yet we are left to ponder exactly what kind of value has been attributed to these "[p]oor sacrifices" (5.3.304). By promising to erect gold statues of each other's children, do Montague and Capulet prove that former enemies can "tender" each other's names as "dearly as [their] own," as Romeo had failed to assure Tybalt (3.1.68, 69)? Or are they still competing for social preeminence, crudely associating the value of their children's lives with the value of gold?

The Prince locates the lasting value of the couple's "true and faithful" love not in their golden statues, but in the legacy of their tragic narrative: "For never was a story of more woe / Than this of Juliet and her Romeo" (5.3.302, 309–310). Although sympathetic to the couple's suffering, the Prince's closing statement attempts to mold the play's messily concatenated series of errors, accidents, deceptions, and rash actions into an artfully shaped, purposeful, and thereby consoling "story of . . . woe." The Prince, that is, directs us to find the meaning of the tragedy in the deaths of Romeo and Juliet, not in the deaths of his own kinsmen, Mercutio and Paris, or of Tybalt, or of Montague's wife. Yet it should not escape our notice that, in a significant departure from his source, Shakespeare has loaded this final scene of carnage with not two but three dead bodies: "the County Paris slain, / And Romeo dead, and Juliet, dead before, / Warm and new killed" (5.3.195–197). Capulet's wife has begun to tell the much less artful story of social chaos and pointless loss that this bloody spectacle seems to demand: "Oh, the people in the street cry 'Romeo,' / Some 'Juliet,' and some 'Paris,' and all run / With open outcry toward our monument" (5.3.191–193). The authoritative Prince, however, has the last word. And it is his more palatable romantic version of the woeful story that most of us have preferred to regard as Shakespeare's own.

Shakespeare and His England

by David Scott Kastan

S hakespeare is a household name, one of those few that don't need a first name to be instantly recognized. His first name was, of course, William, and he (and it, in its Latin form, *Gulielmus*) first came to public notice on April 26, 1564, when his baptism was recorded in the parish church of Stratford-upon-Avon, a small market town about ninety miles northwest of London. It isn't known exactly when he was born, although traditionally his birthday is taken to be April 23rd. It is a convenient date (perhaps too convenient) because that was the date of his death in 1616, as well as the date of St. George's Day, the annual feast day of England's patron saint. It is possible Shakespeare was born on the 23rd; no doubt he was born within a day or two of that date. In a time of high rates of infant mortality, parents would not wait long after a baby's birth for the baptism. Twenty percent of all children would die before their first birthday.

Life in 1564, not just for infants, was conspicuously vulnerable. If one lived to age fifteen, one was likely to live into one's fifties, but probably no more than 60 percent of those born lived past their mid-teens. Whole towns could be ravaged by epidemic disease. In 1563, the year before Shakespeare was born, an outbreak of plague claimed over one third of the population of London. Fire, too, was a constant threat; the thatched roofs of many houses were highly flammable, as well as offering handy nesting places for insects and rats. Serious crop failures in several years of the decade of the 1560s created food short-ages, severe enough in many cases to lead to the starvation of the elderly and the infirm, and lowering the resistances of many others so that between 1536 and 1560 influenza claimed over 200,000 lives.

Shakespeare's own family in many ways reflected these unsettling realities. He was one of eight children, two of whom did not survive their first year, one of whom died at age eight; one lived to twenty-seven, while the four surviving siblings died at ages ranging from Edmund's thirty-nine to William's own fifty-two years. William married at an unusually early age. He was only eighteen, though his wife was twenty-six, almost exactly the norm of the day for women, though men normally married also in their mid- to late twenties. Shakespeare's wife Anne was already pregnant at the time that the marriage was formally confirmed, and a daughter, Susanna, was born six months later, in May 1583. Two years later, she gave birth to twins, Hamnet and Judith. Hamnet would die in his eleventh year.

If life was always at risk from what Shakespeare would later call "the thousand natural shocks / That flesh is heir to" (*Hamlet*, 3.1.61–62), the incessant threats to peace were no less unnerving, if usually less immediately life threatening. There were almost daily rumors of foreign invasion and civil war as the Protestant Queen Eliz-abeth assumed the crown in 1558 upon the death of her Catholic half sister, Mary. Mary's reign had been marked by the public burnings of Protestant "heretics," by the seeming subordination of England to Spain, and by a commitment to a ruinous war with France, that, among its other effects, fueled inflation and encouraged a debasing of the currency. If, for many, Elizabeth represented the hopes for a peaceful and prosperous Protestant future, it seemed unlikely in the early days of her rule that the young monarch could hold her England together against the twin menace of the powerful Catholic monarchies of Europe and the significant part of her own population who were reluctant to give up their old faith. No wonder the Queen's principal secretary saw England in the early years of Elizabeth's rule as a land surrounded by "perils many, great and imminent."

In Stratford-upon-Avon, it might often have been easy to forget what threatened from without. The simple rural life, shared by about 90 percent of the English populace, had its reassuring natural rhythms and delights. Life was structured by the daily rising and setting of the sun, and by the change of seasons. Crops were planted and harvested; livestock was bred, its young delivered; sheep were sheared, some livestock slaughtered. Market days and fairs saw the produce and crafts of the town arrayed as people came to sell and shop—and be entertained by musicians, dancers, and troupes of actors. But even in Stratford, the lurking tensions and dangers could be daily sensed. A few months before Shakespeare was born, there had been a shocking "defacing" of images in the church, as workmen, not content merely to whitewash over the religious paintings decorating the interior as they were ordered, gouged large holes in those felt to be too "Catholic"; a few months after Shakespeare's birth, the register of the same church records another deadly outbreak of plague. The sleepy market town on the northern bank of the gently flowing river Avon was not immune from the menace of the world that surrounded it.

This was the world into which Shakespeare was born. England at his birth was still poor and backward, a fringe nation on the periphery of Europe. English itself was a minor language, hardly spoken outside of the country's borders. Religious tension was inescapable, as the old Catholic faith was trying determinedly to hold on, even as Protestantism was once again anxiously trying to establish itself as the national religion. The country knew itself vulnerable to serious threats both from without and from within. In 1562, the young Queen, upon whom so many people's hopes rested, almost fell victim to smallpox, and in 1569 a revolt of the Northern earls tried to remove her from power and restore Catholicism as the national religion. The following year, Pope Pius V pronounced the excommunication of "Elizabeth, the pretended queen of England" and forbade Catholic subjects obedience to the monarch on pain of their own excommunication. "Now we are in an evil way and going to the devil," wrote one clergyman, "and have all nations in our necks."

It was a world of dearth, danger, and domestic unrest. Yet it would soon dramatically change, and Shakespeare's literary contribution would, for future generations, come to be seen as a significant measure of England's remarkable transformation. In the course of Shakespeare's life, England, hitherto an unsophisticated and underdeveloped backwater acting as a bit player in the momentous political dramas taking place on the European continent, became a confident, prosperous, global presence. But this new world was only accidentally, as it is often known today, "The Age of Shakespeare." To the degree that historical change rests in the hands of any individual, credit must be given to the Queen. This new world arguably was "The Age of Elizabeth," even if it was not the Elizabethan Golden Age, as it has often been portrayed.

The young Queen quickly imposed her personality upon the nation. She had talented councilors around her, all with strong ties to her of friendship or blood, but the direction of government was her own. She was strong willed and cautious, certain of her right to rule and convinced that stability was her greatest responsibility. The result may very well have been, as historians have often charged, that important issues facing England were never dealt with head-on and left to her successors to settle, but it meant also that she was able to keep her England unified and for the most part at peace.

Religion posed her greatest challenge, though it is important to keep in mind that in this period, as an official at Elizabeth's court said, "Religion and the commonwealth cannot be parted asunder." Faith then was not the largely voluntary commitment it is today, nor was there any idea of some separation of church and state. Religion was literally a matter of life and death, of salvation and damnation, and the Church was the Church of England. Obedience to it was not only a matter of conscience but also of law. It was the single issue on which the nation was most likely to be torn apart.

Elizabeth's great achievement was that she was successful in ensuring that the Church of England became formally a Protestant Church, but she did so without either driving most of her Catholic subjects to sedition or alienating the more radical Protestant community. The so-called "Elizabethan Settlement" forged a broad Christian community of what has been called prayer-book Protestantism, even as many of its practitioners retained, as a clergyman said, "still a smack and savor of popish principles." If there were forces on both sides who were uncomfortable with the Settlement—committed Protestants, who wanted to do away with all vestiges of the old faith, and convinced Catholics, who continued to swear their allegiance to Rome—the majority of the country, as she hoped, found ways to live comfortably both within the law and within their faith. In 1571, she wrote to the Duke of Anjou that the forms of worship she recommended would "not properly compel any man to alter his opinion in the great matters now in controversy in the Church." The official toleration of religious ambiguity, as well as the familiar experience of an official change of state religion accompanying the crowning of a new monarch, produced a world where the familiar labels of Protestant and Catholic failed to define the forms of faith that most English people practiced. But for Elizabeth, most matters of faith could be left to individuals, as long as the Church itself, and Elizabeth's position at its head, would remain unchallenged.

In international affairs, she was no less successful with her pragmatism and willingness to pursue limited goals. A complex mix of prudential concerns about religion, the economy, and national security drove her foreign policy. She did not have imperial ambitions; in the main, she wanted only to be sure there would be no invasion of England and to encourage English trade. In the event, both goals brought England into conflict with Spain, determining the increasingly anti-Catholic tendencies of English foreign policy and, almost accidentally, England's emergence as a world power. When Elizabeth came to the throne, England was in many ways a mere satellite nation to the Netherlands, which was part of the Hapsburg Empire that the Catholic Philip II (who had briefly and unhappily been married to her predecessor and half sister, Queen Mary) ruled from Spain; by the end of her reign England was Spain's most bitter rival.

The transformation of Spain from ally to enemy came in a series of small steps (or missteps), no one of which was intended to produce what in the end came to pass. A series of posturings and provocations on both sides led to the rupture. In 1568, things moved to their breaking point, as the English confiscated a large shipment of gold that the Spanish were sending to their troops in the Netherlands. The following year saw the revolt of the Catholic earls in Northern England, followed by the papal excommunication of the Queen in 1570, both of which were by many in England assumed to be at the initiative, or at very least with the tacit support, of Philip. In fact he was not involved, but England under Elizabeth would never again think of Spain as a loyal friend or reliable ally. Indeed, Spain quickly became its mortal enemy. Protestant Dutch rebels had been opposing the Spanish domination of the Netherlands since the early 1560s, but, other than periodic financial support, Elizabeth had done little to encourage them. But in 1585, she sent troops under the command of the Earl of Leicester to support the Dutch rebels against the Spanish. Philip decided then to launch a full-scale attack on England, with the aim of deposing Elizabeth and restoring the Catholic faith. An English assault on Cadiz in 1587 destroyed a number of Spanish ships, postponing Philip's plans, but in the summer of 1588 the mightiest navy in the world, Philip's grand armada, with 132 ships and 30,493 sailors and troops, sailed for England.

By all rights, it should have been a successful invasion, but a combination of questionable Spanish tactics and a fortunate shift of wind resulted in one of England's greatest victories. The English had twice failed to intercept the armada off the coast of Portugal, and the Spanish fleet made its way to England, almost catching the English ships resupplying in Plymouth. The English navy was on its heels, when conveniently the Spanish admiral decided to anchor in the English Channel off the French port of Calais to wait for additional troops coming from the Netherlands. The English attacked with fireships, sinking four Spanish galleons, and strong winds from the south prevented an effective counterattack from the Spanish. The Spanish fleet was pushed into the North Sea, where it regrouped and decided its safest course was to attempt the difficult voyage home around Scotland and Ireland, losing almost half its ships on the way. For many in England the improbable victory was a miracle, evidence of God's favor for Elizabeth and the Protestant nation. Though war with Spain would not end for another fifteen years, the victory over the armada turned England almost overnight into a major world power, buoyed by confidence that they were chosen by God and, more tangibly, by a navy that could compete for control of the seas.

From a backward and insignificant Hapsburg satellite, Elizabeth's England had become, almost by accident, the leader of Protestant Europe. But if the victory over the armada signaled England's new place in the world, it hardly marked the end of England's travails. The economy, which initially was fueled by the military buildup, in the early 1590s fell victim to inflation, heavy taxation to support the war with Spain, the inevitable wartime disruptions of trade, as well as crop failures and a general economic downturn in Europe. Ireland, over which England had been attempting to impose its rule since 1168, continued to be a source of trouble and great expense (in some years costing the crown nearly one fifth of its total revenues). Even when the most organized of the rebellions, begun in 1594 and led by Hugh O'Neill, Earl of Tyrone, formally ended in 1603, peace and stability had not been achieved.

But perhaps the greatest instability came from the uncertainty over the succession, an uncertainty that marked Elizabeth's reign from its beginning. Her near death from smallpox in 1562 reminded the nation that an unmarried queen could not insure the succession, and Elizabeth was under constant pressure to marry and produce an heir. She was always aware of and deeply resented the pressure, announcing as early as 1559: "this shall be for me sufficient that a marble stone shall declare that a queen, having reigned such a time, lived and died a virgin." If, however, it was for her "sufficient," it was not so for her advisors and for much of the nation, who hoped she would wed. Arguably Elizabeth was the wiser, knowing that her unmarried hand was a political advantage, allowing her to diffuse threats or create alliances with the seeming possibility of a match. But as with so much in her reign, the strategy bought temporary stability at the price of longer-term solutions.

By the mid 1590s, it was clear that she would die unmarried and without an heir, and various candidates were positioning themselves to succeed her. Enough anxiety was produced that all published debate about the succession was forbidden by law. There was no direct descendant of the English crown to claim rule, and all the claimants had to reach well back into their family history to find some legitimacy. The best genealogical claim belonged to King James VI of Scotland. His mother, Mary, Queen of Scots, was the granddaughter of James IV of Scotland and Margaret Tudor, sister to Elizabeth's father, Henry VIII. Though James had right on his side, he was, it must be remembered, a foreigner. Scotland shared the island with England but was a separate nation. Great Britain, the union of England and Scotland, would not exist formally until 1707, but with Elizabeth's death early in the morning of March 24, 1603, surprisingly uneventfully the thirty-seven-year-old James succeeded to the English throne. Two nations, one king: King James VI of Scotland, King James I of England.

Most of his English subjects initially greeted the announcement of their new monarch with delight, relieved that the crown had successfully been transferred without any major disruption and reassured that the new King was married with two living sons. However, quickly many became disenchanted with a foreign King who spoke English with a heavy accent, and dismayed even further by the influx of Scots in positions of power. Nonetheless, the new King's greatest political liability may well have been less a matter of nationality than of temperament: he had none of Elizabeth's skill and ease in publicly wooing her subjects. The Venetian ambassador wrote back to the doge that the new King was unwilling to "caress the people, nor make them that good cheer the late Queen did, whereby she won their loves."

He was aloof and largely uninterested in the daily activities of governing, but he was interested in political theory and strongly committed to the cause of peace. Although a steadfast Protestant, he lacked the reflexive anti-Catholicism of many of his subjects. In England, he achieved a broadly consensual community of Protestants. The so-called King James Bible, the famous translation published first in 1611, was the result of a widespread desire to have an English Bible that spoke to all the nation, transcending the religious divisions that had placed three different translations in the hands of his subjects. Internationally, he styled himself *Rex Pacificus* (the peace-loving king). In 1604, the Treaty of London brought Elizabeth's war with Spain formally to an end, and over the next decade he worked to bring about political marriages that might cement stable alliances. In 1613, he married his daughter to the leader of the German Protestants, while the following year he began discussions with Catholic Spain to marry his son to the Infanta Maria. After some ten years of negotiations, James's hopes for what was known as the Spanish match were finally abandoned, much to the delight of the nation, whose long-felt fear and hatred for Spain outweighed the subtle political logic behind the plan.

But if James sought stability and peace, and for the most part succeeded in his aims (at least until 1618, when the bitter religio-political conflicts on the European continent swirled well out of the

King's control), he never really achieved concord and cohesion. He ruled over two kingdoms that did not know, like, or even want to understand one another, and his rule did little to bring them closer together. His England remained separate from his Scotland, even as he ruled over both. And even his England remained self divided, as in truth it always was under Elizabeth, ever more a nation of prosperity and influence but still one forged out of deep-rooted divisions of means, faiths, and allegiances that made the very nature of English identity a matter of confusion and concern. Arguably this is the very condition of great drama—sufficient peace and prosperity to support a theater industry and sufficient provocation in the troubling uncertainties about what the nation was and what fundamentally mattered to its people to inspire plays that would offer tentative solutions or at the very least make the troubling questions articulate and moving.

Nine years before James would die in 1625, Shakespeare died, having returned from London to the small market town in which he was born. If London, now a thriving modern metropolis of well over 200,000 people, had, like the nation itself, been transformed in the course of his life, the Warwickshire market town still was much the same. The house in which Shakespeare was born still stood, as did the church in which he was baptized and the school in which he learned to read and write. The river Avon still ran slowly along the town's southern limits. What had changed was that Shakespeare was now its most famous citizen, and, although it would take more than another 100 years to fully achieve this, he would in time become England's, for having turned the great ethical, social, and political issues of his own age into plays that would live forever.

William Shakespeare: A Chronology

1558	**November 17: Queen Elizabeth crowned**
1564	April 26: Shakespeare baptized, third child born to John Shakespeare and Mary Arden
1564	**May 27: Death of Jean Calvin in Geneva**
1565	John Shakespeare elected alderman in Stratford-upon-Avon
1568	**Publication of the Bishops' Bible**
1568	September 4: John Shakespeare elected Bailiff of Stratford-upon-Avon
1569	**Northern Rebellion**
1570	**Queen Elizabeth excommunicated by the Pope**
1572	**August 24: St. Bartholomew's Day Massacre in Paris**
1576	**The Theatre is built in Shoreditch**
1577–1580	**Sir Francis Drake sails around the world**
1582	November 27: Shakespeare and Anne Hathaway married (Shakespeare is 18)
1583	Queen's Men formed
1583	May 26: Shakespeare's daughter, Susanna, baptized
1584	**Failure of the Virginia Colony**

1585   February 2: Twins, Hamnet and Judith, baptized (Shakespeare is 20)

1586   Babington Plot to dethrone Elizabeth and replace her with Mary, Queen of Scots

1587   February 8: Execution of Mary, Queen of Scots

1587   Rose Theatre built

1588   August: Defeat of the Spanish armada (Shakespeare is 24)

1588   September 4: Death of Robert Dudley, Earl of Leicester

1590   First three books of Spenser's *Faerie Queene* published; Marlowe's *Tamburlaine* published

1592   March 3: *Henry VI, Part One* performed at the Rose Theatre (Shakespeare is 27)

1593   February–November: Theaters closed because of plague

1593   Publication of *Venus and Adonis*

1594   Publication of *Titus Andronicus*, first play by Shakespeare to appear in print (though anonymously)

1594   Lord Chamberlain's Men formed

1595   March 15: Payment made to Shakespeare, Will Kemp, and Richard Burbage for performances at court in December, 1594

1595   Swan Theatre built

1596   Books 4–6 of *The Faerie Queene* published

1596   August 11: Burial of Shakespeare's son, Hamnet (Shakespeare is 32)

1596–1599   Shakespeare living in St. Helen's, Bishopsgate, London

1596   October 20: Grant of Arms to John Shakespeare

1597	May 4: Shakespeare purchases New Place, one of the two largest houses in Stratford (Shakespeare is 33)
1598	Publication of *Love's Labor's Lost*, first extant play with Shakespeare's name on the title page
1598	Publication of Francis Meres's *Palladis Tamia*, citing Shakespeare as "the best for Comedy and Tragedy" among English writers
1599	**Opening of the Globe Theatre**
1601	**February 7: Lord Chamberlain's Men paid 40 shillings to play *Richard II* by supporters of the Earl of Essex, the day before his abortive rebellion**
1601	**February 17: Execution of Robert Devereaux, Earl of Essex**
1601	September 8: Burial of John Shakespeare
1602	May 1: Shakespeare buys 107 acres of farmland in Stratford
1603	**March 24: Queen Elizabeth dies; James VI of Scotland succeeds as James I of England** (Shakespeare is 39)
1603	May 19: Lord Chamberlain's Men reformed as the King's Men
1604	Shakespeare living with the Mountjoys, a French Huguenot family, in Cripplegate, London
1604	**First edition of Marlowe's *Dr. Faustus* published (written c. 1589)**
1604	March 15: Shakespeare named among "players" given scarlet cloth to wear at royal procession of King James
1604	Publication of authorized version of *Hamlet* (Shakespeare is 40)
1605	**Gunpowder Plot**
1605	June 5: Marriage of Susanna Shakespeare to John Hall
1608	Publication of *King Lear* (Shakespeare is 44)
1608–1609	Acquisition of indoor Blackfriars Theatre by King's Men

PE
2019

1609   *Sonnets* published

1611   **King James Bible published** (Shakespeare is 47)

1612   **November 6: Death of Henry, eldest son of King James**

1613   **February 14: Marriage of King James's daughter Elizabeth to Frederick, the Elector Palatine**

1613   March 10: Shakespeare, with some associates, buys gatehouse in Blackfriars, London

1613   **June 29: Fire burns the Globe Theatre**

1614   **Rebuilt Globe reopens**

1616   February 10: Marriage of Judith Shakespeare to Thomas Quiney

1616   March 25: Shakespeare's will signed

1616   April 23: Shakespeare dies (age 52)

1616   **April 23: Cervantes dies in Madrid**

1616   April 25: Shakespeare buried in Holy Trinity Church in Stratford-upon-Avon

1623   August 6: Death of Anne Shakespeare

1623   **October: Prince Charles, King James's son, returns from Madrid, having failed to arrange his marriage to Maria Anna, Infanta of Spain**

1623   First Folio published with 36 plays (18 never previously published)

Words, Words, Words: Understanding Shakespeare's Language
by David Scott Kastan

I t is silly to pretend that it is easy to read Shakespeare. Reading Shakespeare isn't like picking up a copy of *USA Today* or *The New Yorker*, or even F. Scott Fitzgerald's *Great Gatsby* or Toni Morrison's *Beloved*. It is hard work, because the language is often unfamiliar to us and because it is more concentrated than we are used to. In the theater it is usually a bit easier. Actors can clarify meanings with gestures and actions, allowing us to get the general sense of what is going on, if not every nuance of the language that is spoken. "Action is eloquence," as Volumnia puts it in *Coriolanus*, "and the eyes of th' ignorant / More learnèd than the ears" (3.276–277). Yet the real greatness of Shakespeare rests not on "the general sense" of his plays but on the specificity and suggestiveness of the words in which they are written. It is through language that the plays' full dramatic power is realized, and it is that rich and robust language, often pushed by Shakespeare to the very limits of intelligibility, that we must learn to understand. But we can come to understand it (and enjoy it), and this essay is designed to help.

Even experienced readers and playgoers need help. They often find that his words are difficult to comprehend. Shakespeare sometimes uses words no longer current in English or with meanings that have changed. He regularly multiplies words where seemingly one might do as well or even better. He characteristically writes sentences that are syntactically complicated and imaginatively dense. And it isn't just we, removed by some 400 years from his world, who find him difficult to read; in his own time, his friends and fellow actors knew Shakespeare was hard. As two of them, John Hemings and Henry Condell, put it in their prefatory remarks to Shakespeare's First Folio in 1623, "read him, therefore, and again and again; and if then you do not like him, surely you are in some manifest danger not to understand him."

From the very beginning, then, it was obvious that the plays both deserve and demand not only careful reading but continued re-reading—and that not to read Shakespeare with all the attention a reader can bring to bear on the language is almost to guarantee that a reader will not "understand him" and remain among those who "do not like him." But Shakespeare's colleagues were nonetheless confident that the plays exerted an attraction strong enough to ensure and reward the concentration of their readers, confident, as they say, that in them "you will find enough, both to draw and hold you." The plays do exert a kind of magnetic pull, and have successfully drawn in and held readers for over 400 years.

Once we are drawn in, we confront a world of words that does not always immediately yield its delights; but it will—once we learn to see what is demanded of us. Words in Shakespeare do a lot, arguably more than anyone else has ever asked them to do. In part, it is because he needed his words to do many things at once. His stage had no sets and few props, so his words are all we have to enable us to imagine what his characters see. And they also allow us to see what the characters don't see, especially about themselves. The words are vivid and immediate, as well as complexly layered and psychologically suggestive. The difficulties they pose are not the "thee's" and "thou's" or "prithee's" and "doth's" that obviously mark the chronological distance between Shakespeare and us. When

Gertrude says to Hamlet, "thou hast thy father much offended" (3.4.8), we have no difficulty understanding her chiding, though we might miss that her use of the "thou" form of the pronoun expresses an intimacy that Hamlet pointedly refuses with his reply: "Mother, *you* have my father much offended" (3.4.9; italics mine).

Most deceptive are words that look the same as words we know but now mean something different. Words often change meanings over time. When Horatio and the soldiers try to stop Hamlet as he chases after the Ghost, Hamlet pushes past them and says, "I'll make a ghost of him that lets me" (1.4.85). It seems an odd thing to say. Why should he threaten someone who "lets" him do what he wants to do? But here "let" means "hinder," not, as it does today, "allow" (although the older meaning of the word still survives, for example, in tennis, where a "let serve" is one that is hindered by the net on its way across). There are many words that can, like this, mislead us: "his" sometimes means "its," "an" often means "if," "envy" means something more like "malice," "cousin" means more generally "kinsman," and there are others, though all are easily defined. The difficulty is that we may not stop to look thinking we already know what the word means, but in this edition a ° following the word alerts a reader that there is a gloss in the left margin, and quickly readers get used to these older meanings.

Then, of course, there is the intimidation factor—strange, polysyllabic, or Latinate words that not only are foreign to us but also must have sounded strange even to Shakespeare's audiences. When Macbeth wonders whether all the water in all the oceans of the world will be able to clean his bloody hands after the murder of Duncan, he concludes: "No; this my hand will rather / The multitudinous seas incarnadine, / Making the green one red" (2.2.64–66). Duncan's blood staining Macbeth's murderous hand is so offensive that, not merely does it resist being washed off in water, but it will "the multitudinous seas incarnadine": that is, turn the sea-green oceans blood-red. Notes will easily clarify the meaning of the two odd words, but it is worth observing that they would have been as odd to Shakespeare's readers as they are to us. The *Oxford English Dictionary* (*OED*) shows no use of "multitudinous" before this, and it records no use of "incarnadine" before 1591 (*Macbeth* was written about 1606). Both are new words, coined from the Latin, part of a process in Shakespeare's time where English adopted many Latinate words as a mark of its own emergence as an important vernacular language. Here they are used to express the magnitude of Macbeth's offense, a crime not only against the civil law but also against the cosmic order, and then the simple monosyllables of turning "the green one red" provide an immediate (and needed) paraphrase and register his own sickening awareness of the true hideousness of his deed.

As with "multitudinous" in *Macbeth*, Shakespeare is the source of a great many words in English. Sometimes he coined them himself, or, if he didn't invent them, he was the first person whose writing of them has survived. Some of these words have become part of our language, so common that it is hard to imagine they were not always part of it: for example, "assassination" (*Macbeth*, 1.7.2), "bedroom" (*A Midsummer Night's Dream*, 2.2.57), "countless" (*Titus Andronicus*, 5.3.59), "fashionable" (*Troilus and Cressida*, 3.3.165), "frugal" (*The Merry Wives of Windsor*, 2.1.28), "laughable" (*The Merchant of Venice*, 1.1.56), "lonely" (*Coriolanus*, 4.1.30), and "useful" (*King John*, 5.2.81). But other words that he originated were not as, to use yet another Shakespearean coinage, "successful" (*Titus Andronicus*, 1.1.66). Words like "crimeless" (*Henry VI, Part Two*, 2.4.63, meaning "innocent"), "facinorous" (*All's Well That Ends Well*, 2.3.30, meaning "extremely wicked"), and "recountment" (*As You Like It*, 4.3.141, meaning "narrative" or "account") have, without much resistance, slipped into oblivion. Clearly Shakespeare liked words, even unwieldy ones. His working vocabulary, about 18,000 words, is staggering, larger than almost any other English writer, and he seems to be the first person to use in print about

1,000 of these. Whether he coined the new words himself or was intrigued by the new words he heard in the streets of London doesn't really matter; the point is that he was remarkably alert to and engaged with a dynamic language that was expanding in response to England's own expanding contact with the world around it.

But it is neither new words nor old ones that are the source of the greatest difficulty of Shakespeare's language. The real difficulty (and the real delight) comes in trying to see how he uses the words, how he endows them with more than their denotative meanings. Why, for example, does Macbeth say that he hopes that the "sure and firm-set earth" (2.1.56) will not hear his steps as he goes forward to murder Duncan? Here "sure" and "firm-set" mean virtually the same thing: stable, secure, fixed. Why use two words? If this were a student paper, no doubt the teacher would circle one of them and write "redundant." But the redundancy is exactly what Shakespeare wants. One word would do if the purpose were to describe the solidity of the earth, but here the redundancy points to something different. It reveals something about Macbeth's mind, betraying through the doubling how deep is his awareness of the world of stable values that the terrible act he is about to commit must unsettle.

Shakespeare's words usually work this way: in part describing what the characters see and as often betraying what they feel. The example from *Macbeth* is a simple example of how this works. Shakespeare's words are carefully patterned. How one says something is every bit as important as what is said, and the conspicuous patterns that are created alert us to the fact that something more than the words' lexical sense has been put into play. Words can be coupled, as in the example above, or knit into even denser metaphorical constellations to reveal something about the speaker (which often the speaker does not know), as in Prince Hal's promise to his father that he will outdo the rebels' hero, Henry Percy (Hotspur):

Percy is but my factor, good my lord,
To engross up glorious deeds on my behalf.
And I will call him to so strict account
That he shall render every glory up,
Yea, even the slightest worship of his time,
Or I will tear the reckoning from his heart.

(Henry IV, Part One, 3.2.147–152)

The Prince expresses his confidence that he will defeat Hotspur, but revealingly in a reiterated language of commercial exchange ("factor," "engross," "account," "render," "reckoning") that tells us something important both about the Prince and the ways in which he understands his world. In a play filled with references to coins and counterfeiting, the speech demonstrates not only that Hal has committed himself to the business at hand, repudiating his earlier, irresponsible tavern self, but also that he knows it is a business rather than a glorious world of chivalric achievement; he inhabits a world in which value (political as well as economic) is not intrinsic but determined by what people are willing to invest, and he proves himself a master of producing desire for what he has to offer.

Or sometimes it is not the network of imagery but the very syntax that speaks, as when Claudius announces his marriage to Hamlet's mother:

Therefore our sometime sister, now our Queen,
Th' imperial jointress to this warlike state,
Have we—as 'twere with a defeated joy,
With an auspicious and a dropping eye,
With mirth in funeral and with dole in marriage,
In equal scale weighing delight and dole—
Taken to wife.   *(Hamlet, 1.2.8–14)*

All he really wants to say here is that he has married Gertrude, his former sister-in-law: "Therefore our sometime sister . . . Have we . . . Taken to wife." But the straightforward sentence gets interrupted and complicated, revealing his own discomfort with the announcement. His elaborations and intensifications of Gertrude's role ("sometime sister," "Queen," "imperial jointress"), the self-conscious rhetorical balancing of the middle three lines (indeed "in equal scale weighing delight and dole"), all declare by the all-too obvious artifice how desperate he is to hide the awkward facts behind a veneer of normalcy and propriety. The very unnaturalness of the sentence is what alerts us that we are meant to understand more than the simple relation of fact.

Why doesn't Shakespeare just say what he means? Well, he does—exactly what he means. In the example from *Hamlet* just above, Shakespeare shows us something about Claudius that Claudius doesn't know himself. Always Shakespeare's words will offer us an immediate sense of what is happening, allowing us to follow the action, but they also offer us a counterplot, pointing us to what might be behind the action, confirming or contradicting what the characters say. It is a language that shimmers with promise and possibility, opening the characters' hearts and minds to our view—and all we have to do is learn to pay attention to what is there before us.

Shakespeare's Verse

Another distinctive feature of Shakespeare's dramatic language is that much of it is in verse. Almost all of the plays mix poetry and prose, but the poetry dominates. *The Merry Wives of Windsor* has the lowest percentage (only about 13 percent verse), while *Richard II* and *King John* are written entirely in verse (the only examples, although *Henry VI, Part One* and *Part Three* have only a very few prose lines). In most of the plays, about 70 percent of the lines are written in verse.

Shakespeare's characteristic verse line is a non-rhyming iambic pentameter ("blank verse"), ten syllables with every second one stressed. In *A Midsummer Night's Dream*, Titania comes to her senses after a magic potion has led her to fall in love with an ass-headed Bottom: "Methought I was enamored of an ass" (4.1.76). Similarly, in *Romeo and Juliet*, Romeo gazes up at Juliet's window: "But soft, what light through yonder window breaks" (2.2.2). In both these examples, the line has ten syllables organized into five regular beats (each beat consisting of the stress on the second syllable of a pair, as in "But soft," the da-dum rhythm forming an "iamb"). Still, we don't hear these lines as jingles; they seem natural enough, in large part because this dominant pattern is varied in the surrounding lines.

The play of stresses indeed becomes another key to meaning, as Shakespeare alerts us to what is important. In *Measure for Measure*, Lucio urges Isabella to plead for her brother's life: "Oh, to him, to him, wench! He will relent" (2.2.129). The iambic norm (unstressed-stressed) tells us (and an actor) that the emphasis at the beginning of the line is on "to" not "him"—it is the action not the object that is being emphasized—and at the end of the line the stress falls on "will." Alternatively, the line can play against the established norm. In *Hamlet*, Claudius corrects Polonius's idea of what is bothering the Prince: "Love? His affections do not that way tend" (3.1.161). The iambic norm forces the emphasis onto "that" ("do not *that* way tend"), while the syntax forces an unexpected stress on the opening word, "Love." In the famous line, "The course of true love never did run smooth" (*A Midsummer Night's Dream*, 1.1.134), the iambic expectation is varied in both the middle and at the end of the line. Both "love" and the first syllable of "never" are stressed, as are both syllables at the end: "run smooth," creating a metrical foot in which both syllables are stressed (called a "spondee"). The point to notice is that the "da-dum, da-dum, da-dum, da-dum, da-dum" line is not inevitable; it merely sets an expectation against which many variations can be heard.

In fact, even the ten-syllable norm can be varied. Shakespeare sometimes writes lines with fewer or more syllables. Often there is an extra, unstressed syllable at the end of a line (a so-called "feminine ending"); sometimes there are verse lines with only nine. In *Henry IV, Part One*, King Henry replies incredulously to the rebel Worcester's claim that he hadn't "sought" the confrontation with the King: "You have not sought it. How comes it then?" (5.1.27). There are only nine syllables here (some earlier editors, seeking to "correct" the verse, added the word "sir" after the first question to regularize the line). But the pause where one expects a stressed syllable is dramatically effective, allowing the King's anger to be powerfully present in the silence.

As even these few examples show, Shakespeare's verse is unusually flexible, allowing a range of rhythmical effects. It should not be understood as a set of strict rules but as a flexible set of practices rooted in dramatic necessity. It is designed to highlight ideas and emotions, and it is based less upon rigid syllable counts than on an arrangement of stresses within an understood temporal norm, as one might expect from a poetry written to be heard in the theater rather than read on the page.

Here Follows Prose

Although the plays are dominated by verse, prose plays a significant role. Shakespeare's prose has its own rhythms, but it lacks the formal patterning of verse, and so is printed without line breaks and without the capitals that mark the beginning of a verse line. Like many of his fellow dramatists, Shakespeare tended to use prose for comic scenes, the shift from verse serving, especially in his early plays, as a social marker. Upper-class characters speak in verse; lower-class characters speak in prose. Thus, in *A Midsummer Night's Dream*, the Athenians of the court, as well as the fairies, all speak in verse, but the "rude mechanicals," Bottom and his artisan friends, all speak in prose, except for the comic verse they speak in their performance of "Pyramis and Thisbe."

As Shakespeare grew in experience, he became more flexible about the shifts from verse to prose, letting it, among other things, mark genre rather than class and measure various kinds of intensity. Prose becomes in the main the medium of comedy. The great comedies, like *Much Ado About Nothing*, *Twelfth Night*, and *As You Like It*, are all more than 50 percent prose. But even in comedy, shifts between verse and prose may be used to measure subtle emotional changes. In Act One, scene three of *The Merchant of Venice*, Shylock and Bassanio begin the scene speaking of matters of business in prose, but when Antonio enters and the deep conflict between the Christian and the Jew becomes evident, the scene shifts to verse. But prose may itself serve in moments of emotional intensity. Shylock's famous speech in Act Three, scene one, "Hath not a Jew eyes . . ." is all in prose, as is Hamlet's expression of disgust at the world ("I have of late— but wherefore I know not—lost all my mirth . . .") at 3.1.261–276. Shakespeare comes to use prose to vary the tone of a scene, as the shift from verse subtly alerts an audience or a reader to some new emotional register.

Prose becomes, as Shakespeare's art matures, not inevitably the mark of the lower classes but the mark of a salutary daily-ness. It is appropriately the medium in which letters are written, and it is the medium of a common sense that will at least challenge the potential self-deceptions of grandiloquent speech. When Rosalind mocks the excesses and artifice of Orlando's wooing in Act Four, scene one of *As You Like It*, it is in prose that she seeks something genuine in the expression of love:

> The poor world is almost six thousand years old, and in all this time there was not any man died in his own person, *videlicit* [i.e., namely], in a love cause. . . . Men have died from time to time, and worms have eaten them, but not for love.

Here the prose becomes the sound of common sense, an effective foil to the affectation of pinning poems to trees and thinking that it is real love.

It is not that prose is artless; Shakespeare's prose is no less self-conscious than his verse. The artfulness of his prose is different, of course. The seeming ordinariness of his prose is no less an effect of his artistry than is the more obvious patterning of his verse. Prose is no less serious, compressed, or indeed figurative. As with his verse, Shakespeare's prose performs numerous tasks and displays various, subtle formal qualities; and recognizing the possibilities of what it can achieve is still another way of seeing what Shakespeare puts right before us to show us what he has hidden.

Further Reading

N.F. Blake, *Shakespeare's Language: An Introduction* (New York: St. Martin's Press, 1983).

Jonathan Hope, *Shakespeare's Grammar* (London: Thomson, 2003).

Sister Miriam Joseph, *Shakespeare's Use of the Arts of Language* (New York: Columbia University Press, 1947).

M. M. Mahood, *Shakespeare's Wordplay* (London: Methuen, 1957).

Russ McDonald, *Shakespeare and the Arts of Language* (Oxford: Oxford University Press, 2001).

Brian Vickers, *The Artistry of Shakespeare's Prose* (London: Methuen, 1968).

George T. Wright, *Shakespeare's Metrical Art* (Berkeley: Univ. of California Press, 1991).

Key to the Play Text

Symbols

o   Indicates an explanation or definition in the left-hand margin.

1   Indicates a gloss on the page facing the play text.

[ ]   Indicates something added or changed by the editors (i.e., not in the early printed text that this edition of the play is based on).

Terms

Q1, First Quarto   An edition of the play printed in 1597.

Q2, Second Quarto   An edition of the play printed in 1599, and the basis for this edition (see Editing *Romeo and Juliet*, page 333).

F, Folio, or *First Folio*   The first collected edition of Shakespeare's plays, published in 1623.

Romeo and Juliet

William Shakespeare

List of Roles

Chorus

Montague   *a nobleman of Verona*

Lady Montague   *his wife*

Romeo   *their son*

Benvolio   *a nephew of Montague*

Abram   *Montague's servant*

Balthasar   *Romeo's servingman*

Capulet   *a nobleman of Verona*

Lady Capulet   *his wife*

Juliet   *their daughter*

Nurse

Tybalt   *a nephew of Capulet*

Tybalt's Page

Petruccio

Capulet's cousin

Peter, Sampson, Gregory   *Capulet servingmen*

Prince

Mercutio   *the Prince's kinsman*

Mercutio's Page

Paris   *Juliet's suitor and the Prince's kinsman*

Paris's Page

Friar Laurence

Friar John

Apothecary

Servingmen

Three Musicians

Chief Watchman

Second, Third Watchmen

Officer

Gentlemen, gentlewomen, maskers, torchbearers, citizens, attendants, servants

1 **Chorus**

An actor, usually dressed in black, who delivers the prologue, explaining or commenting on forthcoming events. He reappears between the first and second acts, and both of the speeches are sonnets.

2 *fair Verona*

Verona is the setting of the Romeo and Juliet story in Shakespeare's sources. Although the play is a tragedy set in a city stained with *civil blood*, the Prologue's description of Verona as *fair* introduces the generally comic mood of the first half of the play. Italian cities were often the setting for English Renaissance comedies, including Shakespeare's *The Two Gentlemen of Verona* and *The Merchant of Venice*. The first half of *Romeo and Juliet* follows the conventional pattern of comedy (exemplified in Shakespeare's *A Midsummer Night's Dream*), in which young lovers attempt to evade parental opposition to their marriage. For many Elizabethan Protestants, however, Italy also carried negative associations as the seat of Roman Catholicism. The Act of Uniformity (1559) of the Church of England forbade Catholics from practicing their faith. In *Romeo and Juliet*, the Catholicism of Verona is manifested both in the centrality

of the Friar as an authority figure, and in the references to saints and pilgrims in the young lovers' first conversation.

3 *Where civil blood makes civil hands unclean*

Civil has the meaning "of or belonging to citizens," as distinct from military personnel, and also means "domestic" or "intestine," as in the phrase "civil war." In the sense that it also means "orderly, well-governed, and decent," the word carries a tragic irony.

4 *star-crossed*

Thwarted by the destiny shaped by the stars (See LONGER NOTE on page 329.)

5 *take their life*

(1) derive their being; (2) commit suicide

6 *the two hours' traffic of our stage*

I.e., the two-hour-long performance that will take place on our stage. Elizabethan performances generally lasted between two and three hours. *Traffic* suggests the conveyance of merchandise, just as the word *passage* in line 9 carries the sense of a commercial sea voyage.

7 *What here shall miss, our toil shall strive to mend*

I.e., whatever seems inadequate in our performance, we will do our best to improve in the future.

The Prologue

[*Enter*] **Chorus**.[1]

Chorus

social rank   Two households, both alike in dignity°

In fair Verona,[2] where we lay our scene,

violence   From ancient grudge break to new mutiny,°

Where civil blood makes civil hands unclean.[3]

fateful; ruinous   From forth the fatal° loins of these two foes

A pair of star-crossed[4] lovers take their life,[5]

unfortunate   Whose misadventured° piteous overthrows

Doth with their death bury their parents' strife.

The fearful passage of their death-marked love

And the continuance of their parents' rage,

except for / nothing   Which, but° their children's end, naught° could remove,

Is now the two hours' traffic of our stage[6]—

The which, if you with patient ears attend,

What here shall miss, our toil shall strive to mend.[7]

[*He exits.*]

Handwritten annotations:

fighting again

Italy

Feud that has gone on for so long

proper

Pun

Alliterations

death — children — enemies

suicide

fate

not going well — tragic

Irony

awful to watch

when they die — they stop fighting

bad progression — Suicide

they don't approve of their love

death

Only their children's death would stop their feud

what we will see

If something you don't understand

we will explain it in the play

1. love leads to death
2. Parents' feud continues

1   bucklers

     Small round shields

2   *carry coals*

     **I.e., endure insults (but also
     "perform menial work")**

3   *colliers*

     **Men who *carry coals* for sale, and
     therefore dirty and/or shady
     individuals (as *colliers* were often
     thought to be)**

4   *an we be in choler*

     If we're angry (punning on *colliers*)

5   *draw*

     Pull out (our swords)

6   *while you live, draw your neck out of
     collar*

     **(1) as long as you live, avoid the
     hangman's noose; (2) as long as
     you live, avoid tedious, menial
     work (with *collar* referring to the
     yoke of a draft animal, like an ox or
     a horse).**

7   *moved*

     **Multiple senses, variously
     exploited by Gregory and
     Sampson. *Moved* can mean
     "angered" or "provoked," but it
     can also mean "sexually aroused,"
     as well as, in line 9, "forced to
     retreat."**

8   *to stand*

     **(1) to take up an offensive or
     defensive position against an
     enemy; (2) to present a brave front;
     (3) with a sexual connotation, "to
     have an erection"**

9   *take the wall of*

     **I.e., take a superior position to. *The
     wall* referred to the wall side of a
     thoroughfare in an early modern
     city or town. The wall side would
     have been a great deal less dirty
     than the street side, and therefore
     a more desirable place to walk. To
     take the wall of somebody indicated
     that you were either their social
     superior or had intimidated them
     into ceding that place to you.**

10   *the weakest goes to the wall*

     **The proverbial phrase *the weakest
     goes to the wall* describes someone
     who is defeated and pushed aside
     by a stronger adversary.**

11   *weaker vessels*

     **In the Bible, the apostle Peter calls
     women "the weaker vessels"
     (1 Peter 3:7).**

Act 1, Scene 1

*Enter **Sampson** and **Gregory**, with swords and bucklers,* [1] *of the house of Capulet.*

[handwritten: - Bait the other side so they make a move first]

Sampson

Gregory, on my word, we'll not carry coals. [2]

Gregory

No, for then we should be colliers. [3]

Sampson

if   I mean, an° we be in choler, [4] we'll draw. [5]

Gregory

Ay, while you live, draw your neck out of collar. [6]

Sampson

I strike quickly, being moved. [7]   5

Gregory

But thou art not quickly moved to strike.

Sampson

A dog of the house of Montague moves me. *[handwritten: — makes him mad]*

Gregory

To move is to stir, and to be valiant is to stand; [8]
therefore if thou art moved thou runn'st away.

Sampson

A dog of that house shall move me to stand. I will take   10
the wall of [9] any man or maid of Montague's.

Gregory

to be a   That shows thee a° weak slave, for the weakest goes to
the wall. [10]

Sampson

'Tis true, and therefore women, being the weaker
vessels, [11] are ever thrust to the wall; therefore I will   15
push Montague's men from the wall and thrust his
maids to the wall.

1 *'Tis all one.*

It's all the same thing.

2 *Take it in what sense thou wilt.*

I.e., interpret my words however you wish. Gregory's reply in the following line takes *sense* to mean "physical sensation."

3 *stand*

Continues the bawdy punning, with *stand* meaning "keep an erection"; similar jokes exist with *tool* (line 29) and *naked weapon* (line 31).

4 *a pretty piece of flesh*

I.e., a desirable young man

5 *poor-john*

Dried and salted hake fish (implying that Sampson is shriveled, unable to *stand*)

6 *Fear me not.*

I.e., do not doubt me. Gregory takes the word *fear* to mean "be frightened of."

7 *marry*

A mild oath derived from the name of Mary, the mother of Jesus

8 *Let us take the law of our sides.*

Let us be sure we are legally in the right.

Gregory

The quarrel is between our masters and us their men.

Sampson

'Tis all one.[1] I will show myself a tyrant: when I have
fought with the men, I will be civil with the maids.   20
I will cut off their heads.

Gregory

The heads of the maids?

Sampson

hymens   Ay, the heads of the maids or their maidenheads.° virginity
Take it in what sense thou wilt.[2]

Gregory

They must take it in sense that feel it.   25

Sampson

Me they shall feel while I am able to stand,[3] and 'tis
known I am a pretty piece of flesh.[4]

Gregory

'Tis well thou art not fish. If thou hadst, thou hadst
sword / servants of   been poor-john.[5] Draw thy tool!° Here comes of° the
house of Montagues.   30

Enter [**Abram** *and another servingman*].

Sampson

Pick a fight   My naked weapon is out. Quarrel!° I will back thee.

Gregory

How? Turn thy back and run?

Sampson

Fear me not.[6]

Gregory

No, marry,[7] I fear thee.

Sampson

Let us take the law of our sides.[8] Let them begin.   35

1   *I will bite my thumb at them*

Through the insulting gesture of biting his thumb (roughly equivalent to giving the finger), Sampson provokes Abram without fully commiting to a fight. This gesture, as well as the faux-courteous exchange between Sampson and Abram that follows, parodies established codes of conduct for gentlemen engaging in a duel.

2   *if you do, sir, I am for you*

If you do want to fight, I'm ready.

3   **Benvolio**

The name in Italian means "good will."

Gregory

sneer / like I will frown° as I pass by, and let them take it as they list.°

Sampson

Nay, as they dare. I will bite my thumb at them, [1] which
is disgrace to them if they bear it. [*bites his thumb*] *giving the finger*

Abram

Do you bite your thumb at us, sir?

Sampson

I do bite my thumb, sir.   40

Abram

Do you bite your thumb at us, sir?

Sampson

on [*aside to* **Gregory**] Is the law of° our side if I say "ay"?

Gregory

[*aside to* **Sampson**] No.

Sampson

No, sir. I do not bite my thumb at you, sir, but I bite my
thumb, sir.   45

Gregory

Do you quarrel, sir?

Abram

Quarrel, sir? No, sir.

Sampson

But if you do, sir, I am for you. [2] I serve as good a man as
you.

Abram

No better.   50

Sampson

Well, sir.

Enter **Benvolio**. [3]

1   *Here comes one of my master's kinsmen.*

    I.e., Tybalt, not yet seen by Abram and his companion.

2   *Art thou drawn among these heartless hinds?*

    I.e., have you drawn your sword in the presence of cowardly servants? *Hind* means both "servant" and "female deer;" *heartless* means "cowardly," but also is heard as "hartless," a female deer without a male (hart) for protection.

3   *Have at thee*

    I.e., here I come.

4   clubs

    To summon their peers to a street brawl, London apprentices would cry "Clubs!" or "'Prentices and clubs!" (Apprentices were young men in training for various trades, but the term was often used more broadly to designate low-status youths.) On June 29, 1595, an "Apprentice's Insurrection" took place in London in which one thousand people armed with pikes, bills, clubs, swords, and daggers gathered to protest the government's unsympathetic response to a rapid escalation in food prices. In *Romeo and Juliet*, however, street violence is generated not from the political and economic struggles of the poor but from the clannish pride of idle gentlemen. Moreover, those who cry "Clubs!" are not unruly apprentices attempting to subvert social order but established citizens attempting to quell social disorder.

5   *bills, and partisans*

    Long-handled weapons; *bills* with an axe-like concave blade and *partisans* with a spear head and an additional blade projecting laterally.

Gregory

[*aside to* **Sampson**] Say "better." Here comes one of my
master's kinsmen. [1]

Sampson

Yes, better, sir.

Abram

You lie.   55

Sampson

Draw, if you be men.—Gregory, remember thy

slashing washing° blow.   *They fight.*

Benvolio

away Part, fools! Put up° your swords. You know not what
you do. [*draws sword*]

     Enter **Tybalt**.

Tybalt

What? Art thou drawn among these heartless hinds? [2]   60
Turn thee, Benvolio; look upon thy death. [*draws sword*]

Benvolio

I do but keep the peace. Put up thy sword

use Or manage° it to part these men with me.

Tybalt

What? Drawn and talk of peace? I hate the word
As I hate Hell, all Montagues, and thee.   65
Have at thee, [3] coward!   [*They fight.*]

     Enter three or four **Citizens**, *with clubs* [4] *or partisans.*

Citizens

Clubs, bills, and partisans! [5] Strike! Beat them down!

1   gown

    **Dressing gown, a sign of the feud's
    disruption of civic and domestic
    harmony**

2   *my long sword*

    **An old-fashioned weapon in
    Shakespeare's day. Capulet's
    choice of the long sword indicates
    how outdated he is (and his wife
    reminds him of how old he is, no
    longer capable of wielding the
    heavy weapon).**

3   *in spite of me*

    In order to vex or insult me

4   train

    Entourage; attendants

5   *Profaners of this neighbor-stainèd steel*

    **Those who dirty their swords
    sacrilegiously with the blood of
    fellow citizens**

6   *Will they not hear?*

    **Indicating that the fight hasn't
    stopped, despite the arrival of the
    Prince**

7   *mistempered*

    **Both "poorly made" and "used in
    ill-temper"**

Down with the Capulets! Down with the Montagues!

Enter old **Capulet** *in his gown,* [1] *and his wife* [, **Lady Capulet**].

Capulet

What noise is this? Give me my long sword, [2] ho!

Lady Capulet

A crutch, a crutch. Why call you for a sword?   70

Enter old **Montague** *and his wife* [, **Lady Montague**].

Capulet

My sword, I say! Old Montague is come
And flourishes his blade in spite of me. [3]

Montague

Thou villain Capulet! [*to his wife*]Hold me not. Let me go.

Lady Montague

Thou shalt not stir one foot to seek a foe.

Enter **Prince** *Escalus with his train.* [4]

Prince

Rebellious subjects, enemies to peace,   75
Profaners of this neighbor-stainèd steel! [5]
—Will they not hear? [6]—What ho! You men, you beasts,
That quench the fire of your pernicious rage
i.e., bloody With purple° fountains issuing from your veins,
On pain of torture, from those bloody hands   80
Throw your mistempered [7] weapons to the ground
angry And hear the sentence of your movèd° prince.
empty; insubstantial Three civil brawls bred of an airy° word   ~~3 times they have fought in the streets~~
By thee, Old Capulet and Montague,

1   *ancient citizens*

    (1) aged citizens of Verona; (2) the inhabitants of Verona, who for many years have possessed the rights associated with citizenship. The second sense of the phrase conveys the affront to a venerable tradition of civility that is threatened by the feud between the Montagues and the Capulets.

2   *grave-beseeming ornaments*

    (1) appropriately solemn attire; (2) garments appropriate for the grave (i.e., for burial)

3   *If ever you disturb our streets again, . . . forfeit of the peace.*

    In his *Discourses* (1531), the Italian political theorist Niccolò Machiavelli advises the prince to deal harshly with feuding factions. Machiavelli considers three options for imposing unity on a "divided city": killing the faction leaders, banishing them, or forcing them to reconcile. He recommends execution and banishment as the most effective policies. At the end of the play, the Prince acknowledges that his policy of leniency toward the feuding households has failed to prevent further bloodshed. At various times during her reign, Queen Elizabeth had attempted to limit urban violence by issuing proclamations against carrying

long rapiers and handguns; nonetheless, she largely ignored the kind of violence regularly committed by courtiers and noblemen. Queen Elizabeth did, however, authorize harsh punishments for commoners who took part in the "unlawful great assemblies" that erupted in the streets of London.

4   *new abroach*

    Newly into action

5   *close fighting*

    Fighting at close quarters; brawling

6   *cut the winds, / Who, nothing hurt withal, hissed him in scorn*

    I.e., slashed the air (with his sword) and, failing to be hurt, the air hissed back at him in scorn (the *hiss* being the whistle made by the rapier blade as it passed through the air). Tybalt is depicted here as a blowhard, a braggart who waves his sword about impressively but fails to do any actual harm.

7   *Came more and more and fought on part and part*

    More and more people came and fought on one side or the other.

8   *either part*

    Both sides

Have thrice disturbed the quiet of our streets,   85
And made Verona's ancient citizens [1]
aside Cast by° their grave-beseeming ornaments [2]
To wield old partisans in hands as old,
Rusted / venomous Cankered° with peace, to part your cankered° hate.
If ever you disturb our streets again,   90
Your lives shall pay the forfeit of the peace. [3] *death*
For this time, all the rest depart away.
You, Capulet, shall go along with me,
And, Montague, come you this afternoon
To know our farther pleasure in this case,   95
public To old Freetown, our common° judgment-place.
Once more, on pain of death, all men depart.

> *They exit [except for* **Montague**, **Lady Montague**,
> *and* **Benvolio**.]

Montague

Who set this ancient quarrel new abroach? [4]
nearby Speak, nephew. Were you by° when it began?

Benvolio

Here were the servants of your adversary,   100
before And yours, close fighting [5] ere° I did approach.
I drew to part them. In the instant came
bad tempers The fiery Tybalt, with his sword prepared,
Which, as he breathed defiance to my ears,
He swung about his head and cut the winds,   105
Which Who,° nothing hurt withal, hissed him in scorn. [6]
While we were interchanging thrusts and blows,
Came more and more and fought on part and part, [7]
Till the Prince came, who parted either part. [8]

Lady Montague

Oh, where is Romeo? Saw you him today?   110
fight Right glad I am he was not at this fray.°

1 *before the worshipped sun / Peered forth the golden window of the east*

In Benvolio's metaphor, the sun appears at the eastern horizon as a lady might appear at and peer from her window, peering (or appearing) in order to see and to be seen.

2 *drive*

I.e., drove, but an older form of the past tense, pronounced "driv"

3 *sycamore*

A tree frequently associated with the unfortunate in love (perhaps punning on sick-amour)

4 *I, measuring his affections by my own, / Which then most sought where most might not be found*

I.e., I estimated that his mood, like mine, led him to avoid the company of others at that time.

5 *all so*

Just as

6 *Aurora's*

The Roman goddess of the dawn

7 *heavy*

Dejected; gloomy

8 *Black and portentous must this humor prove*

I.e., something bad will inevitably come from his present mood. Romeo's black or melancholy *humor* suggests that he might be suffering from a condition referred to in the period as *erotomania*, or love madness. A typical account of this malady appears in Jacques Ferrand's treatise *Erotomania* (1623; tr. English 1640), which describes how love enters through the eyes and assails the heart, deranging its victim's reason and causing him to cry, weep, gasp, speak incoherently, and seek solitude. Although Romeo's idolization of Rosaline might seem to be "cured" by his more genuine romantic love for Juliet, a contemporary audience might have regarded the young lovers' antisocial and ultimately self-destructive passion as evidence of mental instability. In *The Anatomy of Melancholy* (1621), an encyclopedic analysis of the different causes and effects of melancholy, Robert Burton cites Romeo and Juliet as examples of love melancholics driven to suicide by this psychological malady.

9 *importuned him*

Urged him (to reveal the cause of his sadness)

Benvolio

Madam, an hour before the worshipped sun

Peered forth the golden window of the east,[1]   *dawn*

outdoors A troubled mind drive[2] me to walk abroad,°

Where, underneath the grove of sycamore[3]   115

grows   That westward rooteth° from this city side,

So early walking did I see your son.   *Romeo wanted to*

aware   Towards him I made, but he was ware° of me   *be alone*

hiding place And stole into the covert° of the wood.

I, measuring his affections by my own,   120

Which then most sought where most might not be found,[4]

Being one too many by my weary self,

mood   Pursued my humor,° not pursuing his,

him who And gladly shunned who° gladly fled from me.

Montague

Many a morning hath he there been seen,   125

With tears augmenting the fresh morning's dew,

Adding to clouds more clouds with his deep sighs.

But all so[5] soon as the all-cheering sun

Should in the farthest east begin to draw   *Romeo is*

The shady curtains from Aurora's[6] bed,   *depressed* 130

Away from light steals home my heavy[7] son

And private in his chamber pens himself,

Shuts up his windows, locks fair daylight out,

And makes himself an artificial night.

Black and portentous must this humor prove,[8]   135

Unless good counsel may the cause remove.

Benvolio

My noble uncle, do you know the cause?

Montague

I neither know it nor can learn of him.

Benvolio

Have you importuned him[9] by any means?

1   *bit with an envious worm*

    **Destroyed from within by a
    malicious grub or bug**

2   *same*

    **Many editors amend this to "sun,"
    but Renaissance gardening texts
    regularly note the importance of
    good air for successful growing.**

3   *I'll know his grievance or be much
    denied.*

    **I'll find out what's troubling him or
    force him to refuse directly to tell
    me.**

4   *But new*

    Just now

Montague

Both by myself and many other friends,   140

But he, his own affections' counselor,

i.e., wisely   Is to himself—I will not say how true,°

hidden   But to himself so secret and so close,°

vestigation/disclosure   So far from sounding° and discovery,°

As is the bud bit with an envious worm [1]

it/petals   Ere he° can spread his sweet leaves° to the air   145

Or dedicate his beauty to the same. [2]

Could we but learn from whence his sorrows grow,

We would as willingly give cure as know.

Enter **Romeo**.

Benvolio

See where he comes. So please you, step aside.   150

I'll know his grievance or be much denied. [3]

Montague

wish/fortunate   I would° thou wert so happy° by thy stay

confession   To hear true shrift.°—Come, madam, let's away.

[**Montague** *and* **Lady Montague**] *exit.*

Benvolio

morning   Good morrow,° cousin.

Romeo

Is the day so young?

Benvolio

But new [4] struck nine.

Romeo

Ay me! Sad hours seem long.   155

Was that my father that went hence so fast?

Benvolio

It was. What sadness lengthens Romeo's hours?

1　*love, so gentle in his view, / Should be so tyrannous and rough in proof*

Love, which is so calm and sweet tempered in appearance, turns out to be domineering and harsh when it is experienced.

2　*love, whose view is muffled still*

I.e., Cupid, whose eyes are always blindfolded. Cupid, the classical god of love, was traditionally depicted as a young, winged boy who was blind or blindfolded. His inability to see was often interpreted as an emblem of the irrational passion.

3　*see pathways to his will*

See ways to realize his (Cupid's) desires (by making human beings fall in love).

4　*Here's much to do with hate but more with love.*

I.e., the two families are responsible for this recent street brawl but, more importantly, also for my love (since Rosaline is a Capulet; see 1.2.70 and 84).

5　*O brawling love, O loving hate, / O anything of nothing first created*

Romeo's oxymora (conjoined opposites such as *loving hate*) were a staple of 16th-century love poetry and identify him as a conventional lover in the Petrarchan

tradition. The 14th-century Italian poet Francesco Petrarca ("Petrarch" in English) was widely known in England primarily for his sonnets, which were addressed to the idealized Laura. The conventions of Petrarchan poetry, many of which are manifested by Romeo, include the male lover's distant adoration of a chaste woman who embodies all the beauties of the universe (hence, the endless comparisons of her features to flowers, stars, perfumes, angels, gold, precious stones, and so on); the definition of genuine love as a divinely inspired passion for the beloved's perfection, not as a desire for sexual consummation; and the lover's experience of his intense passion in terms of illness, religious worship, or war. (See Longer Note on page 329.)

6　*Misshapen chaos of well-seeming forms*

A *chaos* (a disordered mass) made up of *well-seeming forms* (i.e., beautiful objects) is a powerful symbol of sensory confusion, expressive of Romeo's difficulty in understanding what he feels and perceives.

7　*This love feel I, that feel no love in this.*

I.e., I feel this love for Rosaline, but not for this brawling.

Romeo

Not having that, which, having, makes them short.

Benvolio

In love?

Romeo

Out.   160

Benvolio

Of love?

Romeo

with whom   Out of her favor where° I am in love.

He loves someone who doesn't love him back

Benvolio

Alas, that love, so gentle in his view,

Should be so tyrannous and rough in proof. [1]

Romeo

Alas, that love, whose view is muffled still, [2]   165

Should, without eyes, see pathways to his will. [3]

Where shall we dine? O me! What fray was here?

Yet tell me not, for I have heard it all.

Oxymorons

Here's much to do with hate but more with love. [4]

Why then, O brawling love, O loving hate,   170

O anything of nothing first created! [5]

O heavy lightness, serious vanity,

Misshapen chaos of well-seeming forms! [6]

Feather of lead, bright smoke, cold fire, sick health,

Permanently wakeful   Still-waking° sleep that is not what it is!   175

This love feel I, that feel no love in this. [7]

Dost thou not laugh?

Benvolio

cousin (kinsman)   No, coz,° I rather weep.

Romeo

Good heart, at what?

Benvolio

affliction   At thy good heart's oppression.°

1   *Which thou wilt propagate to have it*
    pressed / With more of thine

    I.e., the burden of your concern for
    me only only makes my own
    troubles multiply.

2   *A choking gall, and a preserving sweet*

    I.e., a bitter thing that proves fatal,
    and a sweet thing that sustains

3   *An if*

    If

4   *in sadness*

    Romeo plays on Benvolio's use of
    the phrase in line 193, but here it
    means also: (1) in earnest; and (2)
    unhappily.

5   *A word ill urged to one that is so ill*

    Romeo charges Benvolio with
    insensitively using the word *sadness*
    (in line 193) to Romeo, who is
    seriously lovesick.

6   *aimed so near*

    Figured as much (said sarcastically)

Romeo

Why, such is love's transgression.

Griefs of mine own lie heavy in my breast, 180

Which thou wilt propagate to have it pressed

With more of thine. [1] This love that thou hast shown

Doth add more grief to too much of mine own.

vapor Love is a smoke made with the fume° of sighs: Metaphor

purified Being purged,° a fire sparkling in lovers' eyes; 185

agitated Being vexed,° a sea nourished with loving tears.

judicious What is it else? A madness most discreet,°

A choking gall, and a preserving sweet. [2]

Farewell, my coz.

Benvolio

Wait   Soft!° I will go along.

An if [3] you leave me so, you do me wrong. 190

Romeo

Tut, I have lost myself; I am not here.

This is not Romeo; he's some other where. He's not himself

Benvolio

all seriousness Tell me, in sadness,° who is that you love.

Romeo

What? Shall I groan and tell thee?

Benvolio

Groan? Why, no. But sadly tell me who. 195

Romeo

A sick man in sadness [4] makes his will,

A word ill urged to one that is so ill. [5]

In sadness, cousin, I do love a woman.

Benvolio

I aimed so near [6] when I supposed you loved.

Romeo

A right good markman! And she's fair I love. 200

1   *fair mark*

A worthy target, although *fair* also means "beautiful," while *mark* can refer to the female genitals.

2   *Dian's wit*

I.e., she possesses the wisdom and skill associated with the goddess Diana. Diana was the Roman deity of the hunt and of chastity and would therefore not be easily tricked by a pursuing suitor.

3   *th' encounter of assailing eyes*

Romeo uses military language here. An *encounter* is an armed clash, and the lover's eyes *assail* the lady just as troops would attempt to overthrow a guarded fortress.

4   *Nor ope her lap to saint-seducing gold*

Romeo alludes to the classical myth of Danaë, a mortal woman impregnated when Jove, king of the gods, came to her as a shower of gold poured in her lap.

5   *her store*

I.e., everything that she possesses

6   *in that sparing makes huge waste*

A paradox: by being *sparing* (thrifty) with her sexuality, Rosaline wastes her own beauty by preventing it from being passed on to succeeding generations.

7   *'Tis the way / To call hers, exquisite, in question more.*

It (i.e., looking at other women) would serve only to bring her extraordinary beauty more into his thoughts.

8   *fortunate masks*

I.e., lucky masks. Aristocratic women often wore masks at public events (as at the party in 1.5) to hide their features; Romeo considers those masks *happy* because of their physical intimacy with the women they conceal.

Benvolio

A right fair mark, [1] fair coz, is soonest hit.

Romeo

Well, in that hit you miss. She'll not be hit

With Cupid's arrow. She hath Dian's wit, [2]

armor   And, in strong proof° of chastity well armed,

i.e., Cupid's / unaffected   From love's° weak, childish bow she lives uncharmed.°   205

undergo   She will not stay° the siege of loving terms,

endure   Nor bide° th' encounter of assailing eyes, [3]

Nor ope her lap to saint-seducing gold. [4]

Oh, she is rich in beauty, only poor

That when she dies, with beauty dies her store. [5]   210

Benvolio

always   Then she hath sworn that she will still° live chaste?

Romeo

She hath, and in that sparing makes huge waste, [6]

For beauty, starved with her severity,

future generations   Cuts beauty off from all posterity.°

She is too fair, too wise, wisely too fair,   215

Heaven   To merit bliss° by making me despair.

sworn not   She hath forsworn° to love, and in that vow

Do I live dead that live to tell it now.

Benvolio

Be ruled by me: forget to think of her.

Romeo

Oh, teach me how I should forget to think.   220

Benvolio

By giving liberty unto thine eyes;

Examine other beauties.

Romeo

'Tis the way

To call hers, exquisite, in question more. [7]

These fortunate masks [8] that kiss fair ladies' brows,

1   *puts us in mind*

    Suggest to us

2   *a note / Where I may read who passed*

    that passing fair

    I.e., a reminder of the beauty
    (Rosaline) who surpasses all other
    beautiful women.

3   *I'll pay that doctrine or else die in debt.*

    I.e., I'll teach you that (how to
    forget) or else I will die still trying.
    Benvolio puns on *pay* and *debt*,
    which was pronounced the same as
    "death."

Being black, puts us in mind [1] they hide the fair.   225

struck   He that is strucken° blind cannot forget

The precious treasure of his eyesight lost.

woman/surpassingly   Show me a mistress° that is passing° fair;

What doth her beauty serve but as a note

Where I may read who passed that passing fair? [2]   230

Farewell. Thou canst not teach me to forget.

Benvolio

I'll pay that doctrine or else die in debt. [3]   *They exit.*

Reminds him of Rosaline

1   County

Count

2   *in penalty alike*

With the same liability for violations

3   *But saying o'er*

Only saying again

4   *fourteen years*

Juliet would be young to be married, even by early modern standards. In England, women were not usually married before they were in their early twenties, but see 1.3.71–75.

5   *wither in their pride*

I.e., pass (but compare his eagerness to have her married in 3.4.19–22)

6   *the hopeful lady of my earth*

I.e., the repository of all his earthly hopes, and the heiress of his lands and holdings (death having claimed all his other heirs, see 1.2.14)

7   *within her scope of choice, / Lies my consent and fair according voice*

I.e., my approval goes along with her decision. (For more information on marriage in Elizabethan England, See LONGER NOTE on page 330.)

8   *an old accustomed feast*

It is not entirely clear which traditional (*old accustomed*) feast day Capulet has in mind, but it is a summer celebration, near Lammastide, which was celebrated August 1 (see 1.3.16 and note).

9   *Earth-treading stars*

Referring figuratively to the beautiful women who will attend the feast

Act 1, Scene 2

Enter **Capulet**, *County* [1] **Paris**, *and* [*a servingman*].

Capulet

i.e., to keep the peace   But Montague is bound° as well as I,

In penalty alike, [2] and 'tis not hard, I think,

For men so old as we to keep the peace.

Paris

reputation   Of honorable reckoning° are you both,

And pity 'tis you lived at odds so long.   5

But now, my lord, what say you to my suit?

Capulet

But saying o'er [3] what I have said before.

still   My child is yet° a stranger in the world:

passage   She hath not seen the change° of fourteen years. [4]

Let two more summers wither in their pride [5]   10

Ere we may think her ripe to be a bride.

Paris

Younger than she are happy mothers made.

Capulet

ruined   And too soon marred° are those so early made.

Earth hath swallowed all my hopes but she;

She's the hopeful lady of my earth. [6]   15

But woo her, gentle Paris; get her heart.

My will to her consent is but a part.

consenting   And she agreed,° within her scope of choice,

Lies my consent and fair according voice. [7]

This night I hold an old accustomed feast, [8]   20

Whereto I have invited many a guest

number   Such as I love; and you among the store,°

One more, most welcome, makes my number more.

At my poor house look to behold this night

Earth-treading stars [9] that make dark heaven light.   25

1   *Such comfort as do lusty young men feel /*
     When well-appareled April on the heel /
     Of limping winter treads
     **I.e., the kind of pleasure that
     strong youths feel when the slow-
     passing winter months finally give
     way to the beauties of spring**

2   *fresh fennel buds*
     **Some editors print "fresh female
     buds" (as in Q1). *Fennel* is an herb
     with a light, licorice-like taste and
     a spicy aroma; the dried seeds were
     used to freshen breath. Capulet
     seems to use this phrase to evoke
     the pleasant sensory atmosphere
     of his coming feast and to remind
     Paris that many young women will
     be present there.**

3   *Which one more view of many, mine,*
     being one, / May stand in number,
     though in reckoning none
     **I.e., when you see so many young
     women arrayed together, my
     daughter, being one of them, may
     seem worthy of special
     consideration, though as *one* alone
     she isn't (numerically speaking)
     worth much. ("One is no number"
     was proverbial.)**

4   *sirrah*
     **A term of address usually
     reserved for someone of a lower
     social status.**

5   *Find them out whose names are written*
     here?
     **The servingman is unable to read,
     and therefore can't perform the
     errand Capulet has assigned him.**

6   *meddle with his yard*
     **Busy himself with his measuring
     rod. (*Yard* and *last* are euphemisms
     for penis, but the joke is also that
     in each case, the workers are
     inappropriately matched with the
     tools of their trade.)**

7   *last*
     **A wooden model of the foot, used
     for making shoes**

8   *in good time*
     **(1) "at once"; (2) [upon seeing
     Benvolio and Romeo] "and here
     they are—just at the right time!"**

9   *Turn giddy and be holp by backward*
     turning
     **I.e., if you've spun around so much
     that you're dizzy, correct it by
     spinning in the opposite direction.**

10   *cures with*
     Is cured by

11   *another's languish*
     **I.e., the pain arising from a
     different grief**

Such comfort as do lusty young men feel

When well-appareled April on the heel

Of limping winter treads, [1] even such delight

Among fresh fennel buds [2] shall you this night

Receive Inherit° at my house. Hear all, all see,   30

And like her most whose merit most shall be—

Which one more view of many, mine, being one,

May stand in number, though in reckoning none. [3]

Come, go with me.   [*to* **Servingman**, *giving him paper*]

walk   Go, sirrah, [4] trudge° about

Through fair Verona, find those persons out   35

Whose names are written there, and to them say

wait My house and welcome on their pleasure stay.°

                                   [**Capulet** *and* **Paris**] *exit.*

Servingman

Find them out whose names are written here? [5] It is

written that the shoemaker should meddle with his

yard [6] and the tailor with his last, [7] the fisher with his   40

paintbrush pencil° and the painter with his nets, but I am sent to

find those persons whose names are here writ and can

never find what names the writing person hath here

writ. I must to the learnèd in good time! [8]

                    Enter **Benvolio** *and* **Romeo**.

Benvolio

Tut, man, one fire burns out another's burning;   45

One pain is lessened by another's anguish.

helped Turn giddy and be holp° by backward turning; [9]

One desperate grief cures with [10] another's languish. [11]

Take thou some new infection to thy eye,

And the rank poison of the old will die.   50

1   *For your broken shin.*

The sense of Romeo's comment is that Benvolio has prescribed an inadequate remedy for a serious problem (plantain leaves were supposed to make good bandages for minor wounds). Having a *broken shin* didn't mean having a broken shinbone, but only that one's lower leg had been solidly bashed, i.e., a painful but not truly incapacitating experience.

2   *Good e'en*

Good evening (used anytime after noon)

3   *God gi' good e'en.*

God give you a good evening.

4   *without book*

I.e., from experience (not from a book).

5   *Rest you merry.*

The servingman misinterprets Romeo's joke as a confession of illiteracy, so he starts to leave.

Romeo

Your plantain leaf is excellent for that.

Benvolio

For what, I pray thee?

Romeo

For your broken shin. [1]

Benvolio

Why Romeo, art thou mad?

Romeo

confined Not mad, but bound° more than a madman is:

Shut up in prison, kept without my food,   55

Whipped and tormented and—Good e'en, [2] good fellow.

Servingman

God gi' good e'en. [3] I pray, sir, can you read?

Romeo

Ay, mine own fortune in my misery.

Servingman

Perhaps you have learned it without book. [4] But I pray,

can you read anything you see?   60

Romeo

Ay, if I know the letters and the language.

Servingman

speak Ye say° honestly. Rest you merry. [5]

Romeo

Stay, fellow. I can read. (*He reads the letter.*)

"Signior Martino and his wife and daughters;

County Anselme and his beauteous sisters;   65

The lady widow of Utruvio;

Signor Placentio and his lovely nieces;

Mercutio and his brother Valentine;

Mine uncle Capulet, his wife and daughters;

My fair niece Rosaline and Livia;   70

Signior Valentio and his cousin Tybalt;

1   *Up.*

"Come up" was an expression
indicating amused disdain. The
servingman perhaps repays Romeo
for his earlier wordplay on the
subject of reading, or perhaps *up* is
his proud indication of the nobility
of Capulet's house (anticipating
1.2.80–81).

2   *When the devout religion of mine eye /*
Maintains such falsehood, then turn
tears to fire, / And these, who, often
drowned, could never die, / Transparent
heretics, be burnt for liars.

A complex passage with the
artificial religious language of
much 16th-century love poetry:
i.e., "If my belief in the excellence
of Rosaline should change, then
may my tears turn to fire, and may
my eyes (which have often been
flooded, but not harmed, with
tears), then burn like heretics who
are burned at the stake."

Lucio and the lively Helena."

Where   A fair assembly. Whither° should they come?

Servingman

Up.[1]

Romeo

Whither? To supper?   75

Servingman

To our house.

Romeo

Whose house?

Servingman

My master's.

Romeo

Indeed, I should have asked you that before.

Servingman

Now I'll tell you without asking: my master is the great rich   80
Capulet, and, if you be not of the house of Montagues,

drink   I pray come and crush° a cup of wine. Rest you merry!

[*He exits.*]

Irony

If you aren't that

Benvolio

At this same ancient feast of Capulet's

Sups the fair Rosaline whom thou so loves,

With all the admired beauties of Verona.   85

unbiased   Go thither, and with unattainted° eye

Compare her face with some that I shall show,

And I will make thee think thy swan a crow.

Look at all the girls who will be there and compare them to Rosaline

Rosaline

Romeo

When the devout religion of mine eye

Maintains such falsehood, then turn tears to fire,   90

And these, who, often drowned, could never die,

Transparent heretics, be burnt for liars.[2]

One fairer than my love? The all-seeing sun

Ne'er saw her match since first the world begun.

No one is better than Rosaline

1   *you saw her fair, none else being by*
    **You thought she was beautiful
    because you had nothing with
    which to compare her.**

Benvolio

Tut, you saw her fair, none else being by, [1]   95

weighed — Herself poised° with herself in either eye.

i.e., your eyes — But in that crystal scales° let there be weighed

Your lady's love against some other maid

That I will show you shining at this feast,

barely — And she shall scant° show well that now seems best.   100

Romeo

I'll go along, no such sight to be shown,

i.e., Rosaline — But to rejoice in splendor of mine own.°   [*They exit.*]

[handwritten] I'll go just not for the women

1 *by my maidenhead at twelve year old*

   The Nurse swears by the virginity
   she possessed when she was
   twelve years old (presumably lost
   by the time she was thirteen).

2 *give leave awhile*

   I.e., leave us alone.

3 *a pretty age*

   (1) an age worthy of consideration
   (as an adult); (2) a pleasing age

4 *How long is it now to Lammas-tide?*

   Juliet was born on *Lammas Eve* at
   night, or July 31, when the sun is in
   the sign of the constellation Leo.
   According to Renaissance
   astrological lore, people born
   under the sign of Leo were likely to
   have passionate natures.
   Depending on how much weight
   we give to the notion that the
   play's protagonists are influenced
   by the stars, some degree of Juliet's
   passionate behavior might be
   attributed to her birth in July, an
   origin reflected in her name. The
   play itself is set a few weeks before
   Lammastide, in the *hot days* of July,
   when, as Benvolio warns, the *mad
   blood* [is] *stirring* (3.1.4).

5 *A fortnight and odd days.*

   I.e., two weeks and a few days. In
   the next sentence the Nurse
   understands *odd* as the opposite of
   even.

Act 1, Scene 3

Enter [**Lady Capulet**] *and* **Nurse**.

Lady Capulet

Nurse, where's my daughter? Call her forth to me.

Nurse

Just now Now,° by my maidenhead at twelve year old, [1]

Come I bade her come. —What,° lamb! What, ladybird!

God forbid! —Where's this girl? —What, Juliet!

Enter **Juliet**.

Juliet

How now, who calls?   5

Nurse

Your mother.

Juliet

Madam, I am here. What is your will?

Lady Capulet

This is the matter.—Nurse, give leave awhile, [2]

We must talk in secret.—Nurse, come back again.

thou shalt I have remembered me. Thou's° hear our counsel.   10

Thou knowest my daughter's of a pretty age. [3]

Nurse

Faith, I can tell her age unto an hour.

Lady Capulet

She's not fourteen.

Nurse

irritation I'll lay fourteen of my teeth—and yet, to my teen° be it

spoken, I have but four—she's not fourteen. How long   15

is it now to Lammas-tide? [4]

Lady Capulet

A fortnight and odd days. [5]

1 *Susan*

   Susan must have been the Nurse's daughter, who was born at the same time as Juliet but died, probably in infancy, before the play's action commences.

2 *wormwood*

   A medicinal plant with an unpleasant taste used to wean babies from nursing.

3 *Nay, I do bear a brain.*

   I.e., I've got a good memory.

4 *fool*

   Here, an affectionate term

5 *And she was weaned … fall out with the dug!*

   The Nurse's account of Juliet's infancy provides some perspective on the emotional distance that characterizes the adolescent girl's relationship with her parents. The Nurse and her husband served as surrogate parents for Juliet, who in turn served as a surrogate daughter for them. On the memorable day of Juliet's weaning, her parents are notably absent, sojourning in Mantua, the city to which Romeo flees after his banishment.

6 *"Shake!" quoth the dovehouse. 'Twas no need, I trow, / To bid me trudge.*

   I.e., the dovehouse shook (in an earthquake); you can bet that no one needed to tell me to get out of there quickly. This seems to refer to an earthquake that took place on that day, and scholars have attempted to date the writing of the play or the action it represents on that basis. The reference is too vague, however, to allow a convincing date to be established from her recollection.

7 *by th'rood*

   An oath, meaning "by the cross"

8 *broke her brow*

   Hurt her forehead

9 *fall backward*

   I.e., lie on her back in order to engage in sexual intercourse

Nurse

    Even or odd, of all days in the year,

    Come Lammas Eve at night shall she be fourteen.

    Susan[1] and she—God rest all Christian souls!—   20

    Were of an age. Well, Susan is with God;

    She was too good for me. But, as I said,

    On Lammas Eve at night shall she be fourteen;

    That shall she. Marry, I remember it well.

    'Tis since the earthquake now eleven years,   25

    And she was weaned—I never shall forget it—

    Of all the days of the year, upon that day.

breast   For I had then laid wormwood[2] to my dug,°

    Sitting in the sun under the dovehouse wall.

    My lord and you were then at Mantua.   30

    Nay, I do bear a brain.[3] But, as I said,

i.e., Juliet   When it° did taste the wormwood on the nipple

    Of my dug and felt it bitter, pretty fool,[4]

fretful   To see it tetchy° and fall out with the dug![5]

    "Shake!" quoth the dovehouse. 'Twas no need, I trow, 35

    To bid me trudge.[6]

    And since that time it is eleven years,

upright   For then she could stand high° 'lone. Nay, by th' rood,[7]

    She could have run and waddled all about,

    For even the day before, she broke her brow.[8]   40

    And then my husband—God be with his soul,

He   'A° was a merry man—took up the child.

    "Yea," quoth he, "Dost thou fall upon thy face?

    Thou wilt fall backward[9] when thou hast more wit,

holiness   Wilt thou not, Jule?" and, by my halidam,°   45

stopped   The pretty wretch left° crying and said "ay."

i.e., true   To see now how a jest shall come about!°

if   I warrant, an° I should live a thousand years,

    I never should forget it. "Wilt thou not, Jule?" quoth he.

1   *How stands your dispositions to be*
    married?

    **What do you think about being
    married?**

2   *hour*

    **I.e., moment, time. Q1 (1597)
    prints "honor," and many editors
    follow this, but *hour* makes
    reasonable sense and is used by
    Shakespeare elsewhere with this
    meaning. The Nurse's enthusiasm
    for the word in line 69 is probably a
    bawdy response to imagining an
    hour in the marital bed.**

3   *thy teat*

    **I.e., from the breast you suckled
    from.**

4   *much upon these years*

    At about the same age

ceased (crying)   And, pretty fool, it stinted° and said "ay."   50

Lady Capulet

Enough of this. I pray thee, hold thy peace.

Nurse

Yes, madam, yet I cannot choose but laugh

she   To think it° should leave crying and say "ay."

i.e., its (her)   And yet, I warrant, it had upon it° brow

testicle   A bump as big as a young cock'rel's stone,°   55

A perilous knock, and it cried bitterly.

"Yea," quoth my husband, "fall'st upon thy face?

Thou wilt fall backward when thou comest to age,

Wilt thou not, Jule?" It stinted and said "ay."

Juliet

And stint thou too, I pray thee, Nurse, say I.   60

Nurse

Peace, I have done. God mark thee to his grace,

Thou wast the prettiest babe that e'er I nursed.

If   An° I might live to see thee married once,

I have my wish.

Lady Capulet

Marry, that "marry" is the very theme   65

I came to talk of. Tell me, daughter Juliet,

How stands your dispositions to be married?[1]

Juliet

It is an hour[2] that I dream not of.

Nurse

An hour! Were not I thine only nurse,

I would say thou hadst sucked wisdom from thy teat.[3]   70

Lady Capulet

Well, think of marriage now. Younger than you

Here in Verona, ladies of esteem

Are made already mothers. By my count,

I was your mother much upon these years[4]

1   *a man of wax*

    I.e., a man as perfectly made as you could hope for. Wax was easy to sculpt and therefore conformed quickly to the artist's wishes.

2   *Read o'er the volume of young Paris' face*

    Lady Capulet embarks upon an extended comparison between Paris and an unbound, beautifully handwritten book.

3   *married lineament*

    I.e., harmoniously unified feature

4   *how one another lends content*

    How one (feature), when paired with the other, produces delight

5   *the margin of his eyes*

    Medieval and early modern books, both in print and in manuscript, often included annotations in the margins, which explained difficult points in the main body of the text. Here, we are led to understand that Paris's eyes will, like textual annotations, explain anything that Juliet finds difficult to understand about her would-be suitor.

6   *unbound*

    (1) lacking a binding or cover; (2) unpledged; available for marriage

7   *'tis much pride / For fair without the fair within to hide*

    I.e., it is the best situation when that which is beautiful externally (Juliet, the *fair without*) covers that which is beautiful internally (Paris, the *fair within*); a book so bound exists in its natural habitat, like the *fish* that *lives in the sea* (1.3.91).

8   *That book in many's eyes doth share the glory / That in gold clasps locks in the golden story.*

    I.e., books are judged according to the richness of their clasps and bindings, as well as by the value of the text that lies within (the *golden story*). Lady Capulet is implying that Juliet's beauty (representing the covering of the book) would be as important a factor in the marriage as Paris's status and personality (representing the text, or *story*), a revealing metaphor for her sense of proper gender relations.

9   *Nay, bigger.*

    Referring to the swelling of a woman's belly during pregnancy (a typically bawdy interjection from the Nurse)

10 *like of*

    Find appealing

That you are now a maid. Thus then in brief: 75
The valiant Paris seeks you for his love.
Nurse

A man, young lady! Lady, such a man
As all the world! Why, he's a man of wax.[1] *Perfect*
Lady Capulet

Verona's summer hath not such a flower.
Nurse

Nay, he's a flower, in faith, a very flower.   80
Lady Capulet

What say you? Can you love the gentleman?
This night you shall behold him at our feast.
Read o'er the volume of young Paris' face[2]
And find delight writ there with beauty's pen.
Examine every married lineament[3]   85
And see how one another lends content,[4]
And what obscured in this fair volume lies
Find written in the margin of his eyes.[5]
This precious book of love, this unbound[6] lover,
To beautify him only lacks a cover.   90
The fish lives in the sea, and 'tis much pride
For fair without the fair within to hide.[7]
That book in many's eyes doth share the glory
That in gold clasps locks in the golden story.[8]
So shall you share all that he doth possess   95
By having him, making yourself no less.
Nurse *pregnancy*

No less? Nay, bigger.[9] Women grow by men.
Lady Capulet

Speak briefly: can you like of[10] Paris' love?
Juliet   *I'll check him*
I'll look to like if looking liking move.   *out if you want*

1 *But no more deep will I endart mine eye /*
   Than your consent gives strength to
   make it fly.

   I.e., I won't seriously contemplate
   this courtship unless you decide
   that you approve of the match. It is
   a nice irony that Juliet goes to the
   party to see Paris and that Romeo
   goes to see Rosaline (1.2.101–102).

2 *the Nurse cursed in the pantry*

   I.e., the kitchen workers are angry
   at the Nurse for failing to perform
   some household duty.

3 *I must hence to wait.*

   I.e., I have to go start serving food.

But no more deep will I endart mine eye   100
Than your consent gives strength to make it fly. [1]

Enter **Serving[man]**.

Servingman

Madam, the guests are come, supper served up, you
called, my young lady asked for, the Nurse cursed in the
crisis   pantry, [2] and everything in extremity.° I must hence to
at once wait. [3] I beseech you, follow straight.°   [*He exits.*]   105

Lady Capulet

awaits We follow thee.—Juliet, the County stays.°

Nurse

Go, girl; seek happy nights to happy days.   *They exit.*

1   maskers [and] torchbearers

The maskers and torchbearers are the partygoers, wearing masks—which give Romeo the opportunity to enter the Capulet household anonymously—and carrying torches to light their way.

2   *this speech*

Apparently Romeo and his friends have prepared a speech apologizing for their uninvited appearance.

3   *The date is out of such prolixity.*

I.e., such long-windedness is no longer fashionable.

4   *We'll have no Cupid hoodwinked with a scarf, / Bearing a Tartar's painted bow of lath*

Benvolio says that their speech of introduction should not be a tedious presentation like the prologue to some old play delivered by a blindfolded Cupid with his wooden bow.

5   *We'll measure them a measure*

I.e., we'll provide them a dance.

6   *soar with them above a common bound*

Mercutio encourages Romeo to use Cupid's wings to dance more vigorously than any of the other maskers. A *bound* was a leap, an ordinary element of courtly dance; but a *bound* was also a *limit*, and in this sense Mercutio's comment foreshadows Romeo's future as an unusually intrepid (and tragic) lover.

7   *too sore enpiercèd with his shaft*

I.e., too badly wounded by Cupid's arrow; *sore* puns on *soar* in the previous line.

8   *light*

Punning on *light* exists throughout this exchange, with meanings ranging from "not heavy," "easy," and "joyful" to "worthless" and "immoral."

Act 1, Scene 4

Enter **Romeo**, **Mercutio**, **Benvolio**, *with five or six other maskers [and] torchbearers.* [1]

Romeo

What? Shall this speech [2] be spoke for our excuse,
Or shall we on without apology?

Benvolio

The date is out of such prolixity. [3]
blindfolded We'll have no Cupid hoodwinked° with a scarf,
Bearing a Tartar's painted bow of lath, [4]   5
scarecrow Scaring the ladies like a crowkeeper,°
But let them measure us by what they will.
We'll measure them a measure [5] and be gone.

Romeo

way of walking Give me a torch. I am not for this ambling.°
gloomy Being but heavy,° I will bear the light.   10

Mercutio

noble Nay, gentle° Romeo, we must have you dance.

Romeo

Not I, believe me. You have dancing shoes
With nimble soles; I have a soul of lead
So stakes me to the ground I cannot move.

Mercutio

You are a lover. Borrow Cupid's wings   15
And soar with them above a common bound. [6]

Romeo

I am too sore empiercèd with his shaft [7]
To soar with his light [8] feathers, and, so bound,
height I cannot bound a pitch° above dull woe.
Under love's heavy burden do I sink.   20

1   *And to sink in it, should you burden love—/*
    Too great oppression for a tender thing.

    (1) if you allow yourself to be weighed
    down and to sink into love (as if it were
    an ocean) you will be overburdening
    love with your inert body; (2) if you allow
    yourself to sink onto your partner during
    the act of love, you will be putting too
    much weight on her (and particularly
    onto her genitals, the *tender thing*).

2   *If love be rough with you, be rough with love. /*
    Prick love for pricking, and you beat love down.

    In response to Romeo's complaint that
    Cupid is rough and *pricks like thorn,*
    Mercutio tells his friend to prick love
    back. Mercutio seems to be advising,
    through an obscene image of Romeo
    sexually penetrating Cupid, that Romeo
    release his sexual frustration either with
    Rosaline, or, as the male figure of Cupid
    suggests, with another young man. To
    beat love down refers to the detumescence
    following an orgasm.

3   *case*

    "Cover" or "mask," but can also mean
    "vagina"

4   *beetle brows*

    Projecting eyebrows. Mercutio's mask
    apparently features heavy eyebrows
    and red cheeks.

5   *betake him to his legs*

    Start to dance

6   *rushes*

    Reeds, the stalks of a common marsh
    plant, used as a floor covering

7   *I am proverbed with a grandsire phrase*

    I.e., I am accurately described by an
    old saying.

8   *I'll be a candle-holder and look on. / The*
    game was ne'er so fair, and I am done.

    Both proverbial: "I'll observe my
    limitations and stay safe on the sidelines.
    It's best to quit while you're ahead."

9   *Tut, dun's the mouse, the constable's own word.*

    Mercutio plays impatiently on
    Romeo's use of the word *done*
    (finished). *Dun's the mouse* literally
    means "the mouse is earth toned and
    unnoticeable," which as a proverb
    means to "keep quiet." A *constable* is a
    local law-enforcement official.
    Therefore the sense of this line is: "For
    shame—you say you're *done*? Keep
    quiet, as the constable says."

10 *If thou art dun, we'll draw thee from the*
    mire, / Or—save your reverence—love,
    wherein thou stickest

    A further pun on *done.* The game of
    dun-in-the-mire required players to pull
    and lift a heavy log. Mercutio suggests
    that he and Benvolio will pull Romeo
    out of the mire of love, while *save your*
    reverence is a mock apology for
    mentioning the word *love.*

Mercutio

And to sink in it, should you burden love—

Too great oppression for a tender thing. [1]

Romeo

Is love a tender thing? It is too rough,

stabs   Too rude, too boisterous, and it pricks° like thorn.

Mercutio

If love be rough with you, be rough with love.   25

Prick love for pricking, and you beat love down. [2]

face   Give me a case[3] to put my visage° in!

disguise / ugly face   A visor° for a visor.° What care I

notice   What curious eye doth quote° deformities?

that shall   Here are the beetle brows[4] shall° blush for me.   30

Benvolio

Come; knock and enter. And no sooner in

Than   But° every man betake him to his legs. [5]

Romeo

pleasure seekers   A torch for me. Let wantons° light of heart

Tickle the senseless rushes[6] with their heels,

For I am proverbed with a grandsire phrase:[7]   35

I'll be a candle-holder and look on.

The game was ne'er so fair, and I am done. [8]

Mercutio

Tut, dun's the mouse, the constable's own word. [9]

If thou art dun, we'll draw thee from the mire,

Or—save your reverence—love, wherein thou

stickest[10]   40

1   *Come; we burn daylight, ho!*
    I.e., time's a-wasting!

2   *our judgment sits / Five times in that ere*
    once in our fine wits
    I.e., the truth of what we mean is
    more often arrived at through the
    use of common sense than
    through our other, more
    sophisticated tools of analysis. It is
    possible Q2's *fine* should be "five."

3   *In bed asleep*
    Romeo jokingly takes Mercutio's
    lie in 1.4.49 to mean "lie down."

4   *I see Queen Mab hath been with you*
    Mercutio's account of Queen Mab
    provides one of many thematic
    and imagistic links between *Romeo*
    and Juliet and Shakespeare's
    comedy *A Midsummer Night's Dream*,
    in which fairies serve as agents of
    human sexual desire. Queen Mab
    generates dreams that correspond
    to the desires of particular types of
    people, so that a lawyer, for
    example, will dream of legal cases
    and a soldier of battles. Yet the
    name *Queen Mab* itself emphasizes
    the prominent role dreams play in
    shaping erotic fantasies , since
    both "quean" and "mab" meant a
    promiscuous woman or whore.

Mercutio tells the story of Queen
Mab primarily to mock Romeo for
succumbing to the *vain fantasy* or
imagination that generates empty,
romantic dreams (1.4.96).
Ironically, Mercutio's verbose fairy
tale also indulges another kind of
vain fantasy, that of poetic
imagination. Romeo dismisses
Mercutio's talk as *nothing*, and
Benvolio complains that it delays
their arrival at the party (1.4.103).

5   *In shape no bigger than an agate stone*
    I.e., she is a diminutive figure, no
    larger than the tiny portraits cut
    into the agates mounted in
    seal rings.

Up to the ears. Come; we burn daylight, ho! [1]

Romeo

Nay, that's not so.

Mercutio

                I mean, sir, in delay.

We waste our lights in vain, light lights by day.

i.e., intended Take our good° meaning, for our judgment sits

Five times in that ere once in our fine wits. [2]   45

Romeo

masked ball And we mean well in going to this masque,°

act of cleverness But 'tis no wit° to go.

Mercutio

              Why, may one ask?

Romeo

last night I dreamt a dream tonight.°

Mercutio

              And so did I.

Romeo

Well, what was yours?

Mercutio

           That dreamers often lie.

Romeo

In bed asleep [3] while they do dream things true.   50

Mercutio

Oh, then, I see Queen Mab hath been with you. [4]

She is the fairies' midwife, and she comes

In shape no bigger than an agate stone [5]

On the forefinger of an alderman,

tiny creatures Drawn with a team of little atomi°   55

Over men's noses as they lie asleep.

1   *the lash of film*

The whip (is made) of a strand of a cobweb.

2   *a round little worm / Pricked from the lazy finger of a maid*

A folk warning to young women was that if they sat around idly, worms would breed in their fingers.

3   *joiner squirrel or old grub*

Carpenter squirrel or wood-boring grub

4   *Time out o' mind*

A proverbial expression meaning "for longer than anyone can remember"

5   *dream on curtsies straight*

I.e., dream immediately of bows and other courtly gestures of compliment

6   *suit*

A petition presented at court (for which the petitioner would be paid)

7   *tithe-pig's*

The pig, the tenth of the litter, which was the traditional gift of a parish to its minister

8   *benefice*

A collection of tithes and property taxes allotted to a minister by the church, in order to support him financially

9   *breaches, ambuscadoes, Spanish blades*

Holes made in defensive walls, surprise attacks, well-forged swords

10 *healths five fathom deep*

Toasts involving enormous quantities of alcohol. A *fathom* was a nautical measure of roughly six feet in depth.

spiders'	Her wagon-spokes made of long spinners'° legs,	
i.e., made of	The cover of° the wings of grasshoppers,	
reins	Her traces° of the smallest spider web,	
bridles	Her collars° of the moonshine's wat'ry beams,	60
	Her whip of cricket's bone, the lash of film, [1]	
driver	Her wagoner,° a small gray-coated gnat,	
	Not half so big as a round little worm	
	Pricked from the lazy finger of a maid. [2]	
	Her chariot is an empty hazelnut	65
	Made by the joiner squirrel or old grub, [3]	
	Time out o' mind [4] the fairies' coachmakers.	
splendor	And in this state° she gallops night by night	
	Through lovers' brains, and then they dream of love;	
	On courtiers' knees, that dream on curtsies straight; [5]	70
	O'er lawyers' fingers, who straight dream on fees;	
	O'er ladies' lips, who straight on kisses dream,	
	Which oft the angry Mab with blisters plagues,	
candies	Because their breath with sweetmeats° tainted are.	
	Sometime she gallops o'er a courtier's nose,	75
	And then dreams he of smelling out a suit. [6]	
	And sometime comes she with a tithe-pig's [7] tail,	
he	Tickling a parson's nose as 'a° lies asleep;	
	Then he dreams of another benefice. [8]	
	Sometime she driveth o'er a soldier's neck,	80
	And then dreams he of cutting foreign throats,	
	Of breaches, ambuscadoes, Spanish blades, [9]	
at once	Of healths five fathom deep, [10] and then anon°	
	Drums in his ear, at which he starts and wakes,	
	And, being thus frighted, swears a prayer or two	85
	And sleeps again. This is that very Mab	
braids	That plaits° the manes of horses in the night	
matted tangles / unclean	And bakes the elf-locks° in foul sluttish° hairs,	
	Which once untangled much misfortune bodes.	

1   *That presses them and learns them first*
    to bear

    I.e., Mab gives maidens sexual
    dreams (evoking the sensation of
    being pressed by a man's body)
    and teaches them both to bear the
    weight of their lovers and to bear
    children.

2   *of good carriage*

    (1) of good posture and manners;
    (2) well able to support the weight
    of a man; (3) well able to support
    the weight of a child in the womb;
    (4) in Queen Mab's chariot

3   *vain fantasy*

    Useless imagination

4   *blows us from ourselves*

    (1) distracts us from our present
    business (i.e., going to the
    Capulets' party); (2) unsettles our
    sense of who we are

5   *fearful date*

    Frightening interval (during which
    something exists)

6   *expire the term*

    End the allotted time

7   *some vile forfeit of untimely death*

    I.e., the unfair penalty of an early
    death

8   *hath the steerage of my course*

    Controls my fate

9   [exit].

    Some editions do not mark a scene
    break here, but it seems preferable
    to indicate the distinction between
    the revelers going to the party and
    the party itself in the following
    scene. In any case, the fluidity of
    staging in Shakespeare's theater
    would make the action seem more
    or less continuous, as Romeo and
    his friends meet up with the
    Capulets and their guests, who
    have just eaten.

This is the hag, when maids lie on their backs,   90

teaches That presses them and learns° them first to bear, [1]

Making them women of good carriage. [2]

This is she—

Romeo

                    Peace, peace, Mercutio, peace!

Thou talk'st of nothing.

Mercutio

                              True, I talk of dreams,

Which are the children of an idle brain,   95

Begot of nothing but vain fantasy, [3]

Which is as thin of substance as the air

And more inconstant than the wind, who woos

Even now the frozen bosom of the north,

And, being angered, puffs away from thence,   100

Turning his side to the dew-dropping south.

Benvolio

This wind you talk of blows us from ourselves. [4]

Supper is done, and we shall come too late.

The party might contribute to his untimely death

Romeo

worries that I fear too early, for my mind misgives°

Some consequence yet hanging in the stars   105

its Shall bitterly begin his° fearful date [5]

Foreshadowing

With this night's revels and expire the term [6]

Of a despisèd life closed in my breast

By some vile forfeit of untimely death. [7]

But he that hath the steerage of my course [8]   110

Direct my suit. On, lusty gentlemen.

Benvolio

Strike, drum.   *They march about the stage and [exit].* [9]

1   Servingmen come forth with
    napkins.

    **The beginning of Act 1, scene 5
    focuses on the busy clean up
    following Capulet's dinner.
    Romeo, Mercutio, and Benvolio
    have indeed been delayed by their
    conversation. They have missed
    the meal, and the dancing is about
    to begin.**

2   *take away*

    I.e., clear the dishes

3   *shift a trencher*

    **Remove a wooden platter from the
    table**

4   *joint-stools*

    **Stools assembled by a *joiner* or
    furniture maker**

5   *court-cupboard*

    **Movable sideboard used to store
    and display plates, tableware, and
    utensils**

6   *longer liver*

    I.e., the longest lived among us

7   Enter . . . to the Maskers

    **The exact staging of this scene is
    unclear. Q2 has Romeo enter by
    himself immediately after the
    servingmen at the beginning of the
    scene, but that seems impossible.
    This edition takes the group entry
    marked in the 1599 quarto as the
    beginning of the party. Romeo and
    the friends, together in 1.4, enter
    with other party guests and mill
    about until the family arrives and
    Capulet speaks. All are masked or
    carrying masks.**

8   *walk a bout*

    Take a turn (of a dance)

Act 1, Scene 5

Servingmen come forth with napkins. [1]

Servingman

Where's Potpan, that he helps not to take away? [2] He
shift a trencher? [3] He scrape a trencher?

Second Servingman

When good manners shall lie all in one or two men's

dirty; distasteful   hands, and they unwashed too, 'tis a foul° thing.

Servingman

Away with the joint-stools, [4] remove the court-cupboard, [5]   5
look to the plate. —Good thou, save me a piece of march-

almond cake   pane,° and, as thou loves me, let the porter let in Susan
Grindstone and Nell.—Antony and Potpan!

                       [**Second Servingman** *exits.*]

Third Servingman

Ay, boy, ready.

Servingman

You are looked for and called for, asked for and sought   10
for, in the great chamber.

Fourth Servingman

With enthusiasm   We cannot be here and there too.— Cheerly,° boys; be
brisk awhile, and the longer liver [6] take all.

                                  They exit.

        Enter [**Capulet** *with* **Capulet's Cousin**, **Tybalt**,
        Lady Capulet, **Juliet**, *others of the house and*] *all the
        guests and gentlewomen to the Maskers.* [7]

Capulet

Welcome, gentlemen! Ladies that have their toes
Unplagued with corns will walk a bout [8] with you.   15
—Ah, my mistresses! Which of you all

1   *makes dainty*

Acts fastidiously (hesitating to
accept the invitation)

2   *Am I come near ye now?*

I.e., I've got you there, haven't I?

3   *A hall, a hall; give room!*

I.e., clear the hall; make room for
dancing!

4   *turn the tables up*

Dismantle and put away the dining
tables.

5   *this unlooked-for sport comes well*

This unexpected entertainment
(with the arrival of Mercutio and his
friends) is welcome.

6   *Pentecost*

A religious feast, celebrated on the
seventh Sunday after Easter, that
commemorates the descent of the
Holy Ghost upon the twelve
Apostles

refuse   Will now deny° to dance? She that makes dainty, ¹

She, I'll swear, hath corns. Am I come near ye now? ²

—Welcome, gentlemen! I have seen the day

mask   That I have worn a visor° and could tell   20

whispered   A whispering° tale in a fair lady's ear

Such as would please. 'Tis gone; 'tis gone; 'tis gone.

—You are welcome, gentlemen.—Come, musicians, play.

(Music plays and they dance.)

—A hall, a hall; give room! ³—And foot it, girls.

—More light, you knaves! And turn the tables up ⁴   25

(in the kitchen)   And quench the fire.° The room is grown too hot.

—Ah, sirrah, this unlooked-for sport comes well. ⁵

—Nay, sit, nay, sit, good cousin Capulet,

For you and I are past our dancing days.

How long is 't now since last yourself and I   30

Were in a mask?

Capulet's Cousin

Your   By 'r° Lady, thirty years.

Capulet

What, man? 'Tis not so much; 'tis not so much;

'Tis since the nuptials of Lucentio,

Come Pentecost ⁶ as quickly as it will,

Some five and twenty years, and then we masked.   35

Capulet's Cousin

'Tis more; 'tis more. His son is elder, sir;

His son is thirty.

Capulet

                        Will you tell me that?

legal minor   His son was but a ward° two years ago.

Romeo

[*to a* **Servingman**] What lady's that which doth enrich the hand

Of yonder knight?   40

1   *It seems she hangs upon the cheek of*
     night / As a rich jewel in an Ethiope's ear

     **I.e., her beauty is heightened
     against the dark of night, just as a
     richly jeweled earring shines
     brightly against dark skin.**

2   *Beauty too rich for use, for earth too dear*

     **I.e., beauty too splendid to be
     employed in an ordinary manner;
     beauty too costly for this world
     (and for mortal men) to afford it. A
     more ominous reading is possible,
     as well: Juliet is too beautiful for
     earthly existence.**

3   *The measure done, I'll watch her place of
     stand*

     **I.e., now that the dance is ended,
     I'll watch where she stops to rest.**

4   *rapier*

     A light, sharp-pointed sword

5   *Dares the slave / Come hither, covered
     with an antic face, / To fleer and scorn at
     our solemnity?*

     **I.e., does the villain dare to come
     here, hidden under a grotesque
     mask, to sneer at our celebration
     and to mock us?**

6   *stock and honor*

     I.e., honorable lineage

7   *in spite*

     out of malice

8   *Content thee, gentle coz.*

     Calm down, my dear kinsman.

Servingman

I know not, sir.

Romeo

Oh, she doth teach the torches to burn bright!

It seems she hangs upon the cheek of night

As a rich jewel in an Ethiope's ear, [1]

Beauty too rich for use, for earth too dear. [2]   45

seems / flocking   So shows° a snowy dove trooping° with crows

companions   As yonder lady o'er her fellows° shows.

The measure done, I'll watch her place of stand, [3]

And, touching hers, make blessèd my rude hand.

Deny   Did my heart love till now? Forswear° it, sight,   50

For I ne'er saw true beauty till this night.

Tybalt

This, by his voice, should be a Montague.

—Fetch me my rapier, [4] boy.   [*Page exits.*]

                                        What? Dares the slave

Come hither, covered with an antic face,

sneer   To fleer° and scorn at our solemnity? [5]   55

Now, by the stock and honor [6] of my kin,

To strike him dead I hold it not a sin.

Capulet

Why, how now, kinsman? Wherefore storm you so?

Tybalt

Uncle, this is a Montague, our foe,

A villain that is hither come in spite [7]   60

To scorn at our solemnity this night.

Capulet

Young Romeo is it?

Tybalt

                    'Tis he, that villain Romeo.

Capulet

Content thee, gentle coz. [8] Let him alone.

1   *'A bears him*
    He conducts himself

2   *do him disparagement*
    Dishonor him

3   *It fits when such a villain is a guest.*
    **I.e., my anger is perfectly
    appropriate, if we have to host
    such a despicable person.**

4   *goodman boy*
    **Goodman was used to address men
    who were not members of the
    nobility (and would therefore
    represent an insult to Tybalt, a
    gentleman, as also would *boy*).**

5   *Go to.*
    **A dismissive or impatient
    expression**

6   *You will set cock-a-hoop; you'll be the
    man!*
    **I.e., you'll strut and cause havoc.
    You'll be a big shot!**

7   *Marry, 'tis time.*
    **I.e., by God, it's time I did
    something about your attitude,
    Tybalt. (*Marry* is an oath derived
    from the Virgin Mary.)**

8   *Well said, my hearts!—You are a
    princox, go.*
    **Capulet gets distracted from his
    rebuke of Tybalt by the activity
    around him. A dance is ending, and
    he encourages the dancers with *Well
    said, my hearts!* (Well done, good
    people!) Then, as an aside, he directs
    a further insult toward Tybalt (*princox*
    means "insolent boy"). He then
    addresses the servants (*More light,
    more light*), before turning back to
    Tybalt; and he ends addressing the
    dancers once again.**

9   *Patience perforce with willful choler
    meeting / Makes my flesh tremble in their
    different greeting.*
    **The patience that I must display in
    the face of the uncontrollable
    anger that I feel makes me shake
    from the force of their opposition.**

dignified   'A bears him [1] like a portly° gentleman,

And, to say truth, Verona brags of him   65

To be a virtuous and well-governed youth.

I would not for the wealth of all this town

Here in my house do him disparagement. [2]

Therefore be patient. Take no note of him.

It is my will, the which if thou respect,   70

demeanor   Show a fair presence° and put off these frowns,

appearance   An ill-beseeming semblance° for a feast.

Tybalt

It fits when such a villain is a guest. [3]

I'll not endure him.

Capulet

He shall be endured.

What, goodman boy? [4] I say he shall. Go to. [5]   75

Am I the master here or you? Go to.

You'll not endure him? God shall mend my soul,

You'll make a mutiny among my guests;

You will set cock-a-hoop; you'll be the man! [6]

Tybalt

Why, uncle, 'tis a shame.

Capulet

Go to, go to.   80

You are a saucy boy. Is 't so, indeed?

trait / damage This trick° may chance to scathe° you, I know what.

defy   You must contrary° me? Marry, 'tis time. [7]

—Well said, my hearts!—You are a princox, go. [8]

Be quiet, or—More light, more light!—For shame!   85

I'll make you quiet.—What? Cheerly, my hearts!

Tybalt

Patience perforce with willful choler meeting

Makes my flesh tremble in their different greeting. [9]

1   *If I profane with my unworthiest hand /*
    This holy shrine. . . . Thus from my lips,
    by thine, my sin is purged.

    **Romeo and Juliet's dialogue
    (1.5.91–105) forms a sonnet, a
    fourteen-line poem often
    consisting, as here, of three
    rhyming quatrains and a final
    couplet. The sonnet was the
    characteristic form of European
    romantic poetry at the time, and
    the religious language here is
    characteristic of its imagery. (See
    LONGER NOTE on page 330.)**

2   *This holy shrine*

    I.e., Juliet's hand

3   *My lips, two blushing pilgrims, ready
    stand / To smooth that rough touch with
    a tender kiss.*

    **The sense of this passage is that
    Romeo's *blushing lips* (i.e., lips that
    are bashful but also rosy) hover
    near Juliet's hand just as pilgrims
    hover near a religious shrine where
    they hope to perform an act of
    devotion that will expiate their sin.**

4   *Which mannerly devotion shows in this*

    **That demonstrate proper
    reverance in this act (of taking my
    hand)**

5   *saints*

    **Statues of saints, present in Roman
    Catholic shrines**

6   *grant thou*

    Allow this

7   *Saints do not move, though grant for
    prayers' sake.*

    **I.e., statues of saints don't move,
    but prayers offered to them may be
    granted. Her implication is that,
    although she will not physically
    move to kiss him, she may give
    (*grant*) him a kiss if he attempts to
    take one.**

8   *Then have my lips the sin that they have
    took.*

    **Then my lips will contain the sin
    that they have just *purged* (105)
    from your lips.**

9   *You kiss by th' book.*

    **I.e., you kiss according to lovers'
    conventions (i.e., too formally).**

I will withdraw, but this intrusion shall,   *Foreshadowing*

Now seeming sweet, convert to bitt'rest gall.   *90*

[*He exits.*]

Romeo [1]

If I profane with my unworthiest hand

This holy shrine, [2] the gentle sin is this:

My lips, two blushing pilgrims, ready stand

To smooth that rough touch with a tender kiss. [3]

Juliet

Good pilgrim, you do wrong your hand too much,   *95*

Which mannerly devotion shows in this, [4]

For saints [5] have hands that pilgrims' hands do touch,

pilgrims'   And palm to palm is holy palmers'° kiss.

Romeo

Have not saints lips, and holy palmers too?

Juliet

Ay, pilgrim, lips that they must use in prayer.   *100*

Romeo

Oh, then, dear saint, let lips do what hands do.

They pray; grant thou, [6] lest faith turn to despair.

Juliet

Saints do not move, though grant for prayers' sake. [7]

Romeo

Then move not while my prayer's effect I take. [*kisses her*]

Thus from my lips, by thine, my sin is purged.   *105*

Juliet

Then have my lips the sin that they have took. [8]

Romeo

pleaded; demanded   Sin from my lips? O, trespass sweetly urged!°

Give me my sin again. [*They kiss again.*]

Juliet

                     You kiss by th' book. [9]

1   *bachelor*

    I.e., young gentleman

2   *the chinks*

    A lot of money (with a sexual pun
    on *chinks* as vagina)

3   *O dear account!*

    I.e., there will be a heavy reckoning
    to pay (though *dear*, meaning
    "costly," also carries the sense of
    "loving" or "precious").

4   *My life is my foe's debt.*

    I.e., my life is now in the hands of
    my enemy.

5   *The sport is at the best.*

    I.e., this is as good as it is going to
    get, reiterating Romeo's sentiment
    at 1.4.37: *The game was ne'er so fair,
    and I am done.*

6   *We have a trifling foolish banquet
    towards.*

    I.e., we are about to sit down to a
    little dessert.

7   *Is it e'en so?*

    Romeo and Benvolio make some
    gesture that they intend to leave,
    and it is to that that Capulet
    responds, i.e., "Must you?"

8   *it waxes late*

    It's getting late.

Nurse

Madam, your mother craves a word with you.

[**Juliet** *moves away.*]

Romeo

Who What° is her mother?

Nurse

Marry, bachelor, [1] 110

Her mother is the lady of the house,

And a good lady, and a wise and virtuous.

with I nursed her daughter that you talked withal.°

I tell you, he that can lay hold of her

Shall have the chinks. [2] *They'll have a lot of money*

Romeo

Aside Is she a Capulet? 115

O dear account! [3] My life is my foe's debt. [4]

Benvolio

Away; begone. The sport is at the best. [5]

Romeo

Ay, so I fear. The more is my unrest.

Capulet

Nay, gentlemen, prepare not to be gone.

We have a trifling foolish banquet towards. [6] 120

—Is it e'en so? [7] Why, then, I thank you all.

I thank you, honest gentlemen. Good night.

—More torches here!—Come on then; let's to bed.

faith Ah, sirrah, by my fay,° it waxes late. [8]

I'll to my rest. 125

[*All except* **Juliet** *and* **Nurse** *begin to exit.*]

Juliet

Come hither, Nurse. What is yon gentleman?

Nurse

The son and heir of old Tiberio.

1   *My grave is like to be my wedding bed.*

Juliet's association of her *grave* and her *wedding bed* is one of many statements of a love-death nexus that connects *Romeo and Juliet* to the *Liebestod* (German for "love-death") myth from medieval European literature. The Arthurian legend of Tristan and Isolde is perhaps the best-known example of the myth. The sudden commencement of the love between Romeo and Juliet, as well as repeated references to a personified death as Juliet's husband, belong to this tradition of "courtly love" in which the lovers pursue a forbidden relationship that leads to their destruction. However, *Romeo and Juliet* also significantly departs from the idealistic courtly love tradition, in which the lovers celebrate death's power to preserve their passion. In *Romeo and Juliet,* by contrast, *love-devouring death* does not preserve but rather cuts off the protagonists' love (2.6.7). Preparing to destroy his *world-wearied flesh,* Romeo imagines not that he will achieve a transcendent union with Juliet but that he will forever remain in the Capulet tomb, accompanied with *worms that are [Juliet's] chambermaids* (5.3.109).

2   *Too early seen unknown, and known too late.*

I.e., I was attracted to him before I knew who he was, and now that I know, it is *too late* to stop.

Juliet

Who's What's° he that now is going out of door?

Nurse

Marry, that I think be young Petruccio.

Juliet

What's he that follows here, that would not dance?   130

Nurse

I know not.

Juliet

Go ask his name.[**Nurse** *goes after him.*]—If he be marrièd,
My grave is like to be my wedding bed. [1]   *Foreshadowing*

Nurse

[*returning*]His name is Romeo, and a Montague,
The only son of your great enemy.   135

Juliet

My only love sprung from my only hate,   *It's too late to
not love him*
Too early seen unknown, and known too late. [2]

Unnatural; Ominous   Prodigious° birth of love it is to me,   *She can't believe this
happened*
That I must love a loathèd enemy.

Nurse

What's this? What's this?

Juliet

                              A rhyme I learned even now   140
Of one I danced withal.

                              One calls within: "Juliet!"

Nurse

Right away   Anon,° anon!

Come, let's away. The strangers all are gone.   *They exit.*

1   *love*

    I.e., Romeo

2   *to his foe supposed*

    **I.e., to someone whom he has
thought to be his enemy**

3   *complain*

    **Bewail the pain caused by love
(compare *groaned* in line 3)**

4   *Temp'ring extremities with extreme
sweet*

    **Moderating hardships with intense
delight**

Act 2, Prologue

[*Enter* **Chorus**.]

Chorus

Now old desire doth in his deathbed lie,

yearns   And young affection gapes° to be his heir.

i.e., Rosaline   That fair° for which love[1] groaned for and would die,

compared   With tender Juliet matched,° is now not fair.

in return   Now Romeo is beloved and loves again,°   5

Both equally   Alike° bewitchèd by the charm of looks,

But to his foe supposed[2] he must complain,[3]

And she steal love's sweet bait from fearful hooks.

considered   Being held° a foe, he may not have access

To breathe such vows as lovers use to swear.   10

ability (is)   And she as much in love, her means° much less

To meet her new belovèd anywhere.

i.e., time lends them   But passion lends them power, time° means, to meet,

Temp'ring extremities with extreme sweet.[4]   [*He exits.*]

1   *Turn back, dull earth, and find thy center out.*

I.e., go back, sluggish body, and find Juliet again. Romeo compares his body to *earth* in both its senses. Denoting the Planet Earth, the term casts Juliet as the *center* of his new world: she exerts an inexorable, gravity-like pull on him. Denoting the substance, *earth* echoes the biblical tradition of humans being formed "of the dust of the ground" (Genesis 2:7).

2   *I'll conjure too*

Mercutio's "conjuring" might have reminded Shakespeare's audience of a popular contemporary tragedy, Christopher Marlowe's *Dr. Faustus* (1592). Dr. Faustus sells his soul to the devil for power and knowledge. In a memorable conjuring scene, Dr. Faustus stands within a magic circle filled with holy names and astrological figures. He raises the devil Mephistopheles by reciting a Latin invocation, sprinkling holy water, and making the sign of the cross. Mercutio turns the blasphemous practice of conjuring the devil into an elaborate sexual joke through double entendres on words such as *spirit* (penis), *circle* (vagina), and *raise* (make erect). As with his tale of the nocturnal Queen Mab, Mercutio's taste for the supernatural seems to cast a foreboding shadow over Romeo's romantic pursuits.

3   *my gossip Venus*

My good friend Venus (the goddess of love)

4   *Young Abraham Cupid*

Abraham, the biblical patriarch, lived to be 175 years old. Mercutio's phrase thus conveys the sense that Cupid is an ancient youth, an immortal god who retains immature characteristics. *Abraham*, however, was also used in the phrase "Abraham man" to mean a con artist pretending to be a beggar, so perhaps the phrase means "young, roguish Cupid."

5   *When King Cophetua loved the beggar maid*

Familiar from ballads, King Cophetua and his beloved beggar maid are an example of an unlikely love affair.

6   *The ape is dead, and I must conjure him.*

Ape was sometimes used as a term of familiar affection in early modern England. Mercutio also refers to the fairground practice of training an ape to play dead—only to be resurrected, or *conjured*, by the commands of its trainer.

Act 2, Scene 1

*Enter **Romeo** alone.*

Romeo

Can I go forward when my heart is here?

Turn back, dull earth, and find thy center out. [1]

[*moves away*]

*Enter **Benvolio** with **Mercutio**.*

Benvolio

[*calling*] Romeo! My cousin Romeo! Romeo!

Mercutio

He is wise,

himself And, on my life, hath stol'n him° home to bed.   5

Benvolio

garden He ran this way and leapt this orchard° wall.

Call, good Mercutio.

Mercutio

                Nay, I'll conjure too! [2]

Romeo! Humors, madman, passion, lover!

Appear thou in the likeness of a sigh!

Speak but one rhyme, and I am satisfied.   10

Cry but "Ay me!" Pronounce but "love" and "dove."

Speak to my gossip Venus [3] one fair word,

blind One nickname for her purblind° son and heir,

Young Abraham Cupid, [4] he that shot so true

When King Cophetua loved the beggar maid. [5]   15

—He heareth not; he stirreth not; he moveth not:

The ape is dead, and I must conjure him. [6]

—I conjure thee by Rosaline's bright eyes,

By her high forehead and her scarlet lip,

By her fine foot, straight leg, and quivering thigh,   20

1 *raise a spirit in his mistress' circle*

I.e., to conjure a spirit to appear in a magic circle, but with bawdy wordplay, envisioning the *spirit* as a penis and the *circle* as a vagina

2 *conjured it down*

I.e., caused it to diminish by satisfying it sexually

3 *That were some spite.*

That would be some provocation.

4 *raise up him*

"Bring him out of hiding," but also "arouse him sexually"

5 *To be consorted with the humorous night*

To associate with (or to harmonize with, in its musical sense) the humid night; (*humorous* also means "full of humors," or "moody" (see 2.1.8).

6 *medlar*

A small, hard-skinned brown apple with a large opening at the lower end of the fruit; often used as euphemism for the female genitals

7 *open arse*

An obscene term for the medlar fruit (See LONGER NOTE on page 330.)

8 *popp'rin pear*

A pear taking its name from Poperinghe, in Flanders; making bawdy use of the phonetic joke "Pop her in"

9 *truckle bed*

A child's bed, small enough to be tucked under the master bed

10 *field-bed*

(1) the ground itself; (2) a soldier's portable bed

territories   And the demesnes° that there adjacent lie,

That in thy likeness thou appear to us.

Benvolio

An if he hear thee, thou wilt anger him.

Mercutio

This cannot anger him. 'Twould anger him

To raise a spirit in his mistress' circle [1]   25

i.e., not Romeo's   Of some strange° nature, letting it there stand

Till she had laid it and conjured it down. [2]

That were some spite. [3] My invocation

Is fair and honest. In his mistress' name

I conjure only but to raise up him. [4]   30

Benvolio

Come; he hath hid himself among these trees,

To be consorted with the humorous night. [5]

Blind is his love and best befits the dark.

Mercutio

If love be blind, love cannot hit the mark.

Now will he sit under a medlar [6] tree   35

And wish his mistress were that kind of fruit

As maids call medlars when they laugh alone.

—O Romeo, that she were! Oh, that she were

An open arse, [7] and thou a popp'rin pear. [8]

Romeo, good night. I'll to my truckle bed. [9]   40

sleep upon   This field-bed [10] is too cold for me to sleep.°

—Come, shall we go?

Benvolio

                 Go, then, for 'tis in vain

To seek him here that means not to be found.   *They exit.*

1   *the envious moon*

    The moon was a symbol of the
    goddess Diana, and therefore of
    chastity as well.

2   *Her vestal livery is but sick and green*

    Probably a reference to the
    common early modern
    presumption that *green sickness*—a
    form of anemia that attacked
    pubescent girls—resulted from
    prolonged virginity, though here
    metaphoric for the paleness of the
    moon; (*livery* = uniform).

3   *What of that?*

    I.e., what does that matter?

4   *Having some business*

    I.e., having some important errand
    to run

5   *their spheres*

    I.e., the orbits of the planets
    (*stars*). During Shakespeare's
    lifetime, the teachings of the
    Greek astronomer Ptolemy were
    still widely accepted. The
    Ptolomaic universe consisted of
    concentrically nested, inde-
    pendently revolving crystalline
    spheres, each containing one of
    the major planets, the sun, and
    the moon.

Act 2, Scene 2

[**Romeo** *comes forward.*]

Romeo

i.e., Mercutio He° jests at scars that never felt a wound.

He's never felt what I've felt

[*Enter* **Juliet**, *above*.]

But soft! What light through yonder window breaks?
It is the east, and Juliet is the sun.
Arise, fair sun, and kill the envious moon, [1]
Who is already sick and pale with grief
That thou, her maid, art far more fair than she.   5
Be not her maid since she is envious.

virgin Her vestal° livery is but sick and green, [2]
And none but fools do wear it. Cast it off.
It is my lady. Oh, it is my love.   10
Oh, that she knew she were!
She speaks, yet she says nothing. What of that? [3]
Her eye discourses. I will answer it.
I am too bold. 'Tis not to me she speaks.

planets / sky Two of the fairest stars° in all the heaven,°   15
Having some business, [4] do entreat her eyes
To twinkle in their spheres [5] till they return.
What if her eyes were there, they in her head?
The brightness of her cheek would shame those stars

i.e., the sky As daylight doth a lamp. Her eye in heaven°   20
shine Would through the airy region stream° so bright
That birds would sing and think it were not night.
See how she leans her cheek upon her hand.
Oh, that I were a glove upon that hand
That I might touch that cheek!

(comparing Juliet to the sun, moon, stars)

1   *white, upturnèd, wond'ring eyes*

Eyes turned so far up toward the sky that only their whites are visible

2   *Thou art thyself, though not a Montague.*

You would be yourself even if you weren't a Montague.

3   *I take thee at thy word.*

(1) I agree to what you have said; (2) I'll marry you as you have promised.

Juliet

Ay me!

Romeo

[*aside*] She speaks.   25

Oh, speak again, bright angel, for thou art

As glorious to this night, being o'er my head,

i.e., angel   As is a wingèd messenger° of Heaven

Unto the white, upturnèd, wond'ring eyes [1]

Of mortals that fall back to gaze on him   30

When he bestrides the lazy puffing clouds

And sails upon the bosom of the air.

Juliet

Why   O Romeo, Romeo! Wherefore° art thou Romeo?

Deny thy father and refuse thy name.

only   Or, if thou wilt not, be but° sworn my love,   35

And I'll no longer be a Capulet.

They're just why names, why should they hinder us?

Romeo

[*aside*] Shall I hear more, or shall I speak at this?

Juliet

'Tis but thy name that is my enemy.

Thou art thyself, though not a Montague. [2]

neither   What's Montague? It is nor° hand nor foot,   40

Nor arm nor face, nor any other part

Belonging to a man. Oh, be some other name!

What's in a name? That which we call a rose

By any other word would smell as sweet.

A label doesn't mean anything

So Romeo would, were he not Romeo called,   45

owns   Retain that dear perfection which he owes°

take off   Without that title. Romeo, doff° thy name,

in exchange for   And for° thy name, which is no part of thee,

Take all myself.

Romeo

I take thee at thy word. [3]

1   *Had I it written, I would tear the word.*

If I had my name here, written on a piece of paper, I would tear it in pieces.

2   *if either thee dislike*

If either name causes you displeasure

3   *And what love can do, that dares love attempt.*

And whatever love is capable of doing love will attempt to do.

4   *there lies more peril in thine eye / Than twenty of their swords*

The idea that a woman can kill her lover with a disapproving glance was a cliché of Petrarchan love poetry.

Call me but "love," and I'll be new baptized.   50
Henceforth I never will be Romeo.

Juliet

What man art thou that, thus bescreened in night,

private musings So stumblest on my counsel?°

Romeo

                                   By a name
I know not how to tell thee who I am.
My name, dear saint, is hateful to myself   55
Because it is an enemy to thee.
Had I it written, I would tear the word. ¹

Juliet

My ears have yet not drunk a hundred words
Of thy tongue's uttering, yet I know the sound.
Art thou not Romeo, and a Montague?   60

Romeo

Neither, fair maid, if either thee dislike. ²

Juliet

How camest thou hither, tell me, and wherefore?
The orchard walls are high and hard to climb,
And the place death, considering who thou art,
If any of my kinsmen find thee here.   65

Romeo

fly over With love's light wings did I o'erperch° these walls,
For stony limits cannot hold love out,
And what love can do, that dares love attempt. ³
obstacle Therefore thy kinsmen are no stop° to me.

Juliet

If they do see thee, they will murder thee.   70

Romeo

Alack, there lies more peril in thine eye
Than twenty of their swords. ⁴ Look thou but sweet,
protected And I am proof° against their enmity.

1   *My life were better ended by their hate /*
    Than death proroguèd, wanting of thy love.

    **It would be preferable to die now at
    the hands of your family than to have
    my death deferred (*proroguèd*) and
    go on without (*wanting of*) your love.**

2   *Fain would I dwell on form; fain, fain
    deny / What I have spoke. But farewell
    compliment!*

    **I.e., I wish I could behave more
    conventionally (or appropriately);
    I wish I could pretend I hadn't said
    what I just said. But good-bye to
    meaningless good manners.**

3   *At lovers' perjuries, / They say, Jove
    laughs.*

    **I.e., *Jove*, the king of the classical
    gods, is only amused, not
    outraged, when lovers tell
    falsehoods to one another. The
    idea of Jove's bemused tolerance
    for lovers' deceits is well known
    from Ovid, *Ars Amatoria*, 1.633.**

4   *else*

    Otherwise; for any other reason

5   *more coying to be strange*

    **A greater ability to pretend shyness
    in order to play hard to get (*strange* =
    distant; unapproachable)**

Juliet

I would not for the world they saw thee here.

Romeo

I have night's cloak to hide me from their eyes, 75

unless And, but° thou love me, let them find me here:

My life were better ended by their hate

Than death prorogued, wanting of thy love. [1]

He would rather die with her love

Juliet

By whose direction found'st thou out this place?

Romeo

By love, that first did prompt me to inquire. 80

advice He lent me counsel,° and I lent him eyes.

I am no pilot, yet, wert thou as far

As that vast shore washed with the farthest sea,

undertake the risk I should adventure° for such merchandise.

Juliet

Thou knowest the mask of night is on my face, 85

Else would a maiden blush bepaint my cheek

For that which thou hast heard me speak tonight.

Gladly Fain° would I dwell on form; fain, fain deny

What I have spoke. But farewell compliment! [2]

Dost thou love me? I know thou wilt say "ay," 90

And I will take thy word. Yet if thou swear'st,

Thou mayst prove false. At lovers' perjuries,

They say, Jove laughs. [3] O gentle Romeo,

declare If thou dost love, pronounce° it faithfully;

Or if thou thinkest I am too quickly won, 95

I'll frown and be perverse and say thee "nay,"

So that So° thou wilt woo; but else, [4] not for the world.

infatuated In truth, fair Montague, I am too fond,°

frivolous; wanton And therefore thou mayst think my behavior light.°

But trust me, gentleman, I'll prove more true 100

Than those that have more coying to be strange. [5]

If you love me, I'll love you too

Juliet will play hard to get

1   *And not impute this yielding to light*
    love, / Which the dark night hath so
    discoverèd

    **I.e., and don't think that simply
    because your courtship has met
    with quick success, my love (which
    the night has revealed to you) isn't
    serious.**

2   *circle orb*

    **I.e., revolving sphere; see 2.2.17
    and note.**

3   *gracious*

    **Charming, but also "full of all
    graces"**

I should have been more strange, I must confess,

aware But that thou overheard'st, ere I was ware,°

My true love passion. Therefore pardon me,

And not impute this yielding to light love,   105

Which the dark night hath so discoverèd. [1]

Romeo

Lady, by yonder blessèd moon I vow,

That tips with silver all these fruit-tree tops—

Juliet

It changes too often

Oh, swear not by the moon, th' inconstant moon,

That monthly changes in her circle orb, [2]   110

Lest that thy love prove likewise variable.

Romeo

What shall I swear by?

Juliet

                    Do not swear at all;

Or, if thou wilt, swear by thy gracious [3] self,   *Swear by yourself*

Which is the god of my idolatry,

And I'll believe thee.

Romeo

                    If my heart's dear love—   115

Juliet

Well, do not swear. Although I joy in thee,

mutual attraction I have no joy of this contract° tonight:

thoughtless It is too rash, too unadvised,° too sudden,

Too like the lightning, which doth cease to be   *Going too fast Flash and its gone*

Ere one can say "It lightens." Sweet, good night.   120

This bud of love, by summer's ripening breath,

May prove a beauteous flower when next we meet.

Good night, good night! As sweet repose and rest

Come to thy heart as that within my breast.

Romeo

Oh, wilt thou leave me so unsatisfied?   125

1   *thy bent of love*

The intention of your love

Juliet

What satisfaction canst thou have tonight?

Romeo

Th' exchange of thy love's faithful vow for mine.

Juliet

I gave thee mine before thou didst request it,

remained And yet I would it were° to give again.

Romeo

Wouldst thou withdraw it? For what purpose, love?   130

Juliet

generous But to be frank° and give it thee again,

And yet I wish but for the thing I have.

My bounty is as boundless as the sea,

My love as deep. The more I give to thee,

The more I have, for both are infinite.   135

[**Nurse** *calls within.*]

I hear some noise within. Dear love, adieu.

Right away —Anon,° good Nurse!—Sweet Montague, be true.

Wait Stay° but a little. I will come again.

[*She exits, above.*]

Romeo

O blessèd, blessèd night! I am afeard,

Being in night, all this is but a dream,   140

solid; real Too flattering sweet to be substantial.°

[*Enter **Juliet**, above.*]

Juliet

Three words, dear Romeo, and good night indeed.

If that thy bent of love[1] be honorable,

Thy purpose marriage, send me word tomorrow,

arrange By one that I'll procure° to come to thee,   145

Where and what time thou wilt perform the rite,

1   *if thou mean'st not well*

If your intentions aren't good

2   *By and by*

Immediately

3   *Oh, for a falconer's voice, / To lure this tassel-gentle back again!*

Like other forms of hunting, falconry was a sport of aristocratic males, as is apparent from the title of George Turberville's manual, *The Book of Falconry or Hawking; For the Only Delight and Pleasure of All Noblemen and Gentlemen* (1575). Juliet's image of playing the falconer to Romeo's *tassel-gentle* thus inverts conventional gender roles. Moreover, Juliet's longing for a falconer's voice to call Romeo contradicts her intention to maintain the secrecy of their relationship, since displaying skill at falconry was one way a gentleman could earn public acclaim from his peers. In his comedy *The Taming of the Shrew*, Shakespeare makes more conventional use of falconry as a metaphor for a husband's taming of his wife.

4   *Bondage is hoarse and may not speak aloud*

I, who am constrained by being in my parents' house, must whisper hoarsely and cannot talk loudly.

5   *tear*

Split (with the force of her voice)

6   *Else would I tear the cave where Echo lies, / And make her airy tongue more hoarse than mine / With repetition of "My Romeo!"*

Juliet alludes to the Ovidian myth of Echo and Narcissus, a tale of sexual transgression and self-destructive desire. Echo was a nymph whose chatter distracted Juno from catching her husband Jove in an adulterous liaison. Juno punished Echo by taking away her voice, allowing her only the ability to repeat the final words of others. Echo fell in love with Narcissus, a lovely but proud youth, and his rejection of her caused her body to waste away until only an echo remained. Narcissus subsequently fell in love with his own reflection in a pool, and he also wasted away, transformed into the flower that bears his name.

And all my fortunes at thy foot I'll lay,

i.e., as my And follow thee my° lord throughout the world.

Nurse

[*within*] Madam!

Juliet

I come, anon.—But if thou mean'st not well,¹ 150

I do beseech thee—

Nurse

[*within*] Madam!

Juliet

By and by,² I come.

striving —To cease thy strife° and leave me to my grief.

Tomorrow will I send. 155

Romeo

So thrive my soul—

Juliet

A thousand times good night! [*She exits, above.*]

Romeo

lack A thousand times the worse to want° thy light.

Love goes toward love as schoolboys from their books,

But love from love, toward school with heavy looks. 160

Enter **Juliet** *again* [*, above*].

Juliet

Hist! Romeo, hist!—Oh, for a falconer's voice,

male falcon To lure this tassel-gentle° back again!³

Bondage is hoarse and may not speak aloud,⁴

Else would I tear⁵ the cave where Echo lies,

And make her airy tongue more hoarse than mine 165

With repetition of "My Romeo!"⁶

1 *nyas*

Young hawk that has not yet left the nest (picking up the hawking images in 2.2.161–162, and appropriate for Juliet living at home)

2 *still*

Both "always" and "without motion"; Romeo picks up the ambiguity in line 2.2.177.

Romeo

It is my soul that calls upon my name.

How silver-sweet sound lovers' tongues by night,

Like softest music to attending ears!

Juliet

Romeo!

Romeo

My nyas? [1]

Juliet

What o'clock tomorrow   170

Shall I send to thee?

Romeo

By the hour of nine.

Juliet

I will not fail. 'Tis twenty year till then.

I have forgot why I did call thee back.

Romeo

Let me stand here till thou remember it.

Juliet

I shall forget, to have thee still [2] stand there,   175

Remembering how I love thy company.

Romeo

And I'll still stay, to have thee still forget,

Forgetting any other home but this.

Juliet

'Tis almost morning. I would have thee gone—

spoiled child's   And yet no farther than a wanton's° bird,   180

That lets it hop a little from his hand,

leg irons   Like a poor prisoner in his twisted gyves,°

And with a silken thread plucks it back again,

its   So loving-jealous of his° liberty.

Romeo

wish   I would° I were thy bird.

1 **Romeo**

In Q2 (1599), the line *Sleep dwell upon thine eyes, peace in thy breast* is assigned to Juliet, with a new speech prefix, immediately following her previous speech; most editions assign the entire couplet to Romeo, taking the repeated speech prefix as an error and noting the propriety of the couplet for Romeo.

2 *my ghostly friar's close cell*

My holy confessor's small (or secluded) chamber

3 *dear hap*

Good fortune

Juliet

Sweet, so would I. 185

Yet I should kill thee with much cherishing.

Good night, good night! Parting is such sweet sorrow

That I shall say good night till it be morrow.

[*She exits, above.*]

Romeo [1]

Sleep dwell upon thine eyes, peace in thy breast.

Would I were sleep and peace, so sweet to rest. 190

Hence will I to my ghostly friar's close cell, [2]

His help to crave and my dear hap [3] to tell. *He exits.*

1   *The . . . wheels*

     The first four lines of Friar
     Lawrence's speech are nearly
     duplicated in Q2 (1599) in Romeo's
     final speech in 2.2, between lines
     2.2.190–191. Shakespeare must
     have intended to cancel one of
     these, though scholars debate
     which one. This edition takes the
     lines properly to belong to the
     Friar, as Q1 (1597) also has them
     here and omits them from Romeo's
     speech.

2   *osier cage*

     Basket made of intertwined
     willow branches

3   *children of divers kind*

     I.e., plants of various sorts (or
     natures)

4   *None but for some*

     I.e., every herb or flower has some
     useful quality.

5   *strained from that fair use, / Revolts*
     from true birth, stumbling on abuse

     I.e., perverted from its intended
     use, it turns away from its proper
     nature, becoming destructive.

6   *And vice sometime by action dignified*

     And vice can sometimes be
     ennobled if used for an honest
     end.

7   *with that part cheers each part*

     I.e., with that quality (i.e., its odor)
     soothes every part of the human
     body

Act 2, Scene 3

Enter **Friar** [**Laurence**], *alone with a basket.*

Friar Laurence   *[handwritten: A Pothacary, holy Friar, Romeo's closet confidant, gathering herbs]*

The grey-eyed morn smiles on the frowning night,

Checking the eastern clouds with streaks of light;

streaked with light   And fleckled° darkness, like a drunkard, reels

i.e., the sun god's   From forth day's path and Titan's° burning wheels. [1]

raise up   Now, ere the sun advance° his burning eye,   5

The day to cheer and night's dank dew to dry,

I must upfill this osier cage [2] of ours

destructive; noxious   With baleful° weeds and precious-juicèd flowers.

i.e., nature's   The earth, that's nature's mother, is her° tomb.

What is her burying grave, that is her womb,   10

And, from her womb, children of divers kind [3]

We sucking on her natural bosom find,

curative powers   Many for many virtues° excellent,

None but for some, [4] and yet all different.

great / beneficial power   Oh, mickle° is the powerful grace° that lies   15

In plants, herbs, stones, and their true qualities,

i.e., there is nothing   For naught° so vile that on the Earth doth live

But to the Earth some special good doth give,

anything   Nor aught° so good but, strained from that fair use,

[handwritten: Goodness]   Revolts from true birth, stumbling on abuse. [5]   20

Virtue itself turns vice, being misapplied,   *[handwritten: mishandled, misdirected]*

sometimes is   And vice sometime° by action dignified. [6]

[handwritten: Bad]   *[handwritten: Bad can become good for a certain thing]*

Enter **Romeo**.

Within the infant rind of this weak flower   *[handwritten: Poison but it can be turned into medicine]*

Poison hath residence, and med'cine power.

For this, being smelled, with that part cheers each part; [7]   25

stops   Being tasted, stays° all senses with the heart.

139

1 *encamp them still*

   I.e., are always present

2 *grace and rude will*

   Divine influence and unruly
   human desire

3 Benedicite

   Latin: "God bless you"
   (pronounced with five syllables).

4 *Care*

   (1) sorrow; (2) responsibility

Two such opposèd kings encamp them still, [1]
In man as well as herbs—grace and rude will [2]—
And where the worser is predominant,
worm   Full soon the canker° death eats up that plant.   30
Romeo
Good morrow, Father.
Friar Laurence
                    Benedicite. [3]
What early tongue so sweet saluteth me?
disordered; troubled Young son, it argues a distempered° head
So soon to bid good morrow to thy bed.
Care [4] keeps his watch in every old man's eye,   35
And where care lodges, sleep will never lie.
But where unbruisèd youth with unstuffed brain
Doth couch his limbs, there golden sleep doth reign.
Therefore thy earliness doth me assure
ailment   Thou art uproused by some distemp'rature.°   40
Or, if not so, then here I hit it right:
Our Romeo hath not been in bed tonight.
Romeo
That last is true. The sweeter rest was mine.
Friar Laurence
God pardon sin! Wast thou with Rosaline?
Romeo
holy   With Rosaline, my ghostly° Father? No.   45
I have forgot that name and that name's woe.
Friar Laurence
That's my good son. But where hast thou been, then?
Romeo
I'll tell thee ere thou ask it me again.
I have been feasting with mine enemy,
all of   Where on° a sudden one hath wounded me   50
That's by me wounded. Both our remedies

1 *My intercession likewise steads my foe*
My prayer for help aids my enemy (i.e., Juliet as a Capulet) as well.

2 *homely in thy drift*
Simple in your meaning

3 Jesu Maria, *what a deal of brine*
By Jesus and Mary, how many tears

4 *The sun not yet thy sighs from heaven clears*
The mist raised by your lovesick sighs (for Rosaline) has not yet been burned off by the sun.

5 *Women may fall when there's no strength in men.*
I.e., women must be allowed their weaknesses, since men clearly cannot stay faithful.

medicine   Within thy help and holy physic° lies.

I bear no hatred, blessèd man, for, lo,

My intercession likewise steads my foe. [1]

Friar Laurence

Be plain, good son, and homely in thy drift. [2]   55

absolution   Riddling confession finds but riddling shrift.°

Romeo

Then plainly know my heart's dear love is set

On the fair daughter of rich Capulet.

As mine on hers, so hers is set on mine,

And all combined, save what thou must combine   60

By holy marriage. When and where and how

We met, we wooed, and made exchange of vow,

walk   I'll tell thee as we pass,° but this I pray:

That thou consent to marry us today.

Friar Laurence

Holy Saint Francis, what a change is here!   65

Is Rosaline, that thou didst love so dear,

So soon forsaken? Young men's love then lies

Not truly in their hearts, but in their eyes.

Jesu Maria, what a deal of brine [3]

pale; sickly   Hath washed thy sallow° cheeks for Rosaline?   70

How much salt water thrown away in waste

flavor   To season° love that of it doth not taste.

The sun not yet thy sighs from heaven clears, [4]

still   Thy old groans yet° ringing in mine ancient ears.

Lo, here upon thy cheek the stain doth sit   75

Of an old tear that is not washed off yet.

If e'er thou wast thyself and these woes thine,

Thou and these woes were all for Rosaline.

maxim   And art thou changed? Pronounce this sentence° then:

Women may fall when there's no strength in men. [5]   80

1   *bad'st me*

    Ordered me to

2   *Thy love did read by rote that could*
    not spell

    I.e., your idea of love was merely
    some conventional notion rather
    than something felt. (The image is
    of a child who can recite from
    memory a book often heard but
    cannot as yet read it.)

3   *In one respect*

    For one reason only

Romeo

rebuked Thou chid'st° me oft for loving Rosaline.

Friar Laurence

For doting, not for loving, pupil mine.

Romeo

And bad'st me [1] bury love.

Friar Laurence

Not in a grave

To lay one in, another out to have.

Romeo

I pray thee, chide me not. Her I love now   85

Doth grace for grace and love for love allow;

The other did not so.

Friar Laurence

Oh, she knew well

Thy love did read by rote that could not spell. [2]

But come, young waverer, come; go with me.

In one respect [3] I'll thy assistant be: 90

For this alliance may so happy prove

hatred To turn your households' rancor° to pure love.

Romeo

insist Oh, let us hence. I stand° on sudden haste.

Friar Laurence

Wisely and slow. They stumble that run fast.   *They exit.*

1 *answer it*

   Accept the challenge (to a duel). Mercutio's joking response takes *answer* to mean "reply to."

2 *he will answer the letter's master, how he dares, being dared*

   I.e., Romeo will tell Tybalt how courageously he plans to answer the challenge.

3 *pin*

   The peg or nail placed at the center of an archer's target

4 *butt shaft*

   An unbarbed arrow used for practice-shooting at *butts* (targets)

5 *What is Tybalt?*

   Benvolio is not asking for information but saying that he is of no account.

Act 2, Scene 4

Enter **Benvolio** *and* **Mercutio**.

Ty blt sent a challenge on Romeo's life
Duels were fights to the death

Mercutio

Where the devil should this Romeo be?

last night   Came he not home tonight?°

Benvolio

servant   Not to his father's; I spoke with his man.°

Mercutio

Why, that same pale, hard-hearted wench, that Rosaline,

Torments him so that he will sure run mad.   5

Benvolio

Tybalt, the kinsman to old Capulet,

Hath sent a letter to his father's house.

Mercutio

A challenge, on my life.

Benvolio

Romeo will answer it. [1]

Mercutio

Any man that can write may answer a letter.   10

Benvolio

Nay, he will answer the letter's master, how he dares,

being dared. [2]

Mercutio

Alas, poor Romeo! He is already dead, stabbed with a

white wench's black eye, run through the ear with a

love song, the very pin [3] of his heart cleft with the blind   15

i.e., Cupid's   bow-boy's° butt shaft. [4] And is he a man to encounter

Tybalt?

He's already dead because he can't compete w/ Tybalt in this state

He has all these new tricks

Benvolio

who   Why? What° is Tybalt? [5]

147

1   *Prince of Cats*

    Tybalt (or Tybert) is the name of the Prince of Cats in the fable of "Reynard the Fox."

2   *pricksong*

    Composed and scored music (the opposite of improvisational song)

3   *keeps time, distance, and proportion*

    The terms can be used for both fencing and singing: *keeps time* = "be economical in movement" and "observe the tempo"; *distance* refers to the proper space between fencers and the musical intervals; *proportion* = "balance" and "rhythm."

4   *rests*

    (1) pauses in fighting; (2) intervals of silence in a musical score

5   *a gentleman of the very first house of the first and second cause*

    I.e., a nobleman from the best fencing school, a school that teaches in painstaking detail how to distinguish between different reasons (*causes*) for fighting

6   *the immortal* passado, *the* punto reverso, *the* hai

    Fencing terms. The *passado* is a forward lunge, with one step; the *punto reverso* a backhanded stab. *Hai* is Italian for "you have it" (i.e., "I've stabbed you"), and was uttered when a duelist felt his attack strike home. Benvolio is puzzled by the terminology. (See LONGER NOTE on page 331.)

7   *The pox of*

    (I wish) the plague on

8   *affecting phantasms*

    Fashionable gallants who put on pretentious manners

9   *new tuners of accent*

    Individuals who pompously use fashionable foreign words and phrases

10 *grandsire*

    Mercutio is seemingly mocking his own aversion to new fashions, addressing Benvolio as a fellow fuddy-duddy.

11 *"pardon me's"*

    I.e., individuals indulging in an affected formality

12 *new form*

    (1) current fashions; (2) newly made bench

13 *Without his roe*

    (1) without the syllable *ro*, which, when subtracted from *Romeo*, leaves *me, oh!*—a lover's cry of anguish and self-pity; (2) lacking semen (i.e., sexually inadequate). *Roe* can indicate the reproductive cells of both male and female fish; (3) perhaps also, lacking his Ro(saline).

14 *the numbers that Petrarch flowed in*

    The love poems that Petrarch so copiously produced (See LONGER NOTE on page 331.)

Mercutio

More than Prince of Cats. [1] Oh, he's the courageous cap-

fencing etiquette tain of compliments.° He fights as you sing pricksong, [2]   20

keeps time, distance, and proportion. [3] He rests his

briefest minim° rests [4]—one, two, and the third in your

bosom. The very butcher of a silk button, a duelist, a

duelist, a gentleman of the very first house of the first

and second cause. [5] Ah, the immortal *passado*, the *punto*   25

reverso, the *hai!* [6]

Benvolio

The what?

Mercutio

The pox of [7] such antic, lisping, affecting phantasms, [8]

these new tuners of accent! [9] "By Jesu, a very good

brave blade! A very tall° man! A very good whore!" Why, is not   30

this a lamentable thing, grandsire, [10] that we should be

parasites thus afflicted with these strange flies,° these fashion-

mongers, these "pardon me's," [11] who stand so much

on the new form [12] that they cannot sit at ease on the

old bench? Oh, their bones, their bones!   35

Enter **Romeo**.

Benvolio

Here comes Romeo; here comes Romeo.

Mercutio

Without his roe, [13] like a dried herring. O flesh, flesh,

how art thou fishified! Now is he for the numbers that

compared to Petrarch flowed in. [14] Laura to° his lady was a kitchen-

wench—marry, she had a better love to   40

1   *gypsy*

Gypsies (the nomadic tribes of the
Roma people) were associated
with Egyptians (such as Cleopatra)
in early modern England due to the
similarity between the two words.
The Roma were widely thought of
as tricksters and thieves, so calling
a woman a *gypsy* implied that she
was deceptive and untrustworthy.
It also implied a dusky
complexion, at a time when pale
skin was the cultural ideal.

2   *Dido . . . Thisbe*

Dido, *Cleopatra*, *Helen*, *Hero*, and
Thisbe are the tragic heroines of
love stories from classical
antiquity. The story of Pyramus
and Thisbe, in particular, parallels
the plot of *Romeo and Juliet* and is
parodied in Shakespeare's *A
Midsummer Night's Dream*, a nearly
contemporaneous play.

3   *a grey eye or so, but not to the purpose*

Had a somewhat blue (and
therefore beautiful) eye, but that's
of no consequence

4   *French slop*

Baggy velvet breeches; perhaps
teasing Romeo for continuing to
wear last night's masking clothes

5   *The slip*

Mercutio puns on *slip*, meaning
"evasion" and also a "counterfeit
coin."

6   *strain courtesy*

Forgo the usual demands of
courtesy.

7   *case*

(1) circumstance; (2) vagina (of the
woman with whom Romeo
supposedly spent the night)

8   *to bow in the hams*

To be unable to stand upright. The
ham was the back of the thigh, so
bowing in the hams meant
"crouching," presumably
exhausted by sexual activity.

9   *kindly*

Naturally (but also "exactly," as
well as "graciously")

10 *very pink*

Best possible example (but Romeo
puns on *pink* meaning [1] a flower;
[2] a decorative perforation in
leather; [3] vagina).

11 *pump well flowered*

Shoe well decorated

12 *follow me*

Continue along with me in

write a poem about berhyme° her—Dido a dowdy, Cleopatra a gypsy, [1]
worthless women Helen and Hero hildings° and harlots, Thisbe [2] a grey
eye or so, but not to the purpose. [3]— Signor Romeo,
bonjour! There's a French salutation to your French
slop. [4] You gave us the counterfeit fairly last night.   45

Romeo

Good morrow to you both. What counterfeit did I give
you?

Mercutio

understand The slip, [5] sir, the slip. Can you not conceive?°

Romeo

Pardon, good Mercutio, my business was great, and in
such a case as mine a man may strain courtesy. [6]   50

Mercutio

That's as much as to say, such a case [7] as yours
constrains a man to bow in the hams. [8]

Romeo

Meaning "to curtsy"?

Mercutio

Thou hast most kindly [9] hit it.

Romeo

A most courteous exposition.   55

Mercutio

Nay, I am the very pink [10] of courtesy.

Romeo

"Pink" for flower.

Mercutio

Right.

Romeo

Why, then is my pump well flowered. [11]

Mercutio

Dependable Sure° wit, follow me [12] this jest now till thou hast worn   60
i.e., thin out thy pump, that when the single° sole of it is worn,

1 *solely singular*

Completely unique (but punning further on *sole* as shoe bottom)

2 *O single-soled jest, solely singular for the singleness.*

You have told a thin (weak) joke, which is only notable because it is one of a kind (i.e., so bad it will never be repeated).

3 *Come between us, good Benvolio.*

Mercutio pretends that the battle of wits is a physical duel and that Benvolio should break it up because Mercutio has been wounded.

4 *Switch and spurs*

Spur and whip your wit (like a horse) so that it goes faster

5 *cry a match*

I.e., declare victory

6 *wild-goose chase*

A demanding form of horse race, in which a number of riders follow a lead rider until he is overtaken and the first overtaker then becomes the leader, setting the course.

7 *Was I with you there for the goose?*

I.e., did I catch up with you in the contest of wits with my wordplay on *goose*?

8 *there for the goose*

(1) there to play the role of fool; (2) there because you hoped you would find a prostitute. Prostitutes were known as "Winchester geese" in the London of Shakespeare's day.

9 *bitter-sweeting*

A type of apple, so called because it is both sweet and tart.

10 *cheveril*

Leather made from a young goat which is unusually soft and elastic the jest may remain, after the wearing, solely singular. [1]

Romeo

O single-soled jest, solely singular for the singleness. [2]

Mercutio

Come between us, good Benvolio. [3] My wits faints.

Romeo

Switch and spurs, [4] switch and spurs, or I'll cry a match. [5]   65

Mercutio

Nay, if our wits run the wild-goose chase, [6] I am done,

fool   for thou hast more of the wild-goose° in one of thy wits

than I am sure I have in my whole five. Was I with you

there for the goose? [7]

Romeo

Thou wast never with me for anything when thou wast   70

not there for the goose. [8]

Mercutio

I will bite thee by the ear for that jest.

Romeo

Nay, good goose, bite not.

Mercutio

acidic; witty   Thy wit is a very bitter-sweeting. [9] It is a most sharp°

sauce.   75

Romeo

And is it not then well served into a sweet goose?

Mercutio

Oh, here's a wit of cheveril, [10] that stretches from an

i.e., forty-five inches   inch narrow to an ell° broad!

Romeo

I stretch it out for that word "broad," which, added to

obvious   the goose, proves thee far and wide a broad° goose.   80

Mercutio

Why, is not this better now than groaning for love?

are   Now art° thou sociable. Now art thou Romeo; now

1   *by art as well as by nature*

    By means of learning as well as by
    your innate qualities

2   *a great natural that runs lolling up and
    down to hide his bauble in a hole*

    (1) a mentally impaired person who
    runs around with his tongue
    hanging out, looking for a place to
    hide some worthless trinket; (2) a
    court jester who runs around
    looking for a place to hide his
    jester's staff; (3) an idiot clumsily
    trying to find a woman to have sex
    with. *Bauble* was slang for "penis,"
    hole for "vagina." Mercutio
    continues his bawdy play-on-
    words with *tale* (also slang for
    penis) in the following lines.

3   *against the hair*

    (1) against my wishes; (2) against
    the pubic hair

4   *occupy the argument*

    (1) continue with the discussion;
    (2) penetrate the vagina

5   *A sail, a sail!*

    Nautical exclamation, indicating
    that a ship has been sighted

6   *a shirt and a smock*

    I.e., a man and a woman. Men of
    the period wore plain *shirts* as
    undergarments; women wore
    smocks, or loose dresses.

art thou what thou art—by art as well as by nature, [1] for

drooling; idiotic this driveling° love is like a great natural that runs

lolling up and down to hide his bauble in a hole. [2]   85

Benvolio

Stop there; stop there.

Teasing each other

Mercutio

Thou desirest me to stop in my tale against the hair? [3]

Benvolio

enlarged; lengthy Thou wouldst else have made thy tale large.°

Mercutio

Oh, thou art deceived. I would have made it short, for I

was come to the whole depth of my tale, and meant,   90

indeed, to occupy the argument [4] no longer.

Romeo

business Here's goodly gear.°

Enter **Nurse** *and her man* [**Peter**].

A sail, a sail! [5]

Mercutio

Two, two—a shirt and a smock. [6]

Nurse

Peter.   95

Peter

Right away Anon.°

Nurse

My fan, Peter.

Mercutio

Good, Peter, to hide her face, for her fan's the fairer

face.

Nurse

i.e., give you God ye° good morrow, gentlemen.   100

1   *God ye good e'en*

God give you good evening. The
greeting could be used anytime
after noon (see 1.2.57), and it
suggests that the Nurse is at least
three hours late for the meeting
(see 2.2.170–171 and 2.5.1–2).

2   *One, gentlewoman, that God hath
made, himself to mar.*

I.e., a man that God made, but who
exists to *mar* (damage) himself.

3   *confidence*

Probably the Nurse's mistake for
"conference," though it could
mean "confidential discussion";
Benvolio, however, takes it as an
error.

4   *indite*

Benvolio mocks the Nurse's
seeming mistake by deliberately
substituting *indite* (set down) for
"invite."

5   *bawd*

Procuress (of prostitutes); but also
meaning "hare"

6   *So ho!*

A hunter's cry, upon spotting game

Mercutio

God ye good e'en, [1] fair gentlewoman.

Nurse

Is it good e'en?

Mercutio

sundial 'Tis no less, I tell ye, for the bawdy hand of the dial° is

point; penis now upon the prick° of noon.

Nurse

What kind of Out upon you! What° a man are you? 105

Romeo

One, gentlewoman, that God hath made, himself to
mar. [2]

Nurse

faith By my troth,° it is well said: for "himself to mar," quoth

he 'a.° Gentlemen, can any of you tell me where I may find
the young Romeo? 110

Romeo

I can tell you, but young Romeo will be older when you
have found him than he was when you sought him. I

lack am the youngest of that name, for fault° of a worse.

Nurse

You say well.

Mercutio

interpreted Yea, is the worst well? Very well took,° i' faith, wisely, 115
wisely.

Nurse

If you be he, sir, I desire some confidence [3] with you.

Benvolio

She will indite [4] him to some supper.

Mercutio

A bawd, [5] a bawd, a bawd! So ho! [6]

Romeo

What hast thou found? 120

1 *a hare, sir, in a Lenten pie*

(1) "a piece of old meat." No meat
could be served during the forty
days of Lent, according to Church
law, so a hare pie during Lent
would not be fresh; (2) "lustfulness
hiding under the guise of
propriety." Rabbits were (and are
still) proverbially lusty. Mercutio
pretends he suspects the Nurse of
having sexual designs on Romeo.

2 *stale and hoar*

Old and moldy, but *stale* also
means "prostitute," and *hoar*
suggests its obvious homonym.

3 *Is too much for a score*

I.e., too bad tasting to be paid for

4 *saucy merchant*

Impudent fellow

5 *full of his ropery*

Proud of his (verbal) tricks

6 *stand to*

Defend

7 *take him down*

(1) humble him; (2) satisfy him
sexually. The Nurse doesn't intend
the second meaning, but she
unwittingly suggests it.

8 *skeins-mates*

The word is unexplained, but must
mean something like "tramp." The
phrase is clearly parallel to *flirt-gills*,
and may be derived figuratively from
"skein" meaning threads or yarn
loosely bound up together

9 *use*

(1) treat; (2) copulate with (again, an
unintentional second meaning)

Mercutio

No hare, sir, unless a hare, sir, in a Lenten pie [1]—that

used up is, something stale and hoar [2] ere it be spent.°

    [*sings*] An old hare hoar,

    And an old hare hoar,

    Is very good meat in Lent.   125

    But a hare that is hoar

    Is too much for a score [3]

    When it hoars ere it be spent.

Romeo, will you come to your father's? We'll to dinner,

thither.   130

Romeo

I will follow you.

Mercutio

Farewell, ancient lady. Farewell, lady, lady, lady.

                    [**Mercutio** *and* **Benvolio**] *exit.*

Nurse

I pray you, sir, what saucy merchant [4] was this that was

so full of his ropery? [5]

Romeo

A gentleman, Nurse, that loves to hear himself talk,   135

and will speak more in a minute than he will stand to [6]

in a month.

Nurse

If / he An° 'a° speak anything against me, I'll take him down, [7]

scoundrels an 'a were lustier than he is, and twenty such jacks.°

And if I cannot, I'll find those that shall. Scurvy knave! I   140

loose women am none of his flirt-gills;° I am none of his skeins-

mates. [8] [*to* **Peter**] And thou must stand by too and

suffer every knave to use [9] me at his pleasure?

Peter

I saw no man use you at his pleasure. If I had, my

weapon should quickly have been out. I warrant you, I   145

1   *lead her in a fool's paradise*

     I.e., deceive her; seduce her

2   *commend me*

     Give my regards

3   *I will tell her, sir, that you do protest*

     The Nurse repeats Romeo's word
     ***protest* in line 158, though she seems**
     to think it means "propose."

4   *shrived*

     Confessed; granted absolution (by a
     priest) for her sins

dare draw as soon as another man if I see occasion in
a good quarrel and the law on my side.

Nurse

Now, afore God, I am so vexed that every part about me
quivers. Scurvy knave! [*to* **Romeo**] Pray you, sir, a word,
and, as I told you, my young lady bid me inquire you   *150*
out. What she bid me say, I will keep to myself; but first
let me tell ye, if ye should lead her in a fool's
rude   paradise,¹ as they say, it were a very gross° kind of
behavior, as they say. For the gentlewoman is young,
duplicitously   and therefore, if you should deal double° with her,   *155*
truly it were an ill thing to be offered to any gentle-
inferior   woman, and very weak° dealing.

Romeo

swear   Nurse, commend me² to thy lady and mistress. I protest°
unto thee—

Nurse

Good heart, and i' faith, I will tell her as much! Lord,   *160*
Lord, she will be a joyful woman!

Romeo

pay attention to   What wilt thou tell her, Nurse? Thou dost not mark° me.

Nurse

I will tell her, sir, that you do protest,³ which, as I take
it, is a gentlemanlike offer.

Romeo

confession   Bid her devise some means to come to shrift°
this afternoon.   *165*
And there she shall at Friar Laurence' cell
Be shrived⁴ and married. [*giving her coins*] Here is for thy
pains.

Nurse

No, truly, sir. Not a penny.

1   *cords made like a tackled stair*

    Rope ladder, reminiscent of ships'
    rigging

2   *high top-gallant*

    The enclosed platform at the top of
    the highest mast of a ship. Thus,
    the summit or highest point.

3   *Two may keep counsel, putting one away*

    A proverbial expression: "Two
    people can keep a secret, as long as
    one person doesn't know about it."

4   *fain lay knife aboard*

    Happily lay claim to Juliet
    (seemingly the phrase originates
    with the custom of placing one's
    knife at the dining table to reserve
    a seat)

5   *had as lief*

    Would as willingly

Romeo

Go to; I say you shall.

Nurse

[*taking the money*] This afternoon, sir? Well, she shall be
there. [*starts to leave*]   170

Romeo

And stay, good Nurse. Behind the abbey wall
Within this hour my man shall be with thee
And bring thee cords made like a tackled stair, [1]
Which to the high top-gallant[2] of my joy
means of access   Must be my convoy° in the secret night.   175
reward   Farewell. Be trusty, and I'll quit° thy pains.
Farewell. Commend me to thy mistress.

Nurse

Now God in Heaven bless thee! Hark you, sir.

Romeo

What say'st thou, my dear Nurse?

Nurse

trustworthy   Is your man secret?° Did you ne'er hear say,   180
"Two may keep counsel, putting one away"?[3]

Romeo

i.e., I assure   Warrant° thee, my man's as true as steel.

Nurse

Well, sir, my mistress is the sweetest lady. Lord, Lord,
chattering   when 'twas a little prating° thing—Oh, there is a nobleman in town, one Paris, that would fain lay knife aboard,[4]   185
but she, good soul, had as lief[5] see a toad, a very toad,
as see him. I anger her sometimes and tell her
handsomer   that Paris is the properer° man. But I'll warrant you,
cloth; sheet   when I say so, she looks as pale as any clout° in the
universal   versal° world. Doth not rosemary and Romeo begin   190
i.e., the same   both with a° letter?

1   *the dog's name*

    **Because r sounds like a dog's
    growl, rrr.**

2   *sententious*

    **Probably the Nurse's mistake for
    "sentences," i.e., sayings**

3   *Before and apace.*

    Go ahead, and quickly.

Romeo

Ay, Nurse, what of that? Both with an R.

Nurse

Ah, mocker, that's the dog's name.[1] R is for the—No,
I know it begins with some other letter, and she hath
about the prettiest sententious[2] of° it, of you and rosemary,   195
that it would do you good to hear it.

Romeo

Commend me to thy lady.

Nurse

Ay, a thousand times.—Peter!

Peter

right away Anon!°

Nurse

Before and apace.[3]   *They exit.*   200

1 *Therefore do nimble-pinioned doves draw Love*

   Venus, the Roman goddess of love, rode in a chariot pulled by doves.

2 *upon the highmost hill / Of this day's journey*

   I.e., at its highest point, which it reaches at noon

3 *bandy*

   Drive; Juliet imagines that her words will send the Nurse to Romeo and then his words will quickly send the Nurse back to Juliet with his message, as in an exchange of tennis shots.

Act 2, Scene 5

Enter **Juliet**.

Nurse makes excuses

Juliet

The clock struck nine when I did send the Nurse.

In half an hour she promised to return.

Perchance she cannot meet him. That's not so.

messengers   Oh, she is lame! Love's heralds° should be thoughts,

Which ten times faster glides than the sun's beams,   5

dark; threatening   Driving back shadows over louring° hills.

swift-winged   Therefore do nimble-pinioned° doves draw Love,¹

And therefore hath the wind-swift Cupid wings.

Now is the sun upon the highmost hill

Of this day's journey,² and from nine till twelve   10

Is three long hours, yet she is not come.

feelings   Had she affections° and warm youthful blood,

She would be as swift in motion as a ball;

My words would bandy³ her to my sweet love,

And his to me.   15

act   But old folks, many feign° as they were dead,

Unwieldy, slow, heavy, and pale as lead.

Enter **Nurse** [*and* **Peter**].

O God, she comes.—O honey Nurse, what news?

Hast thou met with him? Send thy man away.

Nurse

wait   Peter, stay° at the gate.   [**Peter** *exits.*]   20

Juliet

Now, good sweet Nurse— O Lord, why lookest thou sad?

Though news be sad, yet tell them merrily;

If good, thou shamest the music of sweet news

1   *Give me leave awhile.*

    Leave me alone for a while.

2   *Say either, and I'll stay the circumstance.*

    Immediately tell me if it's one or
    the other, and I'll wait to hear
    further details.

3   *a body*

    The object of the Nurse's admiration
    varies in the different printed
    versions of the play. In the Q1 (1597),
    the Nurse praises Romeo's "baudie";
    in the Q2 (1599) and in the First Folio
    (1623) his "body"; and in the Second
    Folio (1632) his "bawdy." The *body/
    bawdy* homonym emphasizes the
    sexual titillation conveyed by the
    Nurse's account of Romeo's lower
    parts: the leg, foot, and what is *not to
    be talked on* (2.5.42). The Nurse's
    description of Romeo's lower body
    inverts the Petrarchan convention of
    the *blazon,* in which the male poet-
    lover praises his beloved's (upper)
    body parts, such as the hair, eyes,
    lips, and hands. Mercutio parodies
    the blazon when he conjures Romeo
    by Rosaline's *fine foot, straight leg, and
    quivering thigh,* as well as the
    unnamed *demesnes* (territories) *that
    there adjacent lie* (2.1.19–21). Although
    the Nurse takes offense at the saucy
    sexual language Mercutio uses with
    her in public (2.4.133–143), this scene
    indicates that she enjoys privately
    engaging in sexual banter with
    Juliet.

4   *not to be talked on*

    Not worth mentioning

5   *Go thy ways, wench*

    Do as you please, girl. (The Nurse
    is apparently irritated by some
    gesture of impatience that Juliet
    makes.)

By playing it to me with so sour a face.

Nurse

I am aweary. Give me leave awhile. [1]   25

tiring journey Fie, how my bones ache! What a jaunce° have I!

Juliet

I would thou hadst my bones and I thy news.

Nay, come, I pray thee; speak. Good, good Nurse, speak.

Nurse

wait Jesu, what haste! Can you not stay° awhile?

Do you not see that I am out of breath?   30

Juliet

How art thou out of breath when thou hast breath

To say to me that thou art out of breath?

in regard to The excuse that thou dost make in° this delay

Is longer than the tale thou dost excuse.

Is thy news good or bad? Answer to that.   35

Say either, and I'll stay the circumstance. [2]

Let me be satisfied. Is 't good or bad?

Nurse

foolish Well, you have made a simple° choice. You know not

how to choose a man. Romeo? No, not he, though his

face be better than any man's, yet his leg excels all   40

as regards men's, and for° a hand and a foot and a body, [3] though

they be not to be talked on, [4] yet they are past compare.

very height He is not the flower° of courtesy, but, I'll warrant him,

as gentle as a lamb. Go thy ways, wench; [5] serve God.

What? Have you dined at home?   45

Juliet

No, no. But all this did I know before.

What says he of our marriage? What of that?

Nurse

Lord, how my head aches! What a head have I!

as if It beats as° it would fall in twenty pieces.

1   *a' t' other side*

On the other side. In performance,
Juliet usually rubs the Nurse's
back.

2   *God's lady dear*

I.e., Mary, mother of Jesus

3   *Marry, come up, I trow.*

I.e., heavens, you're getting
pushy, I swear.

My back—a' t' other side [1]—ah, my back, my back!   50

Curse Beshrew° your heart for sending me about,

trudging To catch my death with jauncing° up and down!

Juliet

I' faith, I am sorry that thou art not well.

Sweet, sweet, sweet Nurse, tell me: what says my love?

Nurse

Your love says, like an honest gentleman,   55

And a courteous, and a kind, and a handsome,

And, I warrant, a virtuous—Where is your mother?

Juliet

Where is my mother? Why, she is within.

Where should she be? How oddly thou repliest!

"Your love says, like an honest gentleman,   60

'Where is your mother?'"

Nurse

                 O God's lady dear, [2]

impatient Are you so hot?° Marry, come up, I trow. [3]

Is this the poultice for my aching bones?

Henceforward do your messages yourself.

Juliet

fuss Here's such a coil.° Come; what says Romeo?   65

Nurse   at church

confession Have you got leave to go to shrift° today?

Juliet

I have.

Nurse

hasten Then hie° you hence to Friar Laurence' cell.

There stays a husband to make you a wife.

unruly Now comes the wanton° blood up in your cheeks.   70

immediately They'll be in scarlet straight° at any news.

Hie you to church. I must another way

To fetch a ladder by the which your love

1   *a bird's nest*

    I.e., to your bedroom

2   *you shall bear the burden*

    (1) you'll have to do the work; (2)
    you'll have to support the weight
    of your lover (and eventually
    carry a child in pregnancy).

Must climb a bird's nest[1] soon when it is dark.
I am the drudge and toil in your delight,   75
But you shall bear the burden[2] soon at night.
Go. I'll to dinner; hie you to the cell.
Juliet
Hie to high fortune! Honest Nurse, farewell.   *They exit.*

1   *So smile the heavens*

     May the heavens smile

2   *But come what sorrow can, / It cannot countervail the exchange of joy / That one short minute gives me in her sight.*

     No matter what sorrow comes our way, it cannot match the joy for which it is exchanged when I am in her presence for a single minute.

3   *Is loathsome in his own deliciousness*

     Becomes cloying from its own sweetness

4   *the everlasting flint*

     I.e., the flint cobblestones on which she has walked

5   *so light is vanity*

     That is how insubstantial earthly happiness is.

6   *Good ev'n*

     Good evening (used also, as here, to mean "good afternoon")

7   *thank thee*

     I.e., by offering a kiss of greeting

Act 2, Scene 6

*Enter **Friar [Laurence]** and **Romeo**.*

Friar Laurence

So smile the heavens [1] upon this holy act

So that   That° after-hours with sorrow chide us not.

Romeo

may possibly come   Amen, amen. But come what sorrow can,°

balance   It cannot countervail° the exchange of joy

That one short minute gives me in her sight. [2]   5

join   Do thou but close° our hands with holy words,

Then may   Then° love-devouring death do what he dare;

It is enough I may but call her mine.

Friar Laurence

sudden; intense   These violent° delights have violent ends

fulfillment   And in their triumph° die, like fire and powder,   10

burn away   Which, as they kiss, consume.° The sweetest honey

its   Is loathsome in his° own deliciousness [3]

destroys   And, in the taste, confounds° the appetite.

Therefore love moderately. Long love doth so;

Too swift arrives as tardy as too slow.   15

*Enter **Juliet**.*

Here comes the lady. Oh, so light a foot

Will ne'er wear out the everlasting flint. [4]

cobweb strands   A lover may bestride the gossamers°

That idles in the wanton summer air,

And yet not fall; so light is vanity. [5]   20

Juliet

holy   Good ev'n [6] to my ghostly° confessor.

Friar Laurence

Romeo shall thank thee, [7] daughter, for us both.

1   *As much to him*

    I.e., I'll give him a kiss in return.

2   *Unfold the imagined happiness that both /*
    Receive in either by this dear encounter

    I.e., express the anticipated
    happiness that we will receive
    from each other as a result of this
    precious liaison

3   *Conceit, more rich in matter than in*
    words, / Brags of his substance, not of
    ornament.

    I.e., true imagination, when
    there's something of substance to
    consider, is proud of what is really
    there rather than the words it
    might find to describe it.

4   *I cannot sum up sum of half my wealth*

    I.e., I couldn't count even half my
    wealth.

5   *you shall not stay alone*

    You shall not be left alone
    together.

6   *Till holy church incorporate two in one*

    Until the church has made you one
    through the sacrament of marriage

Juliet

As much to him, [1] else is his thanks too much.

Romeo

amount   Ah, Juliet, if the measure° of thy joy

if   Be heaped like mine, and that° thy skill be more   25

thoroughly describe   To blazon° it, then sweeten with thy breath

This neighbor air, and let rich music's tongue

Unfold the imagined happiness that both

Receive in either by this dear encounter. [2]

Juliet

Conceit, more rich in matter than in words,   30

Brags of his substance, not of ornament. [3]

They are but beggars that can count their worth,

But my true love is grown to such excess

I cannot sum up sum of half my wealth. [4]

Friar Laurence

Come, come with me, and we will make short work,   35

For, by your leaves, you shall not stay alone [5]

Till holy church incorporate two in one. [6]   *[They exit.]*

They'll get married and be quick about it. They really want to be together.

1   *claps me*

    **Slaps down (*me* is an obsolete
    form, similar to the Latin ethical
    dative, functioning mainly to draw
    attention to the speaker)**

2   *by the operation of the second cup,
    draws him on the drawer*

    **When his second cup of beer has
    taken effect, draws his sword on
    the servingman**

3   *as hot a jack*

    As intense and excitable a fellow

4   *as soon moved to be moody, and as soon
    moody to be moved*

    **As easily provoked to anger, and as
    easily made angry at having been
    provoked**

5   *And what to?*

    I.e. moved to do what?

6   *two*

    **Mercutio pretends to mistake
    Benvolio's *to* for *two*.**

7   *What eye but such an eye*

    **I.e., what person but just that kind
    of person (with a pun on *eye* for
    Benvolio's *I* in 3.1.10)**

8   *meat*

    **Edible material (i.e., the yolk and
    the white)**

Act 3, Scene 1

Enter **Mercutio**, **Benvolio**, *[Mercutio's page, and other]* men.

Benvolio

I pray thee, good Mercutio, let's retire.

apulets / in the streets The day is hot; the Capels,° abroad;°

And if we meet we shall not 'scape a brawl,

For now, these hot days, is the mad blood stirring.

Mercutio

Thou art like one of these fellows that, when he enters 5

the confines of a tavern, claps me [1] his sword upon

the table and says "God send me no need of thee!" and,

by the operation of the second cup, draws him on the

drawer, [2] when indeed there is no need.

Benvolio

Am I like such a fellow? 10

Mercutio

Come, come, thou art as hot a jack [3] in thy mood as any

provoked in Italy, and as soon moved° to be moody, and as soon

moody to be moved. [4]

Benvolio

And what to? [5]

Mercutio

if Nay, an° there were two [6] such, we should have none 15

shortly, for one would kill the other. Thou, why, thou

wilt quarrel with a man that hath a hair more or a hair

less in his beard than thou hast. Thou wilt quarrel with

a man for cracking nuts, having no other reason but

because thou hast hazel eyes. What eye but such an 20

eye [7] would spy out such a quarrel? Thy head is as full of

quarrels as an egg is full of meat, [8] and yet thy head

rotten hath been beaten as addle° as an egg for quarreling.

Thou hast quarreled with a man for coughing in the

1   *for wearing his new doublet before Easter*

    **For wearing his new jacket during
    Lent (the period of fasting and
    penance immediately before
    Easter). As part of the Easter
    celebration, people traditionally
    wore new clothes, but Benvolio is
    apparently offended by the tailor's
    jumping the gun.**

2   *With another, for tying his new shoes
    with old ribbon*

    **I.e., with another tradesman, for
    using old ribbon as shoelaces for
    the newly made shoes. The point is
    apparently the triviality of the act
    that provokes Benvolio's anger.**

3   *fee simple*

    Absolute possession (i.e., all of)

4   *Mercutio, thou consortest with Romeo.*

    **A *consort* was a group of professional
    musicians who would have been
    socially classified as menial servants.
    In the lines that follow, the
    aristocratic Mercutio thus seems to
    take offense at the social slur
    implied by Tybalt's claim that he
    consortest with Romeo. However,
    consort (see 3.1.42 and 3.1.43) also had
    a sexual meaning: "to espouse; to
    have sexual commerce with" (*OED*).
    Tybalt might be trying to paint the
    friendship between Mercutio and
    Romeo as a socially disorderly or, in
    Renaissance terms, a "sodomitical"
    relationship.**

street because he hath wakened thy dog that hath lain 25
asleep in the sun. Didst thou not fall out with a tailor
for wearing his new doublet before Easter?[1] With
another, for tying his new shoes with old ribbon?[2] And
yet thou wilt tutor me from quarreling!

Benvolio

If An° I were so apt to quarrel as thou art, any man should 30
buy the fee simple[3] of my life for an hour and a quarter.

Mercutio

how feeble The fee simple? Oh, simple!°

Enter **Tybalt**, **Petruccio**, *and others.*

Benvolio

By my head, here comes the Capulets.

Mercutio

By my heel, I care not.

Tybalt

Follow me close, for I will speak to them. 35

evening —Gentlemen, good e'en.° A word with one of you.

Mercutio *He wants to fight*

And but one word with one of us? Couple it with
something: make it a word and a blow.

Tybalt

You shall find me apt enough to that, sir, an you will

cause; excuse give me occasion.° 40

Mercutio

Could you not take some occasion without giving?

Tybalt

Mercutio, thou consortest with Romeo.[4]

Mercutio

Consort? What? Dost thou make us minstrels? An thou
make minstrels of us, look to hear nothing but discords.

1 *public haunt of men*

   Public place

2 *my man*

   **I.e., the fellow I've been looking
   for. Mercutio mockingly takes the
   phrase to mean "my servingman."**

3 *livery*

   **A servingman's uniform,
   indicating the identity of his
   employer.**

4 *Marry, go before to field, he'll be your
   follower*

   **Servants were sometimes called
   followers. Mercutio puns on this
   sense, but his primary meaning is:
   "Indeed, if you head to the
   dueling place (the *field*) first,
   Romeo will follow you quickly."**

5 *villain*

   **(1) scoundrel; (2) peasant (from the
   French *villein*)**

6 *Doth much excuse the appertaining rage /
   To such a greeting*

   **Excuses the fact that I'm not, as
   would be appropriate, enraged by
   being treated in this fashion**

that which [*indicating his sword*] Here's my fiddlestick. Here's that° 45
God's wounds (an oath) shall make you dance. Zounds,° "consort"! *comp. of musicians*

Benvolio

We talk here in the public haunt of men. [1] *They should*
Either withdraw unto some private place, *fight somewhere*
calmly Or reason coldly° of your grievances, *else*
Or else depart. Here all eyes gaze on us. 50

Mercutio

Men's eyes were made to look, and let them gaze.
I will not budge for no man's pleasure, I.

Enter **Romeo**.

Tybalt

Well, peace be with you, sir. Here comes my man. [2]

Mercutio

But I'll be hanged, sir, if he wear your livery. [3]
Marry, go before to field, he'll be your follower; [4] 55
Your worship in that sense may call him "man."

Tybalt

Romeo, the love I bear thee can afford
No better term than this: thou art a villain. [5]

Romeo

Tybalt, the reason that I have to love thee
Doth much excuse the appertaining rage 60
To such a greeting. [6] Villain am I none.
Therefore, farewell; I see thou knowest me not.

Tybalt *He's mad he showed up at the party*

Boy, this shall not excuse the injuries
That thou hast done me. Therefore turn and draw.

Romeo

I do protest I never injured thee, 65
imagine But love thee better than thou canst devise°

1 Alla stoccata

   A fencing term: Italian for "at the thrust." Mercutio continues his mockery of fashionable duelers, which he began at 2.4.20.

2 *carries it away*

   I.e., wins the day

3 *and, as you shall use me hereafter, dry-beat the rest of the eight*

   And, depending on how you behave toward me from now on, beat the rest of your eight lives soundly (without drawing any blood from them)

4 *Come, sir, your* passado.

   Sarcastic; "come then, sir, and show me your fancy moves"

5 Away **Tybalt**

   Q2's "Away Tybalt" is set as a stage direction, so it is set as a stage direction here as well, meaning "Tybalt exits." Some editors conjecture that it is in fact intended as a spoken line, perhaps spoken by the heretofore silent Petruccio.

Till thou shalt know the reason of my love.

regard And so, good Capulet, which name I tender°

As dearly as mine own, be satisfied.

Mercutio

O calm, dishonorable, vile submission! 70

Alla stoccata ¹ carries it away. ² [*draws his sword*]

withdraw Tybalt, you rat-catcher, will you walk?°

Tybalt

What wouldst thou have with me?

Mercutio

Good King of Cats, nothing but one of your nine lives,

with that I mean to make bold withal,° and, as you shall use 75

me hereafter, dry-beat the rest of the eight. ³ Will you

scabbard / hilt pluck your sword out of his pilcher° by the ears?° Make

haste, lest mine be about your ears ere it be out.

Tybalt

ready for I am for° you. [*draws his sword*]

Romeo

away Gentle Mercutio, put thy rapier up.° 80

Mercutio

Come, sir, your *passado*. ⁴

[**Mercutio** and **Tybalt** *fight.*]

Romeo

[*draws his sword*] Draw, Benvolio. Beat down their weapons.

Gentlemen, for shame! Forbear this outrage.

Tybalt! Mercutio! The Prince expressly hath

fighting Forbid this bandying° in Verona streets. 85

Hold, Tybalt! Good Mercutio!

[**Romeo** *tries to break up the fight,*

and **Tybalt** *stabs* **Mercutio** *under* **Romeo**'*s arm.*]

Away **Tybalt**, ⁵ [*and* **Petruccio**, *and the other Capulets also exit.*]

1 *scratch*

   Mercutio's understatement plays
   on Tybalt's name (see 2.4.18–19
   and note).

2 *grave*

   A morose pun; both "serious-
   minded" and "dead"

3 *by the book of arithmetic*

   I.e., according to the textbook
   diagrams

4 *I have it*

   I.e., I have been hit, echoing
   Mercutio's earlier use of the
   fencing phrase *the hai*, meaning
   "you have it" (i.e., "you've been
   stabbed") at 2.4.26.

Mercutio

I am hurt.

households / done for   A plague o' both houses!° I am sped.°

i.e., no wound   Is he gone and hath nothing?°

Benvolio

                    What? Art thou hurt?

Mercutio

Ay, ay, a scratch,[1] a scratch. Marry, 'tis enough.   90

Where is my page?—Go, villain, fetch a surgeon.

                 [*Mercutio's page exits.*]

Romeo

Courage, man. The hurt cannot be much.

Mercutio

No, 'tis not so deep as a well nor so wide as a church-door,

but 'tis enough; 'twill serve. Ask for me tomorrow and

ruined   you shall find me a grave[2] man. I am peppered,° I   95

warrant, for this world. A plague o' both your houses!

Zounds, a dog, a rat, a mouse, a cat to scratch a man to

death! A braggart, a rogue, a villain that fights by the

book of arithmetic![3] Why the devil came you between

us? I was hurt under your arm.   100

Romeo

I thought all for the best.

Mercutio

Help me into some house, Benvolio,

Or I shall faint. A plague o' both your houses!

They have made worms' meat of me.

thoroughly   I have it,[4] and soundly° too. Your houses!   105

                [**Mercutio** *and* **Benvolio**]*exit*.

Romeo

relative   This gentleman, the Prince's near ally,°

My very friend, hath got this mortal hurt

1   *Thy beauty hath made me effeminate /*
    And in my temper softened valor's steel

In Shakespeare's England, an
effeminate man was one who acted
like a woman, in the pejorative
sense of being weak, irrational, or
self-indulgent. Romantic passion
was often cited as a cause of male
effeminacy, because a lover—
especially a lover of women—
would be more inclined to indulge
those soft and sensual qualities
associated with women. Romeo
here blames his refusal to fight
Tybalt on his susceptibility to
Juliet's beauty, which he feels has
made him soft and cowardly. By
fighting Tybalt, he believes, he can
redeem his masculinity. His use of
temper condenses the concern, as it
means both "temperament" and
also the process by which steel is
hardened ("tempered").

2   *This day's black fate on more days doth*
    depend.

I.e., the sad fortune of this day will
exert itself over the future; *depend* =
"hang."

3   *respective lenity*

Discriminating gentleness, i.e., a
mercifulness that takes account of
particular circumstances (like the
order for no fighting)

In my behalf—my reputation stained
who for With Tybalt's slander—Tybalt, that° an hour
kinsman Hath been my cousin!° O sweet Juliet, 110
Thy beauty hath made me effeminate
disposition And in my temper° softened valor's steel. [1]

Enter **Benvolio**.

Benvolio
O Romeo, Romeo, brave Mercutio is dead!
risen to That gallant spirit hath aspired° the clouds,
Who Which° too untimely here did scorn the earth. 115
Romeo
This day's black fate on more days doth depend. [2]
This but begins the woe others must end.

[*Enter* **Tybalt**.]

Benvolio
Here comes the furious Tybalt back again.
Romeo
Again in triumph, and Mercutio slain?
Away to Heaven, respective lenity, [3] 120
guide And fire-eyed fury be my conduct° now.
Now, Tybalt, take the "villain" back again
That late thou gavest me, for Mercutio's soul
Is but a little way above our heads,
Waiting Staying° for thine to keep him company. 125
Either thou or I, or both, must go with him.

one of us will die, or both will die

Tybalt
Thou, wretched boy, that didst consort him here
Shalt with him hence.

1   *up*

    Agitated; up in arms

2   *doom thee death*

    Sentence you to death

3   *fortune's fool*

    **The butt of fortune's jokes;
    fortune's dupe or plaything.**

Romeo

i.e., This sword   This° shall determine that.

They fight. **Tybalt** *falls.*

Benvolio

Romeo, away; be gone!

The citizens are up, [1] and Tybalt slain.   130

stunned; bewildered   Stand not amazed.° The Prince will doom thee death [2]

If thou art taken. Hence, be gone; away!

Romeo

Oh, I am fortune's fool! [3]

Benvolio

Why dost thou stay?

Romeo *exits.*

Enter **Citizens**.

Citizen

Which way ran he that killed Mercutio?

Tybalt, that murderer, which way ran he?   135

Benvolio

There lies that Tybalt.

Citizen

[*to* **Benvolio**] Up, sir, go with me.

I charge thee in the Prince's name, obey.

Enter **Prince**, *old* **Montague**, **Capulet**, *their wives,
and all.*

Prince

Where are the vile beginners of this fray?

Benvolio

make known   O noble prince, I can discover° all

conduct   The unlucky manage° of this fatal brawl.   140

1   *spoke him fair*

    Spoke to him politely

2   *take truce with the unruly spleen*

    **I.e., make peace with the
    uncontrollable anger**

3   *turns deadly point to point*

    **I.e., turns his sword to parry
    Tybalt's**

4   *with one hand beats / Cold death aside
    and with the other sends / It back*

    **Benvolio describes a sword-and-
    dagger fight, in which the
    combatants hold a blade in each
    hand.**

5   *by and by*

    Immediately

There lies the man, slain by young Romeo,
That slew thy kinsman, brave Mercutio.
Lady Capulet

kinsman   Tybalt, my cousin!° Oh, my brother's child!
O Prince! O cousin! Husband! Oh, the blood is spilled
Of my dear kinsman! Prince, as thou art true,   *145*
For blood of ours shed blood of Montague.
O cousin, cousin!
Prince

Benvolio, who began this bloody fray?
Benvolio

Tybalt, here slain, whom Romeo's hand did slay.

consider   Romeo, that spoke him fair,¹ bid him bethink°   *150*

trivial / also   How nice° the quarrel was and urged withal°
Your high displeasure. All this, utterèd
With gentle breath, calm look, knees humbly bowed,
Could not take truce with the unruly spleen²

charges   Of Tybalt, deaf to peace, but that he tilts°   *155*
With piercing steel at bold Mercutio's breast,

just   Who, all° as hot, turns deadly point to point,³
And, with a martial scorn, with one hand beats
Cold death aside and with the other sends
It back⁴ to Tybalt, whose dexterity   *160*

Returns   Retorts° it. Romeo he cries aloud,
"Hold, friends! Friends, part!" and, swifter than his
    tongue,

i.e., sword   His agile arm° beats down their fatal points,
And 'twixt them rushes—underneath whose arm

malicious   An envious° thrust from Tybalt hit the life   *165*

brave   Of stout° Mercutio; and then Tybalt fled,
But by and by⁵ comes back to Romeo,

thought about   Who had but newly entertained° revenge,
And to 't they go like lightning, for ere I

1   *His fault concludes but what the law*
    should end

    I.e., Romeo's mistake only
    finished what the law would have
    (eventually) ended.

2   *hearts'*

    Many editions print "hate's" here,
    following the "hates" of Q1 (1597),
    but *hearts*, as the seat of emotions,
    is no less intelligible (and Q1
    misreads "heart" as "hate" at
    3.2.74).

3   *My blood*

    A member of my family (i.e.,
    Mercutio)

4   *It*

    Most editions print "I" as in Q1
    (1597), but *It* refers to *My blood* (line
    186), recalling Genesis 4:10 : "The
    voice of thy brother's blood crieth
    unto me from the earth."

5   *purchase out abuses*

    I.e., cancel out the crimes

6   *attend our will*

    Respect our judgment

Could draw to part them was stout Tybalt slain,   *170*

And, as he fell, did Romeo turn and fly.

This is the truth, or let Benvolio die.

Lady Capulet

He is a kinsman to the Montague.

Affection makes him false. He speaks not true.

Some twenty of them fought in this black strife,   *175*

And all those twenty could but kill one life.

I beg for justice, which thou, Prince, must give.

Romeo slew Tybalt; Romeo must not live.

Prince

Romeo slew him; he slew Mercutio.

Who now the price of his dear blood doth owe?   *180*

Montague

Not Romeo, Prince; he was Mercutio's friend.

His fault concludes but what the law should end:[1]

The life of Tybalt.

Prince

          And for that offense

Immediately we do exile him hence.

I have an interest in your hearts'[2] proceeding: *185*

My blood[3] for your rude brawls doth lie a-bleeding.

punish But I'll amerce° you with so strong a fine

That you shall all repent the loss of mine.

It[4] will be deaf to pleading and excuses.

Neither Nor° tears nor prayers shall purchase out abuses;[5]   *190*

depart Therefore use none. Let Romeo hence° in haste,

Else, when he's found, that hour is his last.

Bear hence this body and attend our will.[6]

only Mercy but° murders, pardoning those that kill.

                *They exit [with **Tybalt**'s body].*

1   **Juliet**

Juliet's soliloquy takes the form of an epithalamium, a poem or song to celebrate a wedding. Impatient for the arrival of darkness that will bring Romeo to her bed, Juliet alludes to the classical myth of Phaeton, son of the sun god Phoebus Apollo. Disregarding his father's warnings, Phaeton drove the chariot that pulled the sun through the sky. Phaeton was unable to control the *fiery-footed steeds*, which broke from their usual path and would have set the earth afire had Jupiter not destroyed him with a lightning bolt. Praising Phaeton as a *wagoner* who would make the sun set faster, Juliet ironically evokes a figure associated with destruction, youthful rashness, and fallen pride.

2   *Phaeton*

Pronounced with three syllables; see note 1 above.

3   *runaways'*

Reference unclear. Juliet may be referring to the chariot horses of the sun god, suggesting that daylight should disappear to make it easier for Romeo to visit her.

4   *wink*

(1) close; (2) pretend not to see

5   *how to lose a winning match*

I.e., how, by losing, in fact to win (by giving her heart to Romeo and thus winning her heart's desire)

6   *a pair of stainless maidenhoods*

Both Juliet's and Romeo's virginity

7   *Hood my unmanned blood bating in my cheeks*

I.e., hide my blushes. Juliet compares her evident desire to an *unmanned* (untrained) hawk, anxiously *bating* (flapping its wings) until its handler calms it by placing a hood over its head. Juliet is also *unmanned* in the sense that she is still a virgin without a man.

8   *Think true love acted simple modesty*

I.e., think that acting on one's true love is not immoral but is in fact completely innocent

9   *thou day in night*

I.e., Romeo

10   *and when I shall die*

(See LONGER NOTE on page 331.)

11   *bought the mansion*

Purchased the house; Juliet complains that she has entered into the formal relationship with Romeo but has not had the opportunity to experience their love.

Act 3, Scene 2

Enter **Juliet** *alone.*

Juliet [1]

swiftly Gallop apace,° you fiery-footed steeds,

i.e., in the west Toward Phoebus' lodging.° Such a wagoner

As Phaeton [2] would whip you to the west

And bring in cloudy night immediately.

enclosing Spread thy close° curtain, love-performing night,   5

That runaways' [3] eyes may wink [4] and Romeo

Leap to these arms, untalked of and unseen.

Lovers can see to do their amorous rites

i.e., By the light of By° their own beauties, or, if love be blind,

solemn It best agrees with night. Come, civil° night,   10

Thou sober-suited matron, all in black,

teach And learn° me how to lose a winning match [5]

Played for a pair of stainless maidenhoods. [6]

Hood my unmanned blood bating in my cheeks, [7]

unfamiliar With thy black mantle, till strange° love grow bold,   15

i.e., And think Think° true love acted simple modesty. [8]

Come night. Come Romeo. Come thou day in night, [9]

For thou wilt lie upon the wings of night

Whiter than new snow upon a raven's back.

Come, gentle night. Come, loving, black-browed night;   20

Give me my Romeo. And when I shall die, [10]

Take him and cut him out in little stars,

And he will make the face of heaven so fine

That all the world will be in love with night

harshly bright And pay no worship to the garish° sun.   25

Oh, I have bought the mansion [11] of a love

But not possessed it, and, though I am sold,

Not yet enjoyed. So tedious is this day

As is the night before some festival

197

1   cords

    I.e., the rope ladder Romeo
    requests at 2.4.173

2   *cockatrice*

    A mythological serpent that killed
    with its glance

To an impatient child that hath new robes   *30*
And may not wear them.

Enter **Nurse** *with cords.* ¹

            Oh, here comes my Nurse,
And she brings news, and every tongue that speaks
But Romeo's name speaks heavenly eloquence.
—Now, Nurse, what news? What hast thou there? The
    cords
That Romeo bid thee fetch?   *35*

Nurse

[*dropping the ladder*] Ay, ay, the cords.

Juliet

Ay me, what news? Why dost thou wring thy hands?

Nurse

welladay; alas   Ah, weraday!° He's dead; he's dead; he's dead!
We are undone, lady, we are undone!
Alack the day! He's gone; he's killed; he's dead!   *40*

Juliet

spiteful   Can Heaven be so envious?°

Nurse

            Romeo can,

She thought Romeo was dead

Though Heaven cannot. O Romeo, Romeo,
Whoever would have thought it? Romeo!

Juliet

What devil art thou that dost torment me thus?
This torture should be roared in dismal Hell.   *45*
Hath Romeo slain himself? Say thou but "Ay,"
And that bare vowel "I" shall poison more
Than the death-darting eye of cockatrice. ²
I am not I if there be such an "I,"
i.e., Romeo's   Or those° eyes shut that makes thee answer "Ay."   *50*

1   *God save the mark!*

    An apology for bringing up a
    distasteful or injurious subject
    (though the Nurse goes on to
    describe the scene in great detail)

2   *Vile earth, to earth resign.*

    I.e., my wretched body, which I am
    ready to yield to the grave. The
    phrase derives from the familiar
    thought of Genesis 3:19: "Thou
    art dust, and to dust shalt thou
    return."

3   *dreadful trumpet, sound the general
    doom*

    Juliet refers to the trumpet whose
    terrifying sound signifies the end
    of the world.

4   *with a flow'ring face*

    I.e., by a lovely (and seemingly
    harmless) face

If he be slain, say "Ay," or if not, "No."

well-being   Brief sounds determine of my weal° or woe.

Nurse

I saw the wound; I saw it with mine eyes—

God save the mark![1]—here on his manly breast.

A piteous corpse, a bloody piteous corpse,   55

Pale, pale as ashes, all bedaubed in blood,

swooned   All in gore-blood. I sounded° at the sight.

Juliet

bankrupt   Oh, break, my heart, poor bankrout,° break at once!

To prison, eyes, ne'er look on liberty.

i.e., signs of life   Vile earth, to earth resign.[2] End motion° here,   60

weigh down / coffin   And thou and Romeo press° one heavy bier.°

Nurse

O Tybalt, Tybalt, the best friend I had!

honorable   O courteous Tybalt, honest° gentleman!

That ever I should live to see thee dead.

Juliet

What storm is this that blows so contrary?   65

Is Romeo slaughtered, and is Tybalt dead?

My dearest cousin and my dearer lord?

Then, dreadful trumpet, sound the general doom,[3]

For who is living if those two are gone?

Nurse

Tybalt is gone, and Romeo banishèd.   70

Romeo that killed him—he is banishèd.

Juliet

O God, did Romeo's hand shed Tybalt's blood?

Nurse

It did; it did. Alas the day, it did.

Juliet

O serpent heart hid with a flow'ring face![4]

Did ever dragon keep so fair a cave?   75

1   *Dove-feathered raven, wolvish-ravening lamb!*

    I.e., white-feathered raven, wolf-like predatory lamb. Like Romeo's in 1.1.170–175, Juliet's anguish expresses itself in a series of paradoxes.

2   *Despisèd substance of divinest show*

    Hateful reality with a most heavenly appearance

3   *aqua vitae*

    Brandy or some similarly strong alcoholic drink (the phrase is Latin for "water of life": and pronounced aqua-veet)

Beautiful tyrant; fiend angelical!

Dove-feathered raven, wolvish-ravening lamb![1]   *Oxymoron*

Despisèd substance of divinest show,[2]

Exactly / truly   Just° opposite to what thou justly° seem'st.

A damnèd saint, an honorable villain.   80

O nature, what hadst thou to do in Hell

enclose; shelter   When thou didst bower° the spirit of a fiend

In mortal paradise of such sweet flesh?

subject matter   Was ever book containing such vile matter°

So fairly bound? Oh, that deceit should dwell   85

In such a gorgeous palace!

Nurse

trustworthiness   There's no trust,°

No faith, no honesty in men. All perjured,

wicked   All forsworn, all naught,° all dissemblers.

Ah, where's my man? Give me some aqua vitae.[3]

These griefs, these woes, these sorrows make me old.   90

Shame come to Romeo!

Juliet

Blistered be thy tongue   *She is mad
that Nurse
spoke badly
about Romeo*

For such a wish! He was not born to shame;

Upon his brow shame is ashamed to sit,

For 'tis a throne where honor may be crowned

entire   Sole monarch of the universal° Earth.   95

Oh, what a beast was I to chide at him!

Nurse

Will you speak well of him that killed your cousin?

Juliet

Shall I speak ill of him that is my husband?

i.e., speak well of   Ah, poor my lord, what tongue shall smooth° thy name,

damaged   When I, thy three hours' wife, have mangled° it?   100

why   But wherefore,° villain, didst thou kill my cousin?

That villain cousin would have killed my husband.

1   *native spring*

    Original source

2   *Your tributary drops belong to woe, /*
    Which you, mistaking, offer up to joy.

    **The tears you give as an offering
    (*tributary* = in tribute) should be
    dedicated to sorrow; you have
    made a mistake in thinking they
    were tears of joy.**

3   *And needly will be ranked with other*
    griefs

    **And necessarily must be listed
    together with other sorrows. In its
    military sense, *ranked* suggests that
    sorrows, like soldiers, are lining up
    and preparing to attack Juliet.**

4   *a rearward*

    **I.e., the rear guard, the section of
    an armed force held in reserve,
    which enters the battle last; here
    continuing the military metaphor
    of line 118, and meaning this last
    woe added to the news of Tybalt's
    death.**

5   *that woe sound*

    **(1) measure the depth of such a
    grief; (2) express such a grief**

Back, foolish tears, back to your native spring. [1]
Your tributary drops belong to woe,
Which you, mistaking, offer up to joy. [2]   105
My husband lives, that Tybalt would have slain,
And Tybalt's dead, that would have slain my husband.

Why   All this is comfort. Wherefore° weep I then?
Some word there was, worser than Tybalt's death,
willingly   That murdered me. I would forget it fain,°   110
into   But, oh, it presses to° my memory
Like damnèd guilty deeds to sinners' minds:
"Tybalt is dead, and Romeo banishèd."
That "banishèd," that one word "banishèd,"
Hath slain ten thousand Tybalts. Tybalt's death   115
Was woe enough if it had ended there.
Or, if sour woe delights in fellowship
necessarily   And needly° will be ranked with other griefs, [3]
Why followed not, when she said "Tybalt's dead,"
"Thy father" or "thy mother," nay, or both,   120
ordinary / provoked   Which modern° lamentations might have moved?°
But with a rearward [4] following Tybalt's death,
"Romeo is banishèd." To speak that word
Is father, mother, Tybalt, Romeo, Juliet,
All slain, all dead. "Romeo is banishèd."   125
There is no end, no limit, measure, bound,
In that word's death. No words can that woe sound. [5]
Where is my father and my mother, Nurse?

Nurse

Weeping and wailing over Tybalt's corpse.
Will you go to them? I will bring you thither.   130

Juliet

Wash they his wounds with tears? Mine shall be spent
When theirs are dry, for Romeo's banishment.
cheated   Take up those cords. Poor ropes, you are beguiled,°

1   *he made you for a highway*

**I.e., the rope ladder was intended
to provide access**

Both you and I, for Romeo is exiled.

He made you for a highway [1] to my bed,   135

But I, a maid, die maiden-widowèd.

Come cords; come Nurse. I'll to my wedding bed,

And death, not Romeo, take my maidenhead!

Nurse

Hie to your chamber. I'll find Romeo

know   To comfort you. I wot° well where he is.

Hark ye, your Romeo will be here at night.

I'll to him. He is hid at Laurence' cell.

Juliet

Oh, find him! Give this ring to my true knight,

And bid him come to take his last farewell.   *They exit.*

[handwritten note: You will have your wedding night with Romeo, and then he has to leave]

1   *Affliction is enamored of thy parts, / And*
    thou art wedded to calamity.

    Misery is in love with your good
    qualities, and you and disaster are
    bound together.

2   *craves acquaintance at my hand*

    Desires to know me

3   *world's exile*

    Exile from the world

Act 3, Scene 3

Enter **Friar [Laurence]** *and* **Romeo**, [*hiding*].

Friar Laurence

frightened Romeo, come forth; come forth, thou fearful° man.

Affliction is enamored of thy parts,

And thou art wedded to calamity. [1]

Romeo

sentence; judgment [*comes*] Father, what news? What is the Prince's doom?°

What sorrow craves acquaintance at my hand [2]   5

That I yet know not?

Friar Laurence

Too familiar

Is my dear son with such sour company.

I bring thee tidings of the Prince's doom.

Romeo

i.e., death What less than doomsday° is the Prince's doom?

Friar Laurence

issued A gentler judgment vanished° from his lips: 10

Not body's death, but body's banishment.

Romeo

Ha, banishment? Be merciful: say "death,"

For exile hath more terror in his look,

Much more than death. Do not say "banishment."

Friar Laurence

Here from Verona art thou banishèd.   15

calm Be patient,° for the world is broad and wide.

Romeo

outside of There is no world without° Verona walls

Except But° Purgatory, torture, Hell itself.

Hence "banishèd" is banished from the world,

And world's exile [3] is death. Then "banishèd"   20

wrongly named Is death mistermed.° Calling death "banishèd,"

1   *calls death*

   Demands the death penalty for

2   *courtship*

   **Dignity (of a position at court),
   with a pun on *courtship* as wooing**

3   *carrion-flies*

   **Flies that lay their eggs in rotting
   flesh**

4   *their own kisses*

   **I.e., the kiss that Juliet's top lip
   gives her bottom lip, when she
   closes her mouth**

5   *mean . . . mean*

   Instrument . . . unworthy

Thou cutt'st my head off with a golden ax
And smilest upon the stroke that murders me.
Friar Laurence
O deadly sin! O rude unthankfulness!
Thy fault our law calls death,[1] but the kind Prince,   25
forced Taking thy part, hath rushed° aside the law
And turned that black word "death" to "banishment."
This is dear mercy, and thou see'st it not.
Romeo
'Tis torture and not mercy. Heaven is here,
Where Juliet lives, and every cat and dog   30
And little mouse, every unworthy thing,
Live here in Heaven and may look on her,
value But Romeo may not. More validity,°
More honorable state, more courtship[2] lives
In carrion-flies[3] than Romeo. They may seize   35
On the white wonder of dear Juliet's hand
And steal immortal blessing from her lips,
chaste Who even in pure and vestal° modesty
Still blush, as thinking their own kisses[4] sin.
But Romeo may not; he is banishèd.   40
Flies may do this, but I from this must fly.
They are free men, but I am banishèd.
still And sayest thou yet° that exile is not death?
Hadst thou no poison mixed, no sharp-ground knife,
No sudden mean of death, though ne'er so mean,[5]   45
But "banishèd" to kill me? "Banishèd"!
O Friar, the damned use that word in hell.
goes with Howling attends° it. How hast thou the heart,
priest / holy Being a divine,° a ghostly° confessor,
A sin-absolver, and my friend professed,   50
wound To mangle° me with that word "banishèd"?

1   *Yet "banishèd"? Hang up philosophy!*
    I.e., you're still repeating that word
    "banished"? Forget philosophy!

2   *dispute with thee of thy estate*
    Discuss your situation with you

3   *Taking the measure of an unmade grave*
    By falling on the ground, Romeo
    demonstrates how large his grave
    should be.

Friar Laurence

foolish; doting Thou fond° mad man, hear me a little speak.

Romeo

Oh, thou wilt speak again of banishment.

Friar Laurence

I'll give thee armor to keep off that word—

Adversity's sweet milk, philosophy—   55

To comfort thee though thou art banishèd.

Romeo

Still Yet° "banishèd"? Hang up philosophy! [1]

Unless philosophy can make a Juliet,

Transplant Displant° a town, reverse a prince's doom,

It helps not; it prevails not. Talk no more.   60

Friar Laurence

Oh, then I see that madmen have no ears.

Romeo

How should they, when that wise men have no eyes?

Friar Laurence

Let me dispute with thee of thy estate. [2]

Romeo

that which Thou canst not speak of that° thou dost not feel.

Wert thou as young as I, Juliet thy love,   65

only An hour but° married, Tybalt murderèd,

Loving Doting° like me, and like me banishèd,

Then mightst thou speak, then mightst thou tear thy
    hair

And fall upon the ground, as I do now,

Taking the measure of an unmade grave. [3]   70

knock [within]

Friar Laurence

Arise. One knocks. Good Romeo, hide thyself.

Romeo

Not I, unless the breath of heartsick groans,

1   *Mistlike, infold me from the search of eyes.*

    Enfolds me like a mist, hiding me from the gaze of others

2   *By and by!*

    Just a second!

3   *case*

    Condition (with an unintended pun on *case* as a slang term for "vagina")

4   *rise and stand*

    Another unwitting sexual double entendre, which continues with *O* in line 90, where she means only his groaning expression of grief, but *O* was also slang for vagina.

Mistlike, infold me from the search of eyes. [1]

knock [within]

Friar Laurence

Hark, how they knock!—Who's there?—Romeo, arise.

captured   Thou wilt be taken.°—Stay awhile.—Stand up.   75

knock [within]

Run to my study.—By and by! [2]—God's will,

foolishness   What simpleness° is this!—I come; I come.

knock [within]

Who knocks so hard? Whence come you? What's your will?

Nurse

[*within*] Let me come in, and you shall know my errand.

I come from Lady Juliet.

Friar Laurence

                  Welcome then.   80

Enter **Nurse**.

Nurse

O holy Friar, Oh, tell me, holy Friar,

Where's my lady's lord? Where's Romeo?

Friar Laurence

There on the ground, with his own tears made drunk.

Nurse

precisely   Oh, he is even° in my mistress' case, [3]

Exactly / harmony   Just° in her case. O woeful sympathy,°   85

Piteous predicament! Even so lies she,

Blubb'ring and weeping, weeping and blubb'ring

if   —Stand up, stand up. Stand, an° you be a man.

For Juliet's sake, for her sake, rise and stand. [4]

Why should you fall into so deep an O?   90

Romeo

Nurse!

1   *My concealed lady*

    My secret wife

2   *on Romeo cries*

    **The Nurse means "calls for
    Romeo"; Romeo understands
    "exclaims against Romeo."**

3   *In what vile part of this anatomy / Doth
    my name lodge*

    **Recalling Juliet's question in
    2.2.40–42: *What's Montague? It is nor
    hand nor foot, / Nor arm nor face, nor
    any other part / Belonging to a man.***

4   *The hateful mansion*

    **Recalling Juliet's description in
    3.2.26 of Romeo's body as *the
    mansion of a love.***

5   *And ill-beseeming beast in seeming both*

    **And an unnatural creature, due to
    the fact that you seem to be both
    man and woman**

Nurse

Ah sir, ah sir, death's the end of all.

Romeo

[rising] Spakest thou of Juliet? How is it with her?

experienced Doth she not think me an old° murderer,

Now I have stained the childhood of our joy   95

With blood removed but little from her own?

Where is she? And how doth she? And what says

annulled My concealed lady¹ to our canceled° love?

Nurse

Oh, she says nothing, sir, but weeps and weeps,

And now falls on her bed, and then starts up,   100

And "Tybalt" calls, and then on Romeo cries,²

And then down falls again.

Romeo

                As if that name,

aim Shot from the deadly level° of a gun,

Did murder her, as that name's cursèd hand

Murdered her kinsman. Oh tell me, Friar, tell me,   105

body In what vile part of this anatomy°

Doth my name lodge?³ Tell me, that I may sack

The hateful mansion.⁴ *[draws his dagger]*

Friar Laurence

                Hold thy desperate hand!

shape Art thou a man? Thy form° cries out thou art;

Thy tears are womanish. Thy wild acts denote   110

irrational The unreasonable° fury of a beast.

appropriate / apparent Unseemly° woman in a seeming° man,

And ill-beseeming beast in seeming both.⁵

Thou hast amazed me. By my holy order,

balanced I thought thy disposition better tempered.°   115

Hast thou slain Tybalt? Wilt thou slay thyself,

And slay thy lady that in thy life lives

1   *Why railest thou on*

    Why do you rant against

2   *Which, like a usurer, abound'st in all /*
    And usest none in that true use indeed

    A *usurer* is one who charges interest
    on loans, usually at an excessive
    rate. In the Renaissance, usury was
    sometimes symbolically
    associated with sodomy: usury was
    regarded as a perversion of the *true*
    ***use* of money (a medium of**
    exchange for goods), just as
    sodomy was regarded as a
    perversion of the *true use* of
    sexuality (a means of procreation
    of children). By comparing Romeo
    to a usurer, Friar Laurence intends
    to shame him for indulging
    ***womanish* behavior that perverts**
    the *true use* of his gender, namely
    masculine valor (3.3.110).

3   *Digressing from*

    If it diverges from

4   *Misshapen in the conduct of them both*

    Incompetent in its guidance of
    both (shape and love)

5   *There art thou happy*

    In that are you fortunate

6   *mishavèd*

    (miss-HAYV-ed); misbehaved

7   *till the watch be set*

    Until the time when the city guards
    arrive at their watch posts (and the
    gates are shut)

sinful	By doing damnèd° hate upon thyself?	
	Why railest thou on ¹ thy birth, the Heaven, and Earth?	
	Since birth and Heaven and Earth, all three do meet	120
	In thee at once, which thou at once wouldst lose?	
	Fie, fie, thou shamest thy shape, thy love, thy wit,	
Who	Which,° like a usurer, abound'st in all	
	And usest none in that true use indeed ²	
adorn	Which should bedeck° thy shape, thy love, thy wit.	125
	Thy noble shape is but a form of wax,	
	Digressing from ³ the valor of a man;	
	Thy dear love sworn but hollow perjury,	
	Killing that love which thou hast vowed to cherish.	
	Thy wit—that ornament to shape and love,	130
	Misshapen in the conduct of them both ⁴—	
gunpowder	Like powder° in a skill-less soldier's flask	
	Is set afire by thine own ignorance,	
by	And thou dismembered with° thine own defense.	
	What? Rouse thee, man! Thy Juliet is alive,	135
i.e., willing to die	For whose dear sake thou wast but lately dead°—	
wished to	There art thou happy. ⁵ Tybalt would° kill thee,	
	But thou slewest Tybalt—there art thou happy.	
	The law that threatened death becomes thy friend	
	And turns it to exile—there art thou happy.	140
	A pack of blessings light upon thy back,	
finery	Happiness courts thee in her best array,°	
girl	But, like a mishavèd ⁶ and sullen wench,°	
	Thou pout'st upon thy fortune and thy love.	
i.e., such gloomy people	Take heed, take heed, for such° die miserable.	145
previously arranged	Go; get thee to thy love, as was decreed.°	
	Ascend her chamber; hence and comfort her.	
be sure	But look° thou stay not till the watch be set, ⁷	
	For then thou canst not pass to Mantua,	
	Where thou shalt live, till we can find a time	150

1 *prepare to chide*

I.e., get ready to rebuke him for Tybalt's death.

2 *here stands all your state*

I.e., your future depends on what I'm about to say.

3 *so brief to part with thee*

To part so abruptly from you

blicly proclaim / relatives To blaze° your marriage, reconcile your friends,°

Beg pardon of the Prince, and call thee back

With twenty hundred thousand times more joy

Than thou went'st forth in lamentation.

—Go before, Nurse. Commend me to thy lady   155

And bid her hasten all the house to bed,

Which heavy sorrow makes them apt unto.

Romeo is coming.

Nurse

O Lord, I could have stayed here all the night

To hear good counsel. Oh, what learning is!   160

My lord, I'll tell my lady you will come.

Romeo

Do so, and bid my sweet prepare to chide. [1]

Nurse

Here, sir, a ring she bid me give you, sir.

Hurry Hie° you; make haste, for it grows very late.   [*She exits.*]

Romeo

How well my comfort is revived by this!   165

Friar Laurence

Go hence. Good night. And here stands all your state: [2]

Either be gone before the watch be set,

Or by the break of day, disguised from hence,

servant Sojourn in Mantua. I'll find out your man,°

make known And he shall signify° from time to time   170

event / happens Every good hap° to you that chances° here.

Give me thy hand. 'Tis late. Farewell; good night.

Romeo

Except But° that a joy past joy calls out on me,

It were a grief so brief to part with thee. [3]

Farewell.   *They exit.*   175

1   *mewed up to her heaviness*

    Sequestered with her sorrow (like a
    ***mewed* or "caged" hawk)**

2   *desperate tender*

    Rash offer

3   *son*

    I.e., son-in-law, as Capulet already
    imagines him

4   *keep no great ado*

    Not make a big fuss over it

Act 3, Scene 4

Enter old **Capulet**, *his wife, and* **Paris**.

Capulet

Things have fall'n out, sir, so unluckily

persuade That we have had no time to move° our daughter.

Look you, she loved her kinsman Tybalt dearly,

And so did I. Well, we were born to die.

'Tis very late; she'll not come down tonight. 5

were it not I promise you, but° for your company,

I would have been abed an hour ago.

Paris

These times of woe afford no times to woo.

Madam, good night. Commend me to your daughter.

Lady Capulet

I will, and know her mind early tomorrow. 10

Tonight she's mewed up to her heaviness.[1]

Capulet

Sir Paris, I will make a desperate tender[2]

Of my child's love. I think she will be ruled

In all respects by me. Nay, more, I doubt it not.

—Wife, go you to her ere you go to bed. 15

Acquaint her here of my son[3] Paris' love,

And bid her, mark you me, on Wednesday next

—But, soft! What day is this?

Paris

                Monday, my lord.

Capulet

Monday! Ha, ha. Well, Wednesday is too soon,

O' Thursday let it be.—O' Thursday, tell her, 20

She shall be married to this noble earl.

Will you be ready? Do you like this haste?

We'll keep no great ado,[4] a friend or two,

1   *held him carelessly*

    Did not care much about him

2   *Afore me*

    **A mild interjection, "as God is
    before me"**

3   *by and by*

    Very soon

recently   For, hark you, Tybalt being slain so late,°

It may be thought we held him carelessly,[1]   25

Being our kinsman, if we revel much.

Therefore we'll have some half a dozen friends,

And there an end.—But what say you to Thursday?

Paris

My lord, I would that Thursday were tomorrow.

Capulet

Well, get you gone. O' Thursday be it, then.   30

[*to* **Lady Capulet**] Go you to Juliet ere you go to bed.

in anticipation of   Prepare her, wife, against° this wedding day.

—Farewell, my lord.—Light to my chamber, ho!

Afore me,[2] it is so very late,

That we may call it early by and by.[3]   35

—Good night.   *They exit.*

[handwritten annotation: tell Juliet she will be married on Thursday]

1   *severing*

    Separating (both "separating from
    one another" and, as a result of the
    approaching morning, "separating
    Romeo from Juliet")

2   *It is some meteor that the sun exhales*

    According to Elizabethan
    astronomy, the sun pulled in
    polluted vapors from the Earth's
    atmosphere before exhaling those
    fumes in the form of flaming
    meteors.

3   *the pale reflex of Cynthia's brow*

    The pale reflection of the moon's
    face (*Cynthia's brow*). *Cynthia* was a
    Greek name for Diana, goddess of
    the moon.

Act 3, Scene 5

*Enter **Romeo** and **Juliet** aloft.*

Juliet

Wilt thou be gone? It is not yet near day.

It was the nightingale, and not the lark,

apprehensive That pierced the fearful° hollow of thine ear.

yonder Nightly she sings on yon° pom'granate tree.

Believe me, love, it was the nightingale.   5

Romeo

It was the lark, the herald of the morn,

malicious No nightingale. Look, love, what envious° streaks

Do lace the severing¹ clouds in yonder east.

i.e., stars / cheerful Night's candles° are burnt out, and jocund° day

Stands tiptoe on the misty mountain tops.   10

i.e., if I am to I must be gone and° live, or stay and die.

Juliet

Yon light is not daylight; I know it, I.

It is some meteor that the sun exhales²

To be to thee this night a torchbearer,

And light thee on thy way to Mantua;   15

Therefore stay yet. Thou need'st not to be gone.

Romeo

taken; captured Let me be ta'en.° Let me be put to death.

I am content, so thou wilt have it so.

I'll say yon grey is not the morning's eye.

'Tis but the pale reflex of Cynthia's brow.³   20

i.e., And Nor° that is not the lark, whose notes do beat

arched The vaulty° Heaven so high above our heads.

desire I have more care° to stay than will to go.

Come, death, and welcome. Juliet wills it so.

How is 't, my soul? Let's talk. It is not day.   25

1 *Straining harsh discords and unpleasing
   sharps*

   **Croaking ugly, dissonant melodies
   and unpleasant, shrill notes**

2 *makes sweet division*

   **Sings beautiful passages of short
   notes (punning on *division* as
   "separation," as in 3.5.29)**

3 *Since arm from arm that voice doth us affray, /
   Hunting thee hence with hunt's-up to the day.*

   **Since that voice startles us out of
   each other's arms, driving you
   from here with a *hunt's-up* (a song
   to wake a bride on the morning
   after her wedding, named for a
   similar song to rouse hunters)**

4 *Wilt thou be gone? . . . . more dark and
   dark our woes*

   **This dialogue (beginning at 3.5.1) takes
   the form of an aubade (dawn song), a
   poem about lovers reluctantly
   separating after a night together. In the
   medieval tradition of courtly love,
   which posited that true love could not
   exist within marriage, the male lover
   had to leave his mistress' chamber at
   dawn to preserve the secrecy of their
   adulterous relationship. Although
   Romeo and Juliet are married, the
   secrecy of their marriage and the threat
   to Romeo's life should he be caught
   give a sharp urgency to their parting.
   The reference to the courtly love
   tradition in this dialogue reinforces
   the point that the lovers' clandestine
   marriage transgresses social authority.**

5 *by this count I shall be much in years*

   **By this method of counting, I will
   be very old**

Juliet

It is; it is. Hie hence! Be gone; away!

It is the lark that sings so out of tune,

Straining harsh discords and unpleasing sharps. ¹

Some say the lark makes sweet division. ²

separates   This doth not so, for she divideth° us.   30

exchange   Some say the lark and loathèd toad change° eyes.

Oh, now I would they had changed voices too,

Since arm from arm that voice doth us affray,

Hunting thee hence with hunt's-up to the day. ³

Oh, now be gone. More light and light it grows.   35

Romeo

More light and light, more dark and dark our woes. ⁴

Enter **Nurse**.

Nurse

Madam.

Juliet

Nurse?

Nurse

Your lady mother is coming to your chamber.

The day is broke. Be wary; look about.   [*She exits.*]   40

Juliet

Then, window, let day in and let life out.

Romeo

Farewell, farewell. One kiss, and I'll descend.

[*They kiss.* **Romeo** *descends.*]

Juliet

lover   Art thou gone so? Love, lord, ay, husband, friend.°

I must hear from thee every day in the hour,

For in a minute there are many days.   45

Oh, by this count I shall be much in years ⁵

1   *an ill-divining soul*

     A soul that has premonitions of misfortune

2   *Dry sorrow drinks our blood.*

     Sighs were thought to consume blood and expel vital force from the body, leaving the afflicted drawn and pale.

3   *O fortune, fortune! All men call thee fickle. / If thou art fickle, what dost thou with him / That is renowned for faith? Be fickle, fortune, / For then, I hope, thou wilt not keep him long, / But send him back.*

     Fortune was commonly personified as a fickle goddess who turned a wheel on which individuals rose to and fell from power. Fortune plays an important role in the medieval tradition of tragedy centered on the fall of princes. The tradition is often referred to as *de casibus* tragedy, from the Latin title of an influential work by the 14th-century Italian writer Boccaccio, *De Casibus Virorum Illustrium (Of the Falls of Famous Men)*. Like all of Shakespeare's tragedies, however, *Romeo and Juliet* is not simply a *de casibus* account of fortune's role in bringing about suffering. On the one hand, it shifts attention to two young lovers from tragedy's usual focus on the falls and failings of great men. On the other, and more crucially, however, *Romeo and Juliet* explores the psychological and social conditions that influence protagonists to make decisions that lead to their demise. This play, then, can be regarded as an early working out of the tragic pattern that informs Shakespeare's greatest tragedies of character, including *Hamlet* and *King Lear*.

Ere I again behold my Romeo.

Romeo

[*below*]Farewell! I will omit no opportunity

That may convey my greetings, love, to thee.

Juliet

Oh, think'st thou we shall ever meet again?   50

Romeo

I doubt it not, and all these woes shall serve

For sweet discourses in our times to come.

Juliet

O God, I have an ill-divining soul. [1]

Methinks I see thee now: thou art so low

As one dead in the bottom of a tomb.   55

Either my eyesight fails, or thou lookest pale.

Romeo

And trust me, love, in my eye so do you.

Dry sorrow drinks our blood. [2] Adieu, adieu!   *He exits.*

Juliet

O fortune, fortune! All men call thee fickle.

If thou art fickle, what dost thou with him   60

faithfulness   That is renowned for faith?° Be fickle, fortune,

For then, I hope, thou wilt not keep him long,

But send him back. [3]

Enter [**Lady Capulet** *below*].

Lady Capulet

                         Ho, daughter, are you up?

Juliet

[*aside*] Who is 't that calls? It is my lady mother.

i.e., yet in bed   Is she not down° so late or up so early?   65

brings   What unaccustomed cause procures° her hither?

                         [*She descends.*]

1   *Some grief shows much of love, / But much of grief shows still some want of wit.*

A moderate expression of grief demonstrates that you loved the deceased, but excessive grief always indicates a lack of wisdom.

2   *Yet let me weep for such a feeling loss.*

In the following exchange, Juliet repeatedly speaks ambiguously to her mother in order to mislead her. By not specifying the *feeling loss* for which she weeps, Juliet allows her mother to believe she mourns Tybalt's death rather than Romeo's banishment.

3   *So shall you feel the loss, but not the friend / Which you weep for.*

I.e., then you will only feel your own grief, but that won't bring him for whom you grieve back to life. (Lady Capulet means "kinsman" when she says *friend*, i.e., Tybalt, while Juliet takes it to mean "lover.")

4   *Villain and he be many miles asunder.*

Another equivocation. In an apparent condemnation of Romeo, Juliet's words indicate a wish that "he and his villainy be many miles from here." Secretly, however, she defends Romeo, protesting, "Romeo is far from being a villain."

5   *yet no man like he doth grieve my heart*

(1) but no one makes me angry as much as Romeo does; (2) but no one as much as he makes my heart yearn. Lady Capulet only understands the first meaning.

Lady Capulet

Why, how now, Juliet?

Juliet

                  Madam, I am not well.

Lady Capulet

Continuously Evermore° weeping for your cousin's death?

What? Wilt thou wash him from his grave with tears?

Even An° if thou couldst, thou couldst not make him live.   70

Therefore, have done. Some grief shows much of love,

But much of grief shows still some want of wit.[1]

Juliet

deeply felt Yet let me weep for such a feeling° loss.[2]

Lady Capulet

So shall you feel the loss, but not the friend

Which you weep for.[3]

Juliet

                Feeling so the loss,   75

lover I cannot choose but ever weep the friend.°

Lady Capulet

Well, girl, thou weep'st not so much for his death

As that the villain lives which slaughtered him.

Juliet

What villain, madam?

Lady Capulet

                That same villain, Romeo.

Juliet

Villain and he be many miles asunder.[4]   80

God pardon him. I do, with all my heart,

And yet no man like he doth grieve my heart.[5]

Lady Capulet

That is because the traitor murderer lives.

Juliet

away from Ay, madam, from° the reach of these my hands.

1   *I never shall be satisfied / With Romeo, till I*
    behold him——dead—— / Is my poor heart

    Read one way, this passage implies
    that Juliet wants to see Romeo
    dead; read another, it means "I
    never shall have enough of
    Romeo. Until I see him again, my
    heart is dead." There is a further
    irony in that the next time she will
    see Romeo he will in fact be dead.

2   *kinsman*

    Lady Capulet understands Tybalt as
    the *kinsman*; Juliet means her
    husband Romeo.

3   *temper*

    Another equivocation: (1) mix;
    (2) weaken

4   *sleep in quiet*

    Lady Capulet takes this phrase
    metaphorically (i.e., "sleep the
    quiet sleep of death"), though
    Juliet means the phrase literally
    (i.e., "only sleep, rather than die").

5   *wreak*

    Pay (again, with an ambiguous
    sense): (1) revenge; (2) bestow

6   *in happy time*

    Just at the perfect time

I wish that / avenge Would° none but I might venge° my cousin's death! 85

Lady Capulet

We will have vengeance for it, fear thou not;

Then weep no more. I'll send to one in Mantua,

fugitive Where that same banished runagate° doth live,

who shall / dose (of poison) Shall° give him such an unaccustomed dram°

That he shall soon keep Tybalt company, 90

And then, I hope, thou wilt be satisfied.

Juliet

Indeed, I never shall be satisfied

Her heart is dead

With Romeo, till I behold him—dead—

Is my poor heart[1] so for a kinsman[2] vexed.

Madam, if you could find out but a man 95

To bear a poison, I would temper[3] it

So that That° Romeo should, upon receipt thereof,

Soon sleep in quiet.[4] Oh, how my heart abhors

To hear him named and cannot come to him

To wreak[5] the love I bore my cousin 100

Upon his body that hath slaughtered him.

Lady Capulet

Find thou the means, and I'll find such a man.

But now I'll tell thee joyful tidings, girl.

Juliet

And joy comes well in such a needy time.

What are they, beseech your Ladyship? 105

Lady Capulet

attentive Well, well, thou hast a careful° father, child,

sadness One who, to put thee from thy heaviness,°

imminent Hath sorted out a sudden° day of joy

That thou expects not, nor I looked not for.

Juliet

Madam, in happy time.[6] What day is that? 110

1   *Thou counterfeits a bark, a sea, a wind*

    **You resemble a ship, a sea, and a
    wind.**

2   *Without a sudden calm*

    **Unless soon there is an end to the
    (emotional) storm**

Lady Capulet

Marry, my child, early next Thursday morn,

The gallant, young, and noble gentleman,

The County Paris, at Saint Peter's Church,

Shall happily make thee there a joyful bride.

Juliet

Now, by Saint Peter's Church and Peter too,   115

He shall not make me there a joyful bride.

I wonder at this haste, that I must wed

Ere he, that should be husband, comes to woo.

I pray you, tell my lord and father, madam,

I will not marry yet. And when I do, I swear   120

It shall be Romeo, whom you know I hate,

Rather than Paris. These are news indeed!

Lady Capulet

Here comes your father. Tell him so yourself,

And see how he will take it at your hands.

Enter **Capulet** *and* **Nurse**.

Capulet

When the sun sets, the Earth doth drizzle dew,   125

But for the sunset of my brother's son

intensely   It rains downright.°

fountain   How now? A conduit,° girl? What? Still in tears,

Evermore show'ring? In one little body

Thou counterfeits a bark, a sea, a wind,[1]   130

continually   For still° thy eyes, which I may call the sea,

ship   Do ebb and flow with tears. The bark° thy body is,

i.e., winds (are)   Sailing in this salt flood; the winds° thy sighs,

Which   Who,° raging with thy tears, and they with them,

capsize   Without a sudden calm,[2] will overset°   135

Thy tempest-tossèd body.—How now, wife?

1   *take me with you*

Let me follow your meaning; I
don't understand you.

2   *Not proud you have, but thankful that*
you have.

I.e., I take no pride in the fact that
you have secured Paris for me, but
I am grateful for your efforts.

3   *thankful even for hate that is meant love*

Grateful even for what I hate since
it is intended as a gesture of love

4   *Chopped logic*

Superficially clever arguments and
careful phrasing

5   *Mistress minion*

I.e., spoiled brat

6   *fettle your fine joints 'gainst Thursday*
next

Get your spoiled self ready in
preparation for next Thursday. (To
fettle a horse is to groom it.)

7   *I will drag thee on a hurdle thither*

Evoking the image of a criminal
being dragged through the streets
on a *hurdle*, Capulet describes Juliet's
wedding ceremony in terms of a
public display of state power. The
hurdle was a kind of sled on which
traitors were pulled from the Tower
to the scaffold, where they would
be subjected to a gruesomely
elaborate ritual of execution and
dismemberment. In 1586, at the
public execution of fourteen men

accused of plotting to assassinate
Queen Elizabeth, the chief
conspirator was hurdled, hanged,
disemboweled (his heart thrown
into the fire), decapitated (his
head placed upon a stake), and
quartered. Although Capulet
regards Juliet's disobedience as
analogous to rebellion against his
domestic authority, Juliet herself
assures Friar Laurence that she will
die before her *true heart with*
treacherous revolt / Turn[s] to another
(4.1.58–59).

8   *green sickness carrion*

Immature, anemic bag of bones
(see also 2.2.8 and note)

Have you delivered to her our decree?

Lady Capulet

have none of it   Ay, sir, but she will none.° She gives you thanks.
I would the fool were married to her grave!

Capulet

Soft, take me with you,¹ take me with you, wife.   140
How? Will she none? Doth she not give us thanks?
Is she not proud? Doth she not count her blessed,

produced   Unworthy as she is, that we have wrought°

bridegroom   So worthy a gentleman to be her bride?°

Juliet

Not proud you have, but thankful that you have.²   145
Proud can I never be of what I hate,
But thankful even for hate that is meant love.³

Capulet

How, how, how, how? Chopped logic?⁴ What is this?
"Proud," and "I thank you," and "I thank you not,"
And yet "not proud"? Mistress minion⁵ you,   150
Thank me no thankings, nor proud me no prouds,
But fettle your fine joints 'gainst Thursday next⁶
To go with Paris to Saint Peter's Church,

wooden cart   Or I will drag thee on a hurdle° thither.⁷

worthless woman   Out, you green sickness carrion!⁸ Out, you baggage!°   155

pale   You tallow° face!

Lady Capulet

                    Fie, fie! What? Are you mad?

Juliet

[*kneels*] Good Father, I beseech you on my knees,
Hear me with patience but to speak a word.

Capulet

good-for-nothing   Hang thee, young baggage.° Disobedient wretch,
I tell thee what: get thee to church o' Thursday,   160
Or never after look me in the face.

1   *God 'i' good e'en*

    I.e., God give you a good evening;
    here an expression of irritation

2   *Utter your gravity o'er a gossip's bowl*

    Go speak your thoughts when you
    are drinking with your friends.

3   *God's bread!*

    An oath: "by the consecrated
    Communion bread"

4   *Of fair demesnes*

    With desirable estates

5   *limbed*

    Q2 prints "liand," which has
    provoked much speculation about
    the intended reading. Most editions
    opt for "ligned," an unusual word
    related to "lineage," but Paris's
    family has been mentioned in the
    previous line. It seems more likely
    that Capulet moves from consulting
    the Count's family, to his wealth, and
    finally to his person, and that "liand"
    is a misreading of the manuscript's
    "limd."

scarcely

Speak not. Reply not. Do not answer me.
My fingers itch.—Wife, we scarce° thought us blessed
That God had lent us but this only child,
But now I see this one is one too much   165
And that we have a curse in having her.

worthless woman

Out on her, hilding!°

Nurse

God in Heaven bless her!

berate

You are to blame, my lord, to rate° her so.

Capulet

And why, my Lady Wisdom? Hold your tongue,

Chatter / friends

Good Prudence. Smatter° with your gossips,° go.   170

Nurse

I speak no treason.

Capulet

Oh, God 'i' good e'en.[1]

Nurse

May not one speak?

Capulet

Peace, you mumbling fool!
Utter your gravity o'er a gossip's bowl,[2]
For here we need it not.

Lady Capulet

angry

You are too hot.°

Capulet

God's bread![3] It makes me mad.   175

season

Day, night, hour, tide,° time, work, play,

always / concern

Alone, in company, still° my care° hath been
To have her matched. And having now provided
A gentleman of noble parentage,
Of fair demesnes,[4] youthful and nobly limbed,[5]   180

qualities

Stuffed, as they say, with honorable parts,°
Proportioned as one's thought would wish a man—

1   *A whining mammet, in her fortune's tender*

    A whining baby's doll, at the moment she is offered good fortune

2   *pardon*

    Excuse (but in the next line Capulet shifts the meaning to "give permission to go")

3   *Lay hand on heart; advise.*

    Give this serious thought; consider carefully.

4   *I'll not be forsworn.*

    I.e., I won't change my mind.

5   *My husband is on Earth, my faith in Heaven. /*
    How shall that faith return again to Earth, /
    Unless that husband send it me from Heaven /
    By leaving Earth?

    My husband yet lives; my marriage vows are consecrated to God. How can I be released from those vows, except by Romeo's death?

6   *practice stratagems*

    Contrive plots

whimpering And then to have a wretched, puling° fool,

A whining mammet, in her fortune's tender, [1]

To answer "I'll not wed," "I cannot love," 185

"I am too young," "I pray you, pardon [2] me."

if —But an° you will not wed, I'll pardon you;

Graze where you will, you shall not house with me.

have a tendency Look to 't; think on 't. I do not use° to jest.

Thursday is near. Lay hand on heart; advise. [3] 190

If An° you be mine, I'll give you to my friend.

An you be not, hang, beg, starve, die in the streets,

For, by my soul, I'll ne'er acknowledge thee,

Nor what is mine shall never do thee good.

Trust to 't, bethink you. I'll not be forsworn. [4] *He exits.* 195

Juliet

[*rising*] Is there no pity sitting in the clouds

That sees into the bottom of my grief?

Oh, sweet my mother, cast me not away!

Delay this marriage for a month, a week.

Or, if you do not, make the bridal bed 200

In that dim monument where Tybalt lies.

Lady Capulet

Talk not to me, for I'll not speak a word.

Do as thou wilt, for I have done with thee. *She exits.*

Juliet

O God! O Nurse, how shall this be prevented?

My husband is on Earth, my faith in Heaven. 205

How shall that faith return again to Earth,

Unless that husband send it me from Heaven

By leaving Earth? [5] Comfort me. Counsel me.

—Alack, alack, that Heaven should practice stratagems [6]

Upon so soft a subject as myself. 210

—What sayst thou? Hast thou not a word of joy?

Some comfort, Nurse.

1   *all the world to nothing*

    I.e., I would bet anything

2   *this second match*

    16th-century Christian doctrine did
    not permit divorce. In England,
    however, spouses of low status
    sometimes informally separated
    and remarried by moving to
    another town where their
    identities were unknown. This
    option was not available to nobly
    born spouses such as Juliet, whose
    economic and social status were
    tied to a particular locale and
    family name. Advising Juliet to
    appease her father by committing
    bigamy, the Nurse might be
    attempting to protect her own
    livelihood. In London, a servant
    dismissed as disorderly might be
    imprisoned and whipped.

3   *As living here and you no use of him*

    As you living here and having no
    access to him

4   *Ancient damnation!*

    Possibly an oath, like the modern
    "damn," literally referring to
    original sin, but more likely an
    epithet directed at the Nurse,
    meaning "evil old woman."

5   *wish me thus forsworn*

    Wish me to deny my marriage vows
    in this way

Nurse

                   Faith, here it is.

Romeo is banished, and all the world to nothing[1]

claim That he dares ne'er come back to challenge° you,

Or, if he do, it needs must be by stealth.   215

Then, since the case so stands as now it doth,

Count I think it best you married with the County.°

Oh, he's a lovely gentleman.

shcloth / compared with Romeo's a dishclout° to° him. An eagle, madam,

Hath not so green, so quick, so fair an eye   220

Cursed be As Paris hath. Beshrew° my very heart,

fortunate I think you are happy° in this second match,[2]

even if For it excels your first. Or if° it did not,

Your first is dead, or, 'twere as good he were

As living here and you no use of him.[3]   225

Juliet

Speak'st thou from thy heart?

Nurse

And from my soul too, else beshrew them both.

Juliet

Amen!

Nurse

What?

Juliet

marvelously Well, thou hast comforted me marvelous° much.   230

Go in, and tell my lady I am gone,

Having displeased my father, to Laurence' cell

forgiven To make confession and to be absolved.°

Nurse

Marry, I will, and this is wisely done.   [*She exits.*]

Juliet

Ancient damnation![4] O most wicked fiend!   235

Is it more sin to wish me thus forsworn,[5]

1 *Thou and my bosom henceforth shall be*
   twain.
   **I.e., you shall from here on be kept
   away from my innermost thoughts.**

Or to dispraise my lord with that same tongue
Which she hath praised him with above compare
So many thousand times? Go, counselor.
Thou and my bosom henceforth shall be twain.¹   240
I'll to the Friar to know his remedy.

I myself   If all else fail, myself° have power to die.   *She exits.*

*If the Friar can't help,
I'll kill myself.*

1   *nothing slow to slack his haste*

    Not willing to urge him to delay

2   *Uneven*

    **(1) unequal, one-sided; (2) rough,
    difficult**

3   *Venus smiles not in a house of tears*

    **(1) love doesn't fare well in a
    household dominated by
    mourning; (2) the planet Venus
    doesn't exert a favorable influence
    when it occupies an inauspicious
    astrological *house* (in the heavens).**

4   *put from her by society*

    Driven away by companionship

Act 4, Scene 1

Enter **Friar** [**Laurence**] *and County* **Paris**.

Friar Laurence
On Thursday, sir? The time is very short.
Paris
intended father-in-law My father° Capulet will have it so,
And I am nothing slow to slack his haste. [1]
Friar Laurence
You say you do not know the lady's mind.
Uneven [2] is the course; I like it not.   5
Paris
Immoderately she weeps for Tybalt's death,
And therefore have I little talked of love,
For Venus smiles not in a house of tears. [3]
considers Now, sir, her father counts° it dangerous
influence That she do give her sorrow so much sway,°   10
And in his wisdom hastes our marriage
To stop the inundation of her tears—
brooded on Which, too much minded° by herself alone,
May be put from her by society. [4]
for Now do you know the reason of° this haste.   15
Friar Laurence
[*aside*] I would I knew not why it should be slowed.
—Look, sir, here comes the lady toward my cell.

Enter **Juliet**.

Paris
Fortunately Happily° met, my lady and my wife.
Juliet
That may be, sir, when I may be a wife.

1   *certain text*

    True saying

2   *it was bad enough before their spite*

    My face wasn't much to look at
    even before tears damaged its
    appearance.

3   *to my face*

    (1) openly (playing off 4.1.28);
    (2) about my face

4   *It may be so, for it is not mine own.*

    I.e., you might be right, because I
    am not the owner of it (God is; but
    unspoken is her thought that it
    actually belongs to Romeo).

Paris

That "may be" must be, love, on Thursday next.   20

Juliet

What must be shall be.

Friar Laurence

                          That's a certain text. [1]

Paris

Come you to make confession to this Father?

Juliet

should have to To answer that, I should° confess to you.   *Double meaning*

Paris

Do not deny to him that you love me.

Juliet

I will confess to you that I love him.   25

Paris

So will ye, I am sure, that you love me.

Juliet

value If I do so, it will be of more price°

Being spoke behind your back than to your face.

Paris

Poor soul, thy face is much abused with tears.

Juliet

The tears have got small victory by that,   30

For it was bad enough before their spite. [2]

Paris

assessment Thou wrong'st it more than tears with that report.°

Juliet

That is no slander, sir, which is a truth,

And what I spake, I spake it to my face. [3]

Paris

Thy face is mine, and thou hast slandered it.   35

Juliet

It may be so, for it is not mine own. [4]

1 *rouse*

   **Awaken (in preparation for the
   wedding)**

2 *sealed*

   **Legally contracted; Juliet
   continues the legal language in the
   following line.**

3 *label to another deed*

   **Assent to a second deed (of
   marriage).**

4 *this shall slay them both*

   **This knife shall slay both this hand
   and this heart (i.e., herself).**

5 *long-experienced time*

   Lifetime of experience

—Are you at leisure, holy Father, now,

Or shall I come to you at evening mass?

Friar Laurence

mournful   My leisure serves me, pensive° daughter, now.

ask for   —My lord, we must entreat° the time alone.   *40*

Paris

forbid   God shield° I should disturb devotion!

—Juliet, on Thursday early will I rouse[1] ye.

[*kisses her*] Till then, adieu, and keep this holy kiss.   *He exits.*

Juliet

Oh, shut the door, and, when thou hast done so,

Come weep with me, past hope, past care, past help.   *45*

Friar Laurence

O Juliet, I already know thy grief.

limit   It strains me past the compass° of my wits.

delay   I hear thou must, and nothing may prorogue° it,

Count   On Thursday next be married to this County.°

Juliet

Tell me not, Friar, that thou hearest of this,   *50*

Unless thou tell me how I may prevent it.

If in thy wisdom thou canst give no help,

only / decision   Do thou but° call my resolution° wise,

immediately   And with this knife I'll help it presently.°

God joined my heart and Romeo's, thou our hands;   *55*

before   And ere° this hand, by thee to Romeo sealed,[2]

Shall be the label to another deed,[3]

Or my true heart with treacherous revolt

Turn to another, this shall slay them both.[4]

Therefore out of thy long-experienced time,[5]   *60*

Give me some present counsel, or, behold,

hardships   'Twixt my extremes° and me this bloody knife

1   *arbitrating that / Which the commission*
    of thy years and art / Could to no issue of
    true honor bring

    Making a decision about the
    matter that you, despite the
    authority of your age and
    knowledge, couldn't find a way to
    bring to an honorable conclusion

2   *cop'st with death himself to 'scape*
    from it

    Would face death itself, in order to
    escape from shame

3   *thievish ways*

    Streets haunted by thieves

4   *charnel house*

    A freestanding house or vault in
    which the bones of the dead were
    gathered

5   *reeky shanks and yellow, chapless skulls*

    Foul-smelling leg bones and
    yellow skulls lacking the lower jaw

Shall play the umpire, arbitrating that
Which the commission of thy years and art
Could to no issue of true honor bring. [1]   65
slow   Be not so long° to speak; I long to die
If what thou speak'st speak not of remedy.

Friar Laurence

Hold, daughter. I do spy a kind of hope,

risky / action   Which craves as desperate° an execution°

awful   As that is desperate° which we would prevent.   70
If, rather than to marry County Paris,
Thou hast the strength of will to slay thyself,
Then is it likely thou wilt undertake

drive   A thing like death to chide° away this shame,
That cop'st with death himself to 'scape from it. [2]   75
And if thou darest, I'll give thee remedy.

Juliet

Oh, bid me leap, rather than marry Paris,
From off the battlements of any tower,
Or walk in thievish ways, [3] or bid me lurk
Where serpents are. Chain me with roaring bears,   80
Or hide me nightly in a charnel house, [4]
O'ercovered quite with dead men's rattling bones,
With reeky shanks and yellow, chapless skulls, [5]
Or bid me go into a new-made grave
And hide me with a dead man in his tomb—   85
Things that, to hear them told, have made me tremble—
And I will do it without fear or doubt
To live an unstained wife to my sweet love.

Friar Laurence

Hold, then. Go home, be merry, give consent
To marry Paris. Wednesday is tomorrow.   90

see to it   Tomorrow night look° that thou lie alone;

1   *distilling liquor*

    I.e., distilled liquid; the potion the
    Friar has made

2   *but surcease*

    But it will stop

3   *eyes' windows*

    Eyelids

4   *deprived of supple government*

    Rigid and lacking the ability to
    move

5   *uncovered on the bier*

    I.e., with your face uncovered on
    the litter (for carrying you to the
    burial site)

6   *inconstant toy*

    Whim that weakens your resolve

Let not the Nurse lie with thee in thy chamber.

Take thou this vial, being then in bed,

And this distilling liquor[1] drink thou off,

immediately When presently° through all thy veins shall run 95

fluid A cold and drowsy humor,° for no pulse

natural Shall keep his native° progress, but surcease.[2]

No warmth, no breath shall testify thou livest.

The roses in thy lips and cheeks shall fade

pale To wanny° ashes, thy eyes' windows[3] fall 100

Like death when he shuts up the day of life.

Each part, deprived of supple government,[4]

rigid Shall, stiff and stark° and cold, appear like death,

And in this borrowed likeness of shrunk death

Thou shalt continue two and forty hours, 105

And then awake as from a pleasant sleep.

Now, when the bridegroom in the morning comes

To rouse thee from thy bed, there art thou dead.

Then, as the manner of our country is,

In thy best robes, uncovered on the bier,[5] 110

Thou shall be borne to that same ancient vault

Where all the kindred of the Capulets lie.

in preparation for when In the meantime, against° thou shalt awake,

intention Shall Romeo by my letters know our drift,°

And hither shall he come; and he and I 115

wait for Will watch° thy waking, and that very night

Shall Romeo bear thee hence to Mantua.

And this shall free thee from this present shame,

If no inconstant toy[6] nor womanish fear

Abate thy valor in the acting it. 120

Juliet

Give me; give me! Oh, tell not me of fear. [*takes vial*]

1 *help afford*

Provide me help

Friar Laurence

Enough   Hold.° Get you gone. Be strong and prosperous
In this resolve. I'll send a friar with speed
To Mantua with my letters to thy lord.

Juliet

Love give me strength, and strength shall help afford. [1]   125
Farewell, dear Father.   *They exit.*

1   *'tis an ill cook that cannot lick his own*
    fingers

    A familiar proverb mocking anyone
    who will not test the results of his
    labor

2   *unfurnished*

    Not provided with necessary
    supplies; unready

3   *A peevish self-willed harlotry it is.*

    An ill-tempered, headstrong,
    worthless girl—that's what she
    (Juliet) is.

Act 4, Scene 2

Enter father **Capulet**, [**Lady Capulet**], **Nurse**, *and* [*two or three*] **Servingmen**.

[handwritten note: Juliet comes back and apologizes to Capulet. He wants to do it sooner.]

Capulet

[*giving a paper to* **First Servingman**] So many guests
    invite as here are writ.   [**First Servingman** *exits.*]
[*to* **Second Servingman**] Sirrah, go hire me twenty

expert   cunning° cooks.

Second Servingman

unskilled / test You shall have none ill,° sir, for I'll try° if they can lick
their fingers.

Capulet

How canst thou try them so?   5

Second Servingman

Marry, sir, 'tis an ill cook that cannot lick his own
fingers;¹ therefore he that cannot lick his fingers goes
not with me.

Capulet

Go, be gone.
We shall be much unfurnished² for this time.   10

                  [**Second Servingman** *exits.*]

—What? Is my daughter gone to Friar Laurence?

Nurse

truly; indeed Ay, forsooth.°

Capulet

for Well, he may chance to do some good on° her.
A peevish self-willed harlotry it is.³

       Enter **Juliet**.

1   *tomorrow morning*

Capulet moves up the date of the
wedding to Wednesday, an
impatience that will have terrible
consequences.

Nurse

confession See where she comes from shrift° with merry look. 15

Capulet

wandering How now, my headstrong? Where have you been gadding?°

Juliet

Where I have learned me to repent the sin

Of disobedient opposition

directed To you and your behests, and am enjoined°

By holy Laurence to fall prostrate here 20

To beg your pardon. [*kneeling*] Pardon, I beseech you;

Henceforward I am ever ruled by you.

Capulet

Count Send for the County.° Go tell him of this.

marriage knot I'll have this knot° knit up tomorrow morning. ¹

Juliet

I met the youthful lord at Laurence' cell, 25

suitable And gave him what becomèd° love I might,

Not stepping o'er the bounds of modesty.

Capulet

of Why, I am glad on°'t. This is well. Stand up.

This is as 't should be.—Let me see the County.

Ay, marry, go, I say, and fetch him hither. 30

—Now, afore God, this reverend holy Friar!

indebted All our whole city is much bound° to him.

Juliet

private room Nurse, will you go with me into my closet°

choose / attire To help me sort° such needful ornaments°

adorn As you think fit to furnish° me tomorrow? 35

Lady Capulet

No, not till Thursday. There is time enough.

1   *short in our provision*
     Lacking in what is needed for the
     celebration

Capulet

Go, Nurse. Go with her. We'll to church tomorrow.

[**Juliet** *and* **Nurse**]*exit.*

Lady Capulet

We shall be short in our provision. [1]

'Tis now near night.

Capulet

            Tush, I will stir about,

assure   And all things shall be well, I warrant° thee, wife.   40

dress   Go thou to Juliet; help to deck° up her.

I'll not to bed tonight. Let me alone.

I'll play the housewife for this once.—What, ho?

(i.e., The servants)   They° are all forth?—Well, I will walk myself

To County Paris, to prepare up him   45

In preparation for   Against° tomorrow. My heart is wondrous light

Since this same wayward girl is so reclaimed.   *They exit.*

1   *behooveful for our state*

    Necessary for our celebration

Act 4, Scene 3

Enter **Juliet** *and* **Nurse**.

[handwritten: Juliet asks Nurse to let Juliet sleep alone]

Juliet

garments   Ay, those attires° are best. But, gentle Nurse,

I pray thee, leave me to myself tonight,

prayers   For I have need of many orisons°

condition   To move the heavens to smile upon my state,°

unfavorable   Which, well thou knowest, is cross° and full of sin.   5

Enter [**Lady Capulet**].

Lady Capulet

What, are you busy, ho? Need you my help?

Juliet

gathered   No, madam. We have culled° such necessaries

As are behooveful for our state [1] tomorrow.

So please you, let me now be left alone,

And let the Nurse this night sit up with you;   10

For, I am sure, you have your hands full all

In this so sudden business.

Lady Capulet

                Good night.

Get thee to bed and rest, for thou hast need.

           [**Lady Capulet** *and* **Nurse**] *exit*.

Juliet

Farewell!—God knows when we shall meet again.

shivers   I have a faint cold fear thrills° through my veins   15

That almost freezes up the heat of life.

I'll call them back again to comfort me.

[handwritten: what if it doesn't work]

—Nurse!—What should she do here?

dreadful   My dismal° scene I needs must act alone.

Come, vial. What if this mixture do not work at all?   20

1   *This shall forbid it.*

    **This knife will prevent it (the
    marriage to Paris); Juliet mentions
    she has a knife with her first at
    4.1.54.**

2   *it should not*

    **It (the liquid in the vial) should not
    be poison.**

3   *horrible conceit*

    Terrifying visions

4   *green in earth*

    Newly buried

5   *shrieks like mandrakes torn out of the
    earth*

    **It was thought that, when pulled
    from the ground, the mandrake
    root uttered a piercing shriek that
    would drive the listener mad or
    cause death.**

6   *fears*

    **Things to be feared (rather than
    the emotions felt)**

Shall I be married then tomorrow morning?

No, no. This shall forbid it. [1] Lie thou there.

[puts down her knife]

What if it be a poison, which the Friar

Cunningly   Subtly° hath ministered to have me dead,

Lest in this marriage he should be dishonored   25

Because he married me before to Romeo?

i.e., a poison   I fear it is,° and yet, methinks, it should not, [2]

always / proved   For he hath still° been tried° a holy man.

How if, when I am laid into the tomb,

I wake before the time that Romeo   30

Come to redeem me? There's a fearful point.

Shall I not, then, be stifled in the vault,

wholesome   To whose foul mouth no healthsome° air breathes in,

suffocated   And there die strangled° ere my Romeo comes?

likely that   Or, if I live, is it not very like°   35

The horrible conceit [3] of death and night,

Together with the terror of the place—

As in a vault, an ancient receptacle,

Where for this many hundred years the bones

Of all my buried ancestors are packed,   40

Where bloody Tybalt, yet but green in earth, [4]

Lies fest'ring in his shroud, where, as they say,

At some hours in the night spirits resort—

likely   Alack, alack, is it not like° that I,

So early waking, what with loathsome smells,   45

And shrieks like mandrakes torn out of the earth, [5]

That living mortals, hearing them, run mad—

Oh, if I wake, shall I not be distraught,

Surrounded   Environèd° with all these hideous fears, [6]

And madly play with my forefathers' joints,   50

And pluck the mangled Tybalt from his shroud,

1   [She drinks and falls upon her
     bed within the curtains.]

     **Q1 prints the stage direction
     essentially this way (omitting
     "drinks and"), while Q2 has no
     direction here. The Q1 direction
     seems to suggest that a bed was
     placed behind a curtain at the rear
     of the stage.**

fit of madness   And, in this rage,° with some great kinsman's bone,

As with a club, dash out my desp'rate brains?

Oh, look! Methinks I see my cousin's ghost   Visions of

impale   Seeking out Romeo, that did spit° his body   Tybalt

Stop   Upon a rapier's point. Stay,° Tybalt, stay!   55

Romeo, Romeo, Romeo! Here's drink. I drink to thee.

[*She drinks and falls upon her bed within the curtains.*] [1]

1 *curfew bell*

The bell that signaled the night curfew also rang in the morning, officially commencing the working day.

2 *Angelica*

It is not clear if this is the first name of the Nurse, Lady Capulet, or an unseen servant.

3 *cot-quean*

Meddler, usually referring to a man who officiously involves himself in the management of the household

4 *jealous hood*

Jealous woman, though some editors hyphenate to make it "jealous-hood," a made-up noun on the model of "nationhood," thus meaning "jealousy" itself.

Act 4, Scene 4

Enter [**Lady Capulet**] *and* **Nurse**.

Getting ready for the wedding

Lady Capulet

Hold; take these keys and fetch more spices, Nurse.

Nurse

the pastry kitchen They call for dates and quinces in the pastry.°

Enter old **Capulet**.

Capulet

Come; stir, stir, stir! The second cock hath crowed.

The curfew bell [1] hath rung. 'Tis three o'clock.

meat pies —Look to the baked meats,° good Angelica. [2]   5

Spare not for the cost.

Nurse

                          Go, you cot-quean, [3] go.

Get you to bed. Faith, you'll be sick tomorrow

wakefulness For this night's watching.°

Capulet

No, not a whit. What? I have watched ere now

All night for lesser cause and ne'er been sick.   10

Lady Capulet

womanizer Ay, you have been a mouse-hunt° in your time,

i.e., keep But I will watch° you from such watching now.

                          [**Lady Capulet**] *and* **Nurse** *exit*.

Capulet

A jealous hood, a jealous hood! [4]

Enter three or four [**Servingmen**] *with spits and logs and baskets*.

                          Now, fellow,

273

1   *I have a head, sir, that will find out logs*

    **I.e., since my head is like wood, I
    have a natural affinity to find the
    logs.**

2   *whoreson*

    **Rogue; bastard (here used
    jocularly)**

3   *take your pennyworths*

    **I.e., take what (sleep) you can get;
    pennyworths (pronounced
    "penn'urths") is what you can buy
    for a penny, hence a small amount.**

What is there?

First Servingman

Things for the cook, sir, but I know not what.   15

Capulet

Make haste; make haste, sirrah.

                                        [**First Servingman** *exits.*]

[*to* **Second Servingman**] Fetch drier logs.

Call Peter. He will show thee where they are.

Second Servingman

I have a head, sir, that will find out logs, [1]

And never trouble Peter for the matter.   [*He exits.*] 20

Capulet

By the Mass (an oath) Mass,° and well said. A merry whoreson, [2] ha!

blockhead / God Thou shalt be loggerhead.°—Good Father,° 'tis day.

                                        Play music [*within.*]

very soon The County will be here with music straight,°

For so he said he would. I hear him near.

—Nurse! Wife! What, ho? What, Nurse, I say!

                                                                25

                Enter **Nurse**.

dress Go waken Juliet. Go and trim° her up.

I'll go and chat with Paris. Hie; make haste,

Make haste. The bridegroom he is come already.

Make haste, I say.   [*He exits.*]

Nurse

Fast asleep Mistress! What? Mistress! Juliet!—Fast,° I warrant her,

i.e., she is she.°

—Why, lamb! Why, lady! Fie, you slug-a-bed.   30

Why, love, I say. Madam! Sweetheart! Why, bride!

What? Not a word? You take your pennyworths [3] now.

Sleep for a week; for the next night, I warrant,

1   *set up his rest*

    **Wagered everything, i.e., made up
    his mind (with a bawdy suggestion
    as well)**

2   *take you*

    **(1) surprise you; (2) have
    intercourse with you**

3   *aqua vitae*

    **Brandy (as in 3.2.89, and also
    pronounced aqua-veet)**

The County Paris hath set up his rest[1]   35
That you shall rest but little.—God forgive me,
Marry, and amen. How sound is she asleep.
I needs must wake her.—Madam, madam, madam!
Ay, let the County take you[2] in your bed.
He'll fright you up, i' faith. Will it not be?   [opens the curtains] 40
What? Dressed and in your clothes, and down again?
I must needs wake you. Lady, lady, lady!
—Alas, alas! Help, help! My lady's dead!

alas —Oh weraday° that ever I was born!
—Some aqua vitae,[3] ho!—My lord! My lady!   45

[*Enter* **Lady Capulet**.]

Lady Capulet
What noise is here?
Nurse
             O lamentable day!
Lady Capulet
What is the matter?
Nurse
             Look; look. O heavy day!
Lady Capulet
O me, O me! My child, my only life,
Revive, look up, or I will die with thee!
—Help, help! Call help.   50

Enter [**Capulet**].

Capulet
For shame, bring Juliet forth. Her lord is come.
Nurse
She's dead, deceased; she's dead. Alack the day!

1 *Out alas*

A colloquial phrase of lament,
with *out* functioning as an
intensifier

2 *is settled*

Has ceased to flow

3 *deflow'rèd*

With her virginity taken (by death)

4 *leave him all*

Bequeath everything to him

Lady Capulet

Alack the day. She's dead; she's dead; she's dead!

Capulet

Ha, let me see her! Out alas, [1] she's cold.

Her blood is settled, [2] and her joints are stiff.   55

Life and these lips have long been separated.

Death lies on her like an untimely frost

Upon the sweetest flower of all the field.

Nurse

O lamentable day!

Lady Capulet

            O woeful time.

Capulet

Death, that hath ta'en her hence to make me wail,   60

Ties up my tongue and will not let me speak.

       Enter **Friar** [**Laurence**] *and the County* [**Paris** *with*
       Musicians].

Friar Laurence

Come; is the bride ready to go to church?

Capulet

Ready to go, but never to return.

son-in-law —O son!° The night before thy wedding day

Hath Death lain with thy wife. There she lies,   65

Flower as she was, deflow'rèd [3] by him.

Death is my son-in-law. Death is my heir;

My daughter he hath wedded. I will die

livelihood And leave him all. [4] Life, living,° all is Death's.

Paris

i.e., for so long Have I thought long° to see this morning's face,   70

And doth it give me such a sight as this?

1 *In lasting labor of his pilgrimage*

   **In the unending work of its (i.e.,
   time's) onward journey**

2 *Uncomfortable*

   Offering no consolation; pitiless

Lady Capulet

Accursed, unhappy, wretched, hateful day!

Most miserable hour that e'er time saw

In lasting labor of his pilgrimage. [1]

But one, poor one, one poor and loving child,   75

But one thing to rejoice and solace in,

snatched And cruel death hath catched° it from my sight!

Nurse

O woe! O woeful, woeful, woeful day!

Most lamentable day, most woeful day

That ever, ever, I did yet behold!   80

O day, O day, O day, O hateful day!

Never was seen so black a day as this.

O woeful day, O woeful day!

Paris

Cheated (of hopes) Beguiled,° divorcèd, wrongèd, spited, slain!

Most detestable Death, by thee beguiled,   85

By cruel, cruel thee quite overthrown!

O love! O life! Not life, but love in death.

Capulet

Despised, distressèd, hated, martyred, killed!

Uncomfortable [2] time, why cam'st thou now

celebration To murder, murder our solemnity?°   90

O child, O child! My soul, and not my child!

Dead art thou! Alack, my child is dead,

And with my child my joys are buried.

Friar Laurence

Catastrophe's Peace, ho, for shame! Confusion's° cure lives not

outbursts In these confusions.° Heaven and yourself   95

Had part in this fair maid; now Heaven hath all,

And all the better is it for the maid.

Your part in her you could not keep from death,

But Heaven keeps his part in eternal life.

1   *'twas your Heaven she should be*
    advanced

    **I.e., your idea of perfect
    happiness was that Juliet should
    be advanced in status (by her
    marriage to Paris).**

2   *well*

    **In a state of good fortune (i.e., in
    Heaven)**

3   *rosemary*

    **Rosemary, a token of
    remembrance, was included in
    arrangements for both weddings
    and funerals.**

4   *For though some nature bids us all
    lament, / Yet nature's tears are reason's
    merriment.*

    **Although our natural affection
    tells us to mourn, reason laughs at
    the folly of our instinctive grief
    (since she is in Heaven).**

	The most you sought was her promotion,°	100
betterment	For 'twas your Heaven she should be advanced. [1]	
raised	And weep ye now, seeing she is advanced°	
	Above the clouds, as high as Heaven itself?	
	Oh, in this love you love your child so ill	
	That you run mad, seeing that she is well. [2]	105
	She's not well married that lives married long,	
	But she's best married that dies married young.	
	Dry up your tears and stick your rosemary [3]	
	On this fair corpse, and, as the custom is,	
	And in her best array, bear her to church;	110
	For though some nature bids us all lament,	
	Yet nature's tears are reason's merriment. [4]	

Capulet

	All things that we ordainèd festival	
proper function	Turn from their office° to black funeral:	
	Our instruments to melancholy bells,	115
	Our wedding cheer to a sad burial feast,	
mournful / funeral songs	Our solemn hymns to sullen° dirges° change.	
	Our bridal flowers serve for a buried corpse,	
	And all things change them to the contrary.	

Friar Laurence

	Sir, go you in, and, madam, go with him,	120
	And go, Sir Paris. Every one prepare	
	To follow this fair corpse unto her grave.	
frown / evil deed	The heavens do lour° upon you for some ill.°	
Anger	Move° them no more by crossing their high will.	

*They all exit [except **Nurse** and the **Musicians**].*

First Musician

| | Faith, we may put up° our pipes and be gone. | 125 |
| away | | |

1   *case*

    (1) situation; (2) instrument case

2   *may be amended*

    (1) the situation could be
    improved; (2) the instrument case
    could be fixed up

3   *"Heart's Ease"*

    Title of a popular song

4   *soundly*

    Thoroughly, though with a pun on
    soundly pointing to the sounds the
    musicians make; Peter's word *note*
    in line 144 puns similarly.

5   *I will give you the minstrel.*

    I will insult you by calling you
    minstrel (instead of "musician").

6   *I will give you the serving creature.*

    I will insult you by calling you
    servant (with the disdainful
    implication that you are a *creature*
    rather than a "man").

Nurse

Honest good fellows, ah, put up, put up,

For, well you know, this is a pitiful case.

First Musician

Ay, by my troth, the case [1] may be amended. [2]

[**Nurse**] *exits.*

Enter [**Peter**].

Peter

Musicians, O musicians, "Heart's Ease," [3] "Heart's

Ease." 130

if Oh, an° you will have me live, play "Heart's Ease."

First Musician

Why "Heart's Ease"?

Peter

O musicians, because my heart itself plays "My Heart Is

song Full." Oh, play me some merry dump° to comfort me.

First Musician

Not a dump, we; 'tis no time to play now.

Peter 135

You will not then?

First Musician

No.

Peter

I will then give it you soundly. [4]

First Musician

What will you give us?

Peter

mockery / call No money, on my faith, but the gleek.° I will give° you 140

the minstrel. [5]

First Musician

Then will I give you the serving creature. [6]

1   *I will carry no crotchets*

    (1) I won't put up with any funny ideas; (2) I won't sing any quarter notes (i.e., I won't follow your tune).

2   *I'll re you, I'll fa you.*

    The syllables *re* and *fa* represent notes on the musical scale. Peter uses them as threatening verbs here to mean something like, "I'll show you some notes!"

3   *you note us*

    (1) you will be giving us musical notes after all; (2) you will be paying attention to us (even though you don't want to give us the satisfaction).

4   *put out*

    Both "display" and "quench" (as one may *put out* a fire)

5   *When griping griefs the heart doth wound…*

    The song (also at lines 162-163) is from a poem by Richard Edwards, published in 1576, in a collection of songs and poems called *The Paradise of Dainty Devices*.

6   *Catling*

    Catgut string, for an instrument such as a lute

7   *Prates.*

    I.e., he speaks nonsense (in response to the First Musician's unsatisfactory answer).

8   *Rebeck*

    Or *rebec*; a fiddle-like instrument with three strings

9   *Soundpost*

    Wooden peg set under the bridge of a violin

10 *I cry you mercy*

    Pardon me.

11 *have no gold for sounding*

    (1) are never paid for their performances; (2) don't have any gold coins to jingle together

Peter

Then will I lay the serving creature's dagger on your

head   pate.° I will carry no crotchets. ¹ I'll *re* you; I'll *fa* you. ²

heed   Do you note° me?

[First] Musician

If   An° you *re* us and *fa* us, you note us. ³   145

Second Musician

Pray you, put up your dagger and put out⁴ your wit.

Peter

soundly thrash   Then have at you with my wit. I will dry-beat° you with an

iron wit and put up my iron dagger. Answer me like men.

    [*sings*] When griping griefs the heart doth wound, ⁵

    Then music with her silver sound—   150

[*speaks*] Why "silver sound"? Why "music with her

silver sound"? What say you, Simon Catling? ⁶

First Musician

Marry, sir, because silver hath a sweet sound.

Peter

Prates. ⁷—What say you, Hugh Rebeck? ⁸

Second Musician

produce sound   I say, "silver sound," because musicians sound° for silver.   155

Peter

Prates too.—What say you, James Soundpost? ⁹

Third Musician

Faith, I know not what to say.

Peter

Oh, I cry you mercy, ¹⁰ you are the singer. I will say for

you. It is "music with her silver sound" because

musicians have no gold for sounding. ¹¹   160

    [*sings*] Then music with her silver sound

    With speedy help doth lend redress.   *He exits.*

1   *stay dinner*

**Wait for dinner (the noontime
meal)**

First Musician

What a pestilent knave is this same!

Second Musician

knave Hang him, jack!° Come; we'll in here, tarry for the
mourners, and stay dinner. ¹ *They exit.* 165

1   *flattering truth of sleep*

    **I.e., the belief that the truth is
    revealed to us while we sleep**

2   *My bosom's lord sits lightly in his throne*

    **I.e., Cupid (love) sits happily in my
    heart**

3   *How sweet is love itself possessed / When
    but love's shadows are so rich in joy!*

    **Love, when enjoyed in reality, must
    be sweet indeed if even dreams of
    it are so delightful!**

4   *Capels' monument*

    The Capulet's family sepulcher

5   *took post*

    **Rode quickly; *post* refers to post-
    horses, which were stationed at
    intervals along major routes in
    order to speed the delivery of
    important messages.**

Act 5, Scene 1

Enter **Romeo**.

Romeo

If I may trust the flattering truth of sleep, [1]

foretell   My dreams presage° some joyful news at hand.

My bosom's lord sits lightly in his throne, [2]

And all this day an unaccustomed spirit

Lifts me above the ground with cheerful thoughts.   5

I dreamed my lady came and found me dead

permission   (Strange dream, that gives a dead man leave° to think)

And breathed such life with kisses in my lips

That I revived and was an emperor.

Ah me! How sweet is love itself possessed   10

When but love's shadows are so rich in joy! [3]

Enter **Romeo**'s *man* [**Balthasar**].

News from Verona!—How now, Balthasar?

Dost thou not bring me letters from the Friar?

How doth my lady? Is my father well?

How doth my lady Juliet? That I ask again,   15

For nothing can be ill if she be well.

Balthasar

Then she is well, and nothing can be ill.

Her body sleeps in Capels' monument, [4]

soul   And her immortal part° with angels lives.

I saw her laid low in her kindred's vault   20

at once   And presently° took post [5] to tell it you.

Oh, pardon me for bringing these ill news,

duty   Since you did leave it for my office,° sir.

Romeo

Is it e'en so? Then I defy you, stars.

1 *see for means*

I.e., figure out how to do so

2 *an apothecary*

Elizabethan apothecaries, who were regarded as respected members of the medical profession, were not necessarily poor. Shakespeare's portrait of the Apothecary might reflect the destitution of a London artificer working in any number of trades during the economic crisis of the mid-1590s. In times of dearth, city and state officials urged the rich to demonstrate charity toward the poor; in 1596, for instance, Lord Burghley issued an order for the Restraint of Eating, which commanded the citizens of London to supply poor relief by reducing their consumption of food and foregoing lavish feasts, such as those held in the Capulet household. Such measures were motivated not only by Christian charity, but also by the fear that extreme poverty would increase crime and social disorder. Romeo urges the Apothecary to break the law against selling poison on the grounds that the law—and the social *world* whose interests it represents (5.1.72)—has done nothing to protect him from falling into destitution and starvation.

3 *overwhelming brows*

Extremely bushy eyebrows (often taken as a sign of a sullen or surly personality)

4 *Culling of simples*

Gathering potent herbs

5 *a tortoise*

Part of the customary display (see *show* in line 48) of exotic commodities in apothecaries' shops, along with the other items mentioned in this passage

6 *beggarly account*

Pitifully small number

7 *cakes of roses*

Compressed bars of dried rose petals, which were sold for their scent

Thou knowest my lodging. Get me ink and paper,   25
leave this place And hire post horses. I will hence° tonight.

Balthasar

I do beseech you, sir, have patience.
Your looks are pale and wild and do import
Some misadventure.

Romeo

                    Tush, thou art deceived.
Leave me and do the thing I bid thee do.   30
Hast thou no letters to me from the Friar?

Balthasar

No, my good lord.

Romeo

                    No matter. Get thee gone
And hire those horses. I'll be with thee straight.

                              [**Balthasar**] *exits.*

Well, Juliet, I will lie with thee tonight.
Let's see for means. ¹ O mischief, thou art swift   35
To enter in the thoughts of desperate men!
I do remember an apothecary²
he / recently —And hereabouts 'a° dwells—which late° I noted
clothing In tattered weeds,° with overwhelming brows, ³
Gaunt Culling of simples. ⁴ Meager° were his looks,   40
Sharp misery had worn him to the bones,
run-down And in his needy° shop a tortoise⁵ hung,
An alligator stuffed, and other skins
Of ill-shaped fishes; and about his shelves
A beggarly account⁶ of empty boxes,   45
Green earthen pots, bladders, and musty seeds,
Remnants of packthread, and old cakes of roses, ⁷
Were thinly scattered to make up a show.
poverty Noting this penury,° to myself I said,
"An if a man did need a poison now,"   50

1   *is present death*

   I.e., carries the penalty of
immediate execution

2   *soon-speeding gear*

   Quickly working substance

3   *hasty powder*

   Volatile gunpowder

4   *hangs upon thy back*

   I.e., breathes down your neck; is
waiting for you

Whose sale is present death [1] in Mantua,

miserable "Here lives a caitiff° wretch would sell it him."

anticipate Oh, this same thought did but forerun° my need,

And this same needy man must sell it me.

As I remember, this should be the house. 55

Being holiday, the beggar's shop is shut.

What, ho! Apothecary!

[*Enter* **Apothecary**.]

Apothecary

Who calls so loud?

Romeo

Come hither, man. I see that thou art poor.

(gold coins) Hold; there is forty ducats.° Let me have

A dram of poison, such soon-speeding gear [2] 60

As will disperse itself through all the veins

So that That° the life-weary taker may fall dead,

body And that the trunk° may be discharged of breath

suddenly As violently° as hasty powder [3] fired

Doth hurry from the fatal cannon's womb. 65

Apothecary

lethal Such mortal° drugs I have, but Mantua's law

man / sells Is death to any he° that utters° them.

Romeo

Art thou so bare and full of wretchedness,

And fearest to die? Famine is in thy cheeks;

Need and oppression starveth in thy eyes; 70

Contempt and beggary hangs upon thy back. [4]

The world is not thy friend, nor the world's law.

provides The world affords° no law to make thee rich;

Then be not poor, but break it and take this.

[*holds out coins*]

1   *I pay thy poverty and not thy will.*

Given Romeo's emphasis on the
Apothecary's poverty, most editors
prefer the line as printed in Q1
(1597), "I pay thy poverty," to the
line as printed in Q2 (1599), "I pray
thy poverty." Romeo's offer to "*pay
thy poverty*" emphasizes his
economic advantage over the
destitute Apothecary who
reluctantly sells him poison.
Romeo's offer to "*pray* thy poverty"
would emphasize the ironic
religious subtext of this scene:
Romeo condemns the gold he
gives to the Apothecary as *poison* to
men's souls (5.1.80), yet he will use
the literal poison exchanged for
the metaphorical poison (gold) to
destroy his body and soul in a
sacrilegious act of suicide.

2   *dispatch you straight*

Kill you immediately

3   *get thyself in flesh*

I.e., put on some weight

4   *cordial*

Comforting drink; medicine for the
heart

Apothecary

My poverty, but not my will, consents.

He is starving, so he lets Romeo buy the poison bc. he needs money

Romeo

I pay thy poverty and not thy will. [1]

Apothecary

[*gives him a vial*] Put this in any liquid thing you will

And drink it off, and, if you had the strength

Of twenty men, it would dispatch you straight. [2]

It has the strength of 20 men

75

Romeo

There is thy gold, worse poison to men's souls,

Doing more murder in this loathsome world

Than these poor compounds that thou mayst not sell.

I sell thee poison; thou hast sold me none.

Farewell. Buy food and get thyself in flesh. [3]

—Come, cordial [4] and not poison; go with me

To Juliet's grave, for there must I use thee.   *They exit.*

80

money does evil in the world

85

1   *a barefoot brother*

    I.e., another member of the
    Franciscan order. Franciscan friars
    went barefoot, or with minimal
    protection for their feet, in accord
    with the order's vow of poverty.

2   *Where the infectious pestilence did reign*

    Plague, an extremely deadly
    infectious disease carried by flea-
    bearing rodents, was a major cause
    of mortality in Renaissance cities,
    including London. In 1593, more
    than 10,000 Londoners died of
    plague, and from June 1592 to June
    1594, the theaters were closed to
    prevent its spread. Shutting up
    infected houses was common
    practice, and "warders" would be
    posted at such quarantine sites to
    ensure that no one went in or out.

3   *speed to Mantua there was stayed*

    Journey to Mantua was prevented

4   *dear import*

    Dire consequence

Act 5, Scene 2

Enter **Friar John** [*and*] **Friar Laurence** [*separately*].

Friar John

Holy Franciscan Friar! Brother, ho!

Friar Laurence

This same should be the voice of Friar John.

Welcome from Mantua. What says Romeo?

Or, if his mind be writ, give me his letter.

Friar John

Going to find a barefoot brother[1] out,

One of our order, to associate° me,   *accompany*

Here in this city visiting the sick,

And finding him, the searchers° of the town,   *health officials*

Suspecting that we both were in a house

Where the infectious pestilence did reign,[2]   10

Sealed up the doors and would not let us forth,

So that my speed to Mantua there was stayed.[3]

Friar Laurence

Who bare my letter, then, to Romeo?

Friar John

I could not send it—here it is again—

[*hands him the letter*]

Nor get a messenger to bring it thee,   15

So fearful were they of infection.

Friar Laurence

Unhappy fortune! By my brotherhood,

The letter was not nice° but full of charge,°   *trivial / significance*

Of dear import,[4] and the neglecting it

May do much danger.° Friar John, go hence;   20   *harm*

5 appears beside line "Going to find a barefoot brother out,"

1 *notice of these accidents*

Notification of what has occured

crowbar Get me an iron crow° and bring it straight
Unto my cell.

Friar John

                    Brother, I'll go and bring it thee.   *He exits.*

Friar Laurence

Now must I to the monument alone.   *she will wake up*
Within this three hours will fair Juliet wake;

blame She will beshrew° me much that Romeo   25
Hath had no notice of these accidents. ¹
But I will write again to Mantua,   *She will be safe*
And keep her at my cell till Romeo come.   *in his cell*
Poor living corpse, closed in a dead man's tomb!   *He exits.*

1   *Hence, and stand aloof.*

    Leave, and stay some distance off.

2   *lay thee all along*

    **Lie down, stretching yourself out
    on the ground.**

3   *The obsequies that I for thee will keep*

    **The mourning rituals that I will
    observe in honor of you**

Act 5, Scene 3

Enter **Paris** *and his* **Page**.

[handwritten: Juliet's tomb]

Paris

Give me thy torch, boy. Hence, and stand aloof.¹

Yet put it out, for I would not be seen.

Under yon yew trees lay thee all along,²

Holding thy ear close to the hollow ground,

So shall no foot upon the churchyard tread,   5

(The soil) Being° loose, unfirm, with digging up of graves,

But thou shalt hear it. Whistle then to me,

As signal that thou hearest something approach.

Give me those flowers. Do as I bid thee. Go.

Page *[handwritten: – stay and whistle if someone comes]*

[*aside*] I am almost afraid to stand alone   10

take the risk Here in the churchyard. Yet I will adventure.°

[handwritten: He's bringing flowers]   [**Page** *moves away*.]

Paris

Sweet flower, with flowers thy bridal bed I strew

—O woe! Thy canopy is dust and stones—

perfumed Which with sweet° water nightly I will dew,

lacking Or, wanting° that, with tears distilled by moans.   15

The obsequies that I for thee will keep³

Nightly shall be to strew thy grave and weep.

[**Page** *whistles*.]

The boy gives warning something doth approach.

What cursèd foot wanders this way tonight

interrupt To cross° my obsequies and true love's rite?   20

What? With a torch? Muffle me, night, awhile.

[**Paris** *hides*.]

Enter **Romeo** *and* [**Balthasar**].

1   *wrenching iron*

     I.e., crowbar

2   *dear employment*

     Important business, though *dear*
     carries other relevant meanings,
     including "precious" and "costly."
     Romeo, however, has made up a
     story for Balthasar to hide his
     actual *dear employment* (i.e., his
     planned suicide).

Romeo

pickaxe Give me that mattock° and the wrenching iron. [1]

Hold; take this letter. Early in the morning

See thou deliver it to my lord and father.

Give me the light. Upon thy life I charge thee,   25

Whate'er thou hearest or see'st, stand all aloof

And do not interrupt me in my course.

Why I descend into this bed of death

Is partly to behold my lady's face,

But chiefly to take thence from her dead finger   30

A precious ring, a ring that I must use

In dear employment. [2] Therefore hence; be gone.

suspicious But if thou, jealous,° dost return to pry

In what I farther shall intend to do,

By Heaven, I will tear thee joint by joint   35

And strew this hungry churchyard with thy limbs.

The time and my intents are savage, wild,

More fierce, and more inexorable far

hungry Than empty° tigers or the roaring sea.

Balthasar

I will be gone, sir, and not trouble ye.   40

Romeo

So shalt thou show me friendship. Take thou that.

[gives him money]

Live and be prosperous, and farewell, good fellow.

Balthasar

[aside] For all this same, I'll hide me hereabout.

suspect His looks I fear, and his intents I doubt.°

*[**Balthasar** hides.]*

Romeo

stomach *[opening the tomb]* Thou detestable maw,° thou womb of

death,   45

Gorged with the dearest morsel of the earth,

1   *in despite*

    **To spite you (because the tomb is
    already filled with dead bodies)**

2   *more food*

    I.e., Romeo's own body

force Thus I enforce° thy rotten jaws to open,

And in despite[1] I'll cram thee with more food![2]

Paris

[*aside*] This is that banished haughty Montague

That murdered my love's cousin, with which grief   50

It is supposèd the fair creature died,

dishonor And here is come to do some villainous shame°

To the dead bodies. I will apprehend him.

[*to* **Romeo**] Stop thy unhallowed toil, vile Montague!

Can vengeance be pursued further than death?   55

Condemnèd villain, I do apprehend thee.

Obey and go with me, for thou must die.

Romeo

I must indeed, and therefore came I hither.

Good gentle youth, tempt not a desp'rate man.

i.e., the corpses Fly hence and leave me. Think upon these° gone.   60

Let them affright thee. I beseech thee, youth,

Put not another sin upon my head

By urging me to fury. Oh, be gone!

By Heaven, I love thee better than myself,

For I come hither armed against myself.   65

Stay not; be gone. Live, and hereafter say

A madman's mercy bid thee run away.

Paris

threat I do defy thy commination°

arrest And apprehend° thee for a felon here.

Romeo

Wilt thou provoke me? Then have at thee, boy!   70

[*They fight.*]

Page

chmen; night guards O Lord, they fight! I will go call the watch.°   [*He exits.*]

Paris

Oh, I am slain! If thou be merciful,

1 *lantern*

   The image is architectural; a *lantern*
   is a many-windowed tower at the
   top of a building that allows light
   into it.

2 *feasting presence*

   Presence chamber, a formal room
   where a monarch entertains guests

3 *light'ning before death*

   A lifting (i.e., *lightening*) of spirits
   before death, though it is
   impossible not to hear "lightning"

Open the tomb. Lay me with Juliet.

[He dies.]

Romeo

In faith, I will.—Let me peruse this face.

Mercutio's kinsman, noble County Paris. 75

i.e., Balthasar What said my man,° when my betossèd soul

listen to Did not attend° him as we rode? I think

was supposed to He told me Paris should° have married Juliet.

Said he not so? Or did I dream it so?

i.e., Paris Or am I mad, hearing him° talk of Juliet, 80

To think it was so?—Oh, give me thy hand,

One writ with me in sour misfortune's book.

glorious I'll bury thee in a triumphant° grave.

[He opens the tomb to reveal **Juliet**.]

A grave? Oh no, a lantern,¹ slaughtered youth;

For here lies Juliet, and her beauty makes 85

This vault a feasting presence² full of light.

[placing **Paris** in the tomb]

i.e., Paris's body Death,° lie thou there, by a dead man interred.

How oft when men are at the point of death

nurses Have they been merry, which their keepers° call

A light'ning before death!³ Oh, how may I 90

Call this a light'ning?—O my love, my wife!

Death, that hath sucked the honey of thy breath,

Hath had no power yet upon thy beauty;

banner Thou art not conquered. Beauty's ensign° yet

Is crimson in thy lips and in thy cheeks, 95

And Death's pale flag is not advancèd there.

—Tybalt, liest thou there in thy bloody sheet?

Oh, what more favor can I do to thee,

Than with that hand that cut thy youth in twain

cut To sunder° his that was thine enemy? 100

Forgive me, cousin.—Ah, dear Juliet,

1   *set up my everlasting rest*
    **(1) bring about a sleep that lasts
    forever; (2) risk my place in Heaven
    (see 4.4.35 and note).**

2   *A dateless bargain to engrossing death*
    **A perpetual contract with all-
    consuming death**

Why art thou yet so fair? Shall I believe

That unsubstantial death is amorous,

And that the lean, abhorrèd monster keeps

lover Thee here in dark to be his paramour?°   105

always For fear of that, I still° will stay with thee

bed And never from this pallet° of dim night

Depart again. Here, here will I remain

With worms that are thy chambermaids. Oh, here

Will I set up my everlasting rest[1]   110

And shake the yoke of inauspicious stars

From this world-wearied flesh. Eyes, look your last;

Arms, take your last embrace; and, lips, (O you

The doors of breath), seal with a righteous kiss

A dateless bargain to engrossing death.[2]   115

Come, bitter conduct; come, unsavoury guide.

Thou desperate pilot, now at once run on

ship The dashing rocks thy seasick, weary bark.°

Here's to my love! [*drinks the poison*] O true apothecary,

Thy drugs are quick. Thus with a kiss I die.   [*He dies.*]   120

Enter **Friar** [**Laurence**] *with lantern, crow, and spade.*

Friar Laurence

aid Saint Francis be my speed!° How oft tonight

Have my old feet stumbled at graves!——Who's there?

Balthasar

Here's one, a friend, and one that knows you well.

Friar Laurence

Bliss be upon you! Tell me, good my friend,

What torch is yon that vainly lends his light   125

maggots To grubs° and eyeless skulls? As I discern,

Romeo and Juliet

1   *knows not but I am gone hence*

Does not know that I have not left
as he ordered (see 5.3.41–42)

It burneth in the Capels' monument.

Balthasar

It doth so, holy sir, and there's my master,
One that you love.

Friar Laurence

Who is it?

Balthasar

Romeo.

Friar Laurence

How long hath he been there?

Balthasar

Full half an hour.   130

Friar Laurence

Go with me to the vault.

Balthasar

I dare not, sir.
My master knows not but I am gone hence, [1]
And fearfully did menace me with death
If I did stay to look on his intents.

Friar Laurence

Stay, then; I'll go alone. Fear comes upon me.   135

unfortunate   Oh, much I fear some ill unthrifty° thing.

Balthasar

As I did sleep under this yew tree here,
I dreamed my master and another fought,
And that my master slew him.

Friar Laurence

Romeo!

—Alack, alack, what blood is this which stains   140
The stony entrance of the sepulcher?
What mean these masterless and gory swords

i.e., with blood   To lie discolored° by this place of peace?
Romeo! Oh, pale! Who else? What? Paris too?

1   *in thy bosom*

Apparently, Romeo's body has fallen across Juliet's, and she has not yet awakened fully enough to notice.

2   *I dare no longer stay.*

The Friar's fear of being caught resonates with the peril faced in Elizabethan England by Catholic priests, who were regarded as spies in allegiance with the pope, and who could be tortured or executed if captured.

3   *timeless*

(1) eternal; (2) untimely

4   *To make me die with a restorative*

(1) to kill me with a cure (i.e. a kiss that under ordinary circumstances would restore me); (2) to kill me, thus restoring Romeo and me to each another

unnatural   And steeped in blood? Ah, what an unkind° hour   145
                  Is guilty of this lamentable chance!   [**Juliet** *wakes.*]
                  The lady stirs.

Juliet

comfort-giving O comfortable° Friar, where is my lord?
                  I do remember well where I should be,
                  And there I am. Where is my Romeo?   150

Friar Laurence

                  I hear some noise. Lady, come from that nest
                  Of death, contagion, and unnatural sleep.
                  A greater power than we can contradict
                  Hath thwarted our intents. Come, come away.
                  Thy husband in thy bosom[1] there lies dead,   155
                  And Paris too. Come; I'll dispose of thee
                  Among a sisterhood of holy nuns.
                  Stay not to question, for the watch is coming.
                  Come; go, good Juliet. I dare no longer stay.[2]   *He exits.*

Juliet

                  Go; get thee hence, for I will not away.   160
                  What's here? A cup, closed in my true love's hand?
                  Poison, I see, hath been his timeless[3] end.
                  O churl! Drunk all and left no friendly drop
                  To help me after? I will kiss thy lips.
Perhaps   Haply° some poison yet doth hang on them,   165
                  To make me die with a restorative.[4]

                                              [*She kisses* **Romeo**.]

                  Thy lips are warm.

                      Enter [**Page**] *and* Watch[*men*].

Chief Watchman

                  [*to* **Page**] Lead, boy. Which way?

1 *ground*

   **Cause (but punning on *ground* or
   earth in the previous line)**

2 *We cannot without circumstance descry*

   **We cannot discover without
   knowing more details.**

3 *in safety*

   I.e., under guard

Juliet

fortunate   Yea, noise? Then I'll be brief. [*takes Romeo's dagger*] O happy°
        dagger,

        This is thy sheath. [*stabs herself*] There rust and let me die.   170

Page   *They give what happened*

        This is the place, there, where the torch doth burn.

Chief Watchman

        The ground is bloody.—Search about the churchyard.

arrest   Go, some of you. Whoe'er you find, attach.°

                             [*Some of the* **Watchmen** *exit.*]

        Pitiful sight! Here lies the County slain,

        And Juliet bleeding, warm and newly dead,   175

        Who here hath lain this two days burièd.

        —Go; tell the Prince. Run to the Capulets.

        Raise up the Montagues. Some others search.

                             [*Other* **Watchmen** *exit.*]

i.e., murdered bodies   We see the ground whereon these woes° do lie,

griefs   But the true ground [1] of all these piteous woes°   180

        We cannot without circumstance descry. [2]

           Enter [**Watchmen** *with*] *Romeo's man,* [**Balthasar**].

Second Watchman

        Here's Romeo's man. We found him in the churchyard.

Chief Watchman

        Hold him in safety [3] till the Prince come hither.

          Enter **Friar** [**Laurence**] *and another* **Watchman**.

Third Watchman

        Here is a Friar that trembles, sighs, and weeps.

pickaxe   We took this mattock° and this spade from him   185

        As he was coming from this churchyard's side.

1   *A great suspicion.*

    I.e., that is very suspicious.

2   *This dagger hath mista'en, for, lo, his
    house / Is empty on the back of
    Montague*

    **This dagger has been misplaced;
    look, its sheath, which Romeo is
    wearing, is empty.**

Chief Watchman

Detain A great suspicion. [1] Stay° the Friar too.

Enter the **Prince** [*with attendants*].

Prince

What misadventure is so early up

That calls our person from our morning rest?

Enter [**Capulet** *and* **Lady Capulet**].

Capulet

in the streets What should it be that is so shrieked abroad?°   190

Lady Capulet

Oh, the people in the street cry "Romeo,"

Some "Juliet," and some "Paris," and all run

With open outcry toward our monument.

Prince

causes shock What fear is this which startles° in your ears?

Chief Watchman

Sovereign, here lies the County Paris slain,   195

And Romeo dead, and Juliet, dead before,

Warm and new killed.

Prince

Search, seek, and know how this foul murder comes.

Chief Watchman

Here is a Friar and slaughtered Romeo's man,

With instruments upon them fit to open   200

These dead men's tombs.

Capulet

O heavens! O wife, look how our daughter bleeds!

sheath This dagger hath mista'en, for, lo, his house°

Is empty on the back of Montague, [2]

1   *is dead tonight*
    Died last night

2   *Grief of my son's exile hath stopped her*
    breath.

    In Q1 (1597), Montague reports the
    death not only of his wife, but also
    of "*yong Benvolto*" (Benvolio). The
    line there provides an explanation
    for the notable absence of
    Benvolio at the conclusion of the
    play. Benvolio's absence has been
    explained on the pragmatic
    grounds of the play's original
    casting, since the same actor might
    have played both Benvolio and
    Paris, who plays an important role
    in the last scene. However,
    Benvolio's absence might be
    symbolic as well as pragmatic,
    since by the end of the play all the
    youthful protagonists (Romeo,
    Juliet, Mercutio, Tybalt, and Paris)
    have died, and only members of
    the older generation remain.

3   *press before*
    Hurry ahead of

4   *Seal up the mouth of outrage*

    (1) close the doors of the tomb
    (where this *outrage* has taken place);
    (2) silence these passionate cries.

5   *even to death*

    (1) even if sorrow would kill me; (2)
    justly to the death penalty for the
    guilty parties; (3) to the very cause
    of the deaths

6   *let mischance be slave to patience*

    **I.e., be calm and control your
    reaction to this misfortune.**

7   *impeach and purge*

    Accuse and exonerate

And it mis-sheathèd in my daughter's bosom.   205

Lady Capulet

O me! This sight of death is as a bell

summons That warns° my old age to a sepulcher.

Enter **Montague**.

Prince

Come, Montague, for thou art early up

To see thy son and heir now early down.

Montague

Alas, my liege, my wife is dead tonight.[1]   *She died from grief*   210

Grief of my son's exile hath stopped her breath.[2]

What further woe conspires against mine age?

Prince

Look, and thou shalt see.

Montague

rude boy [*to* **Romeo**] O thou untaught!° What manners is in this,

To press before[3] thy father to a grave?   215

Prince

Seal up the mouth of outrage[4] for a while,

Till we can clear these ambiguities

origin And know their spring,° their head, their true descent,

commander And then will I be general° of your woes

And lead you even to death.[5] Meantime forbear   220

subservient And let mischance be slave° to patience.[6]

under —Bring forth the parties of° suspicion.   *He tells everything they did + the plan*

Friar Laurence

i.e., prime suspect I am the greatest,° able to do least,

Yet most suspected, as the time and place

i.e., accusation against Doth make against° me, of this direful murder.   225

And here I stand, both to impeach and purge,[7]

Myself condemnèd and myself excused.

1   *date of breath*

    Interval of life

2   *borrowed grave*

    **It is merely *borrowed* since Juliet
    was not then dead.**

Prince

Then say at once what thou dost know in this.

Friar Laurence

I will be brief, for my short date of breath[1]

Is not so long as is a tedious tale.   230

Romeo, there dead, was husband to that Juliet,

And she, there dead, that's Romeo's faithful wife.

secret   I married them, and their stol'n° marriage day

day of death   Was Tybalt's doomsday,° whose untimely death

Banished the new-made bridegroom from this city,   235

For whom, and not for Tybalt, Juliet pined.

i.e., the Capulets   You,° to remove that siege of grief from her,

by compulsion   Betrothed and would have married her perforce°

To County Paris. Then comes she to me,

And with wild looks bid me devise some mean   240

To rid her from this second marriage,

Or in my cell there would she kill herself.

medical knowledge   Then gave I her, so tutored by my art,°

A sleeping potion, which so took effect

As I intended, for it wrought on her   245

appearance   The form° of death. Meantime I writ to Romeo

on   That he should hither come as° this dire night,

To help to take her from her borrowed grave,[2]

Being the time the potion's force should cease.

who   But he which° bore my letter, Friar John,   250

stopped   Was stayed° by accident, and yesternight

Returned my letter back. Then all alone,

prearranged   At the prefixèd° hour of her waking,

Came I to take her from her kindred's vault,

secretly   Meaning to keep her closely° at my cell   255

Till I conveniently could send to Romeo;

But when I came, some minute ere the time

Of her awakening, here untimely lay

1   *what made your master*

    What was your master doing

2   *by and by*

    Immediately

    faithful   The noble Paris and true° Romeo dead.

        She wakes, and I entreated her come forth   260

        And bear this work of Heaven with patience.

        But then a noise did scare me from the tomb,

    despairing   And she, too desperate,° would not go with me,

        But, as it seems, did violence on herself.

        All this I know (and to the marriage   265

  secretly informed   Her Nurse is privy°), and if aught in this

        Miscarried by my fault, let my old life

    its   Be sacrificed some hour before his° time

        Unto the rigor of severest law.

        Prince

    always   We still° have known thee for a holy man.   270

        —Where's Romeo's man? What can he say to this?

        Balthasar

        I brought my master news of Juliet's death,

    haste   And then in post° he came from Mantua

        To this same place, to this same monument.

        This letter he early bid me give his father,   275

        And threatened me with death, going in the vault,

        If I departed not and left him there.

        Prince

        Give me the letter. I will look on it.

        Where is the County's page that raised the watch?

        —Sirrah, what made your master¹ in this place?   280

        Page

        He came with flowers to strew his lady's grave,

  at a distance   And bid me stand aloof,° and so I did.

        Anon comes one with light to ope the tomb,

  drew his sword   And by and by² my master drew° on him,

        And then I ran away to call the watch.   285

        Prince

        This letter doth make good the Friar's words,

1   *to kill your joys with love*

    I.e., to kill your children by means
    of their love for one another

2   *raise her statue*

    Have an effigy carved (not an upright
    statue but a recumbent figure, see
    5.3.303, like those that often appear
    on Renaissance tombs)

3   *at such rate*

    Of such esteem (but suggests also
    "of such cost," introducing a
    disturbing materialism, echoed in
    Capulet's word *rich* in line 303)

4   *Some shall be pardoned and some*
    punishèd.

    Shakespeare's primary source,
    Arthur Brooke's *Tragical History of*
    Romeus and Juliet (1562), leaves no
    ambiguity about who is pardoned
    and who is punished. Whereas the
    Friar is exonerated, harsh
    punishments are meted out to
    figures of lower status: the Nurse is
    banished and the Apothecary is
    hanged.

Their course of love, the tidings of her death.

And here he writes that he did buy a poison

with that poison Of a poor 'pothecary, and therewithal°

Came to this vault to die and lie with Juliet. 290

Where be these enemies?—Capulet! Montague!

punishment See what a scourge° is laid upon your hate,

That Heaven finds means to kill your joys with love! [1]

closing my eyes And I, for winking° at your discords, too

pair (Mercutio and Paris) Have lost a brace° of kinsmen. All are punished. 295

Capulet

O brother Montague, give me thy hand.

dowry This is my daughter's jointure,° for no more

Can I demand.

Montague

But I can give thee more,

For I will raise her statue [2] in pure gold,

That whiles Verona by that name is known, 300

statue There shall no figure° at such rate [3] be set

As that of true and faithful Juliet.

Capulet

As rich shall Romeo's by his lady's lie,

Poor sacrifices of our enmity.

Prince

gloomy; clouded A glooming° peace this morning with it brings. 305

The sun, for sorrow, will not show his head.

Go hence to have more talk of these sad things.

Some shall be pardoned and some punishèd. [4]

For never was a story of more woe

Than this of Juliet and her Romeo. *[They all exit.]* 310

Longer Notes

PAGE 45

Prologue 0.6   *star-crossed*

The play's many references to the stars and to fortune suggest that fate plays a role in the protagonists' tragedy. Yet the idea that Romeo and Juliet are *star-crossed* raises more questions than it answers, in that a variety of factors—misjudgment, bad timing, coincidence, ignorance, rashness—contributes to the lovers' demise. The phrase is also ambiguous: are they *crossed* (thwarted) by the stars or have they crossed (acted in opposition to) the stars? Moreover, according to Renaissance astrology lore, the stars could directly affect only the body's "lower" physical faculties—the senses and passions—not its "higher" mental faculties, such as reason. Romeo and Juliet are not simply passive victims of fate, then, since in yielding to passion they make themselves vulnerable to disruptive astrological influences. For instance, Romeo decides to attend the Capulet feast despite a premonition

that his presence there will initiate a mortal *consequence yet hanging in the stars* (1.4.105).

PAGE 63

1.1.170–171   *O brawling love, O loving hate, / O anything of nothing first created*

The most famous Elizabethan sonneteer in the Petrarchan tradition was the courtier-poet Sir Philip Sidney, whose immensely influential *Astrophil and Stella* (1591) comprises a series of over one hundred poems in which Astrophil ("star-lover") describes the fluctuations of joy and despair he experiences in his unfulfilled love for a married woman, Stella ("star").

By the mid-1590s, when *Romeo and Juliet* was first performed, the sonnet tradition in England had already reached its peak and was ripe for parody. Shakespeare's own sonnet sequence, probably begun during this period, significantly modifies the Petrarchan tradition. Instead of praising a fair and chaste lady, Shakespeare's sonnets explore the dynamics of an erotic triangle composed of the male speaker, a fair young man, and a sexually promiscuous "black" (dark-haired or dark-complexioned) woman.

1.2.18—19   *within her scope of choice, / Lies my consent and fair according voice*

The legal age of consent for marriage in Elizabethan England was twelve for girls and fourteen for boys. In aristocratic and wealthy families, parents often arranged marriages for their children in order to forge politically and financially beneficial alliances. There was some debate about the age at which a girl was *ripe to be a bride*, however, since a fourteen-year-old girl might face a difficult childbirth. Even among the wealthiest, the mean age of marriage in the late 16th century was approximately twenty for daughters and twenty-five for sons.

Shakespeare's contemporaries were also engaged in a vigorous debate about the relative claims of parents and children in choosing marriage partners. On the one hand, parental wisdom, authority, and financial resources (particularly in the form of the dowry a father bestowed on his son-in-law) were acknowledged as playing an important role in determining an appropriate partner. On the other hand, the Protestant emphasis on marriage as a bond of "perpetual friendly fellowship" stressed the importance of love as a source of joy and harmony within

marriage. Of course, the ideal situation, which all the members of the Capulet household initially work toward, was one in which the romantic desires of the child accorded with the prudent judgment of the parents.

1.5.91—105   *If I profane with my unworthiest hand / This holy shrine. . . Thus from my lips, by thine, my sin is purged.*

Romeo and Juliet initiate their romance through Catholic imagery of shrines, pilgrims, saints, and statues of saints. Since English Protestantism condemned the Catholic practices of visiting shrines and praying to saints as superstitious idolatry, some members of Shakespeare's audience might have regarded this dialogue as a sign that Romeo and Juliet were indulging an excessively sensual passion. However, many Elizabethans (including, possibly, Shakespeare's father) remained attached to traditional Catholic rituals and beliefs, and might have been more likely to regard the religious imagery in this dialogue as elevating instead of degrading the protagonists' love.

2.1.39   *open arse*

The two different published versions of the play, one in 1597 (the First Quarto or Q1, *An Excellent Conceited Tragedy of Romeo and Juliet*) and the other in 1599 (the Second Quarto or Q2, *The Most Excellent and Lamentable Tragedy of Romeo and Juliet*) print different versions of this line, creating a problem for modern editors. Q1 reads "open *Et caetera*" and Q2 reads "open, or." This textual crux illustrates the difficulty of deriving performance practices from printed texts, especially in the case of provocative sexual language such as *open arse*.

Modern editors usually print *open arse*, the bawdy nickname for the medlar fruit Mercutio has been discussing as an image of female genitalia. However, Mercutio's overt reference to the *arse* might also suggest that he is thinking of a more transgressive sexual act: anal intercourse. Although anal intercourse can be practiced by a man and a woman (such as Romeo and Rosaline), the evident delight Mercutio takes in imagining Romeo in a sexual act may suggest Mercutio's own erotic interest in his friend. By conjuring Rosaline, Mercutio desires to *raise up* Romeo—to make him appear and to make him erect.

PAGE 149

2.4.25–26 *the immortal* passado, *the* punto reverso, *the* hai

Elizabethan gentlemen's fascination with dueling is indicated by the publication of three fencing manuals between 1590 and 1595. Mercutio mocks the pretensions of men who fight according to the formal codes and rules spelled out in books such as Vincentio Saviolo's *Practice of the Rapier and Dagger* (1595).

PAGE 149

2.4.38–39 *the numbers that Petrarch flowed in*

Characteristically mocking, Mercutio makes the play's only direct reference to Petrarch, the poet who inspired the tradition of love sonnets whose conventions flow through Romeo's early speeches. Laura is the name of the idealized woman in Petrarch's poems; Dido, Cleopatra, Helen, Hero, and Thisbe (see lines 41–42) are tragic figures from classical literature. If Laura harks back to Rosaline, the object of Romeo's first, Petrarchan love, the list of classical heroines looks forward to Juliet, the object of his last, romantic love.

PAGE 197

3.2.21 *and when I shall die*

In the Second Quarto (1599) and the First Folio (1623) of *Romeo and Juliet*, Juliet says "when I shall die," but editors often substitute the reading of the Fourth Quarto (1622), "when he shall die." The reference to Romeo's death in "when he shall die" seems logically to precede the subsequent image of Romeo's metamorphosis into *little stars*. In Ovid's *Metamorphoses*, Julius Caesar is transformed into a shining star after his death. However, for Juliet to say "when I shall die" makes sense when we recall the familiar Renaissance pun on orgasm as death. Juliet provocatively imagines that her own "death" (sexual climax) will effect a bodily transformation in Romeo that is at once violent (*cut him out in little stars*) and elevating (*he will make the face of heaven so fine*).

THE MOST EX-
cellent and lamentable
Tragedie, of *Romeo* and *Iuliet*.

Enter Sampson *and* Gregorie, *with Swords and Bucklers, of the house of* Capulet.

Samp. Gregorie, on my word weele not carrie Coles.
Greg. No, for then we fhould be Collyers.
Samp. I meane, and we be in choller, weele draw.
Greg. I while you liue, draw your necke out of choller.
Samp. I ftrike quickly being moued.
Greg. But thou art not quickly moued to ftrike.
Samp. A dog of the houfe of *Mountague* moues me.
Grego. To moue is to ftirre, and to be valiant, is to ftand:
Therefore if thou art moued thou runft away.
Samp. A dog of that houfe fhall moue me to ftand:
I will take the wall of any man or maide of *Mounta-gues.*
Grego. That fhewes thee a weake flaue, for the weakeft goes to the wall.
Samp. Tis true, & therfore women being the weaker veffels are euer thruft to the wall: therfore I wil pufh *Mountagues* men from the wall, and thruft his maides to the wall.
Greg. The quarell is betweene our maifters, and vs their men.
Samp. Tis all one, I will fhew my felfe a tyrant, when I haue fought with the men, I will be ciuil with the maides, I will cut off their heads.

A 3   *Grego.* The

A reproduction of the first page of *Romeo and Juliet* in the Second Quarto (1599).

Editing *Romeo and Juliet*
by David Scott Kastan

omeo and Juliet was a hit in the bookshops, even as it was a great success on stage. Five individual editions of the play appeared between 1597 and 1637, and the play was twice more published in this period in the Folios of 1623 and 1632. The earliest text of *Romeo and Juliet* appeared in 1597 (Q1), published by John Danter and printed by Danter and Edward Allde. Two years later a second edition was published, printed by Thomas Creede for Cuthbert Burby. This announced itself on the title page as "*Newly corrected, augmented, and amended.*" Although title page claims are often mere publisher's puff, in this case they are accurate. Indeed it is this second edition that provides the most authoritative early text of the play, and it is the Second Quarto (Q2) that in later reprints would serve as the text for the Folio of 1623. The play itself was probably written sometime between 1594 and 1596, though it is impossible to date with more precision. The First Quarto title page identifies Lord Hundson's men as the acting company that performed it, a company that came into being in the summer of 1596 and was renamed the Lord Chamberlain's Men in April 1597, setting an outside limit for the date of the play. Most likely the play reached the stage sometime in 1595, although, as stylistic and linguistic evidence suggest, Shakespeare could have been working on it as early as 1592.

The Second Quarto (1599), on which this edition is based, is a generally well-printed text, although it also includes a number of duplications, seemingly derived from the manuscript on which the printing is based in places being unclear about what has been revised and what was intended to be replaced. The manuscript, as this might indicate, was probably in Shakespeare's own hand, a worked-over draft that had not been fully cleaned up either for performance or publication. One section of Q2 (1.2.50–1.3.35) seems to have followed Q1, perhaps because the manuscript that reached Creede's printing house was incomplete or in this section illegible.

In general the editorial work of this present edition is conservative, a matter of normalizing spelling, capitalization, and punctuation, removing superfluous italics, regularizing the names of characters, and rationalizing entrances and exits. A comparison of the edited text of 1.1.1–21 with the facsimile page of Q2 (on p. 332) reveals some of the issues in this modernization. The speech prefixes are expanded and normalized for clarity, so that "*Samp.*" and "*Greg.*" (or "*Grego.*" in one case) become Sampson and Gregory. Spelling, capitalization, and italicization in this edition regularly follow modern practices rather than the habits of the Quarto's printers. As neither spelling nor punctuation in Shakespeare's time had yet been standardized, words were spelled in various ways that indicated their proximate pronunciation; and punctuation, which then was largely a rhythmical pointer rather than predominantly designed, as it is now, to clarify logical relations, was necessarily far more idiosyncratic than today. In any case, as compositors were under no obligation to follow either the spelling or punctuation of their copy, the spelling and punctuation of the Q2 text would not necessarily reflect Shakespeare's own preferences. For most readers, then, there is little advantage in an edition that reproduces the spelling and punctuation of the Quarto. It does not accurately represent Shakespeare's writing habits, and it makes reading difficult, in a way Shakespeare could never have anticipated or desired.

Therefore "weele" in the first line becomes "we'll" and "Coles" becomes the familiar "coals," regularizing the spelling and eliminating the "literary" capitalization of the noun. In line 4 of the facsimile, "liue" becomes "live," though here it is interesting to notice how early modern practice differs from our own. In Shakespeare's time, "u" was regularly used where we would use "v" (see also "moued" in line 5 or "slaue" in line 12), while, oppositely, at the beginning of words "v" was used for "u," as in "vs" in line 18, just as "I" was regularly used for "J" (as in "Iuliet" in the title at the top of the page). The intrusive "e"s in words like "necke" in line 4 or "maide" in line 11 are eliminated, and the spelling of the proper name, *Mountague*, is regularized to "Montague" and the italics removed. Punctuation is changed to modern practice: the colon after "stand" in line 8 becomes here a semicolon, as the comma after "maides" in line 20 is changed to a period. In all these cases, modernizing clarifies rather than alters Shakespeare's intentions. Thus, Sampson's speech at the bottom of the page (1.1.19–21 in this edition) reads in Q2:

Tis all one, I will shew myself a tyrant, when I haue fought with the men, I will be ciuil with the maides, I will cut of their heads.

Modernized this reads:

'Tis all one. I will show myself a tyrant: when I have fought with the men, I will be civil with the maids. I will cut off their heads.

No doubt there is some loss in modernization. Clarity and consistency is admittedly gained at the expense of expressive detail, but normalizing spelling, capitalization, and punctuation allows the text to be read with far greater ease than the original, and essentially as it was intended to be understood. We lose the archaic feel of the text in exchange for clarity of meaning. Old spellings are consistently modernized here, but old *forms* of words (i.e., "art" in line 6) are retained. If, inevitably, in such modernization we lose the historical feel of the text Shakespeare's contemporaries read, it is important to remember that Shakespeare's contemporaries would not have thought the playbook in any sense archaic or quaint, as these details inevitably make it for a reader today. The text would have seemed to them as modern as this one does to us. Modern readers, however, cannot help but be distracted by the different conventions they encounter on the page of the earliest texts. While it is indeed of interest to see how orthography and typography have changed over time, these changes are not primary concerns for most readers of this edition. What little, then, is lost in a careful modernization of the text is more than made up for by the removal of the artificial obstacle of unfamiliar spelling forms and punctuation habits, which Shakespeare never could have intended as interpretive difficulties for his readers.

Textual Notes

The list below records all substantive departures in this edition from the 1599 Second Quarto of the play (Q2). It does not record modernizations of spelling, normalization in the use of capitals, corrections of obvious typographical errors, adjustments of lineation, minor repositioning or rewording of stage directions, or rationalizations of speech prefixes. Four lines in Q2 at the end of 2.2 spoken by Romeo and essentially repeated by Friar Laurence at the beginning of 2.3 are discussed in note 1 on page 138. The adopted reading in this edition is given first in boldface and followed by the original, rejected reading of the Second Quarto, or noted as being absent from the quarto text. Editorial stage directions are not collated but are enclosed within brackets in the text. Latin stage directions are translated (e.g., *They all exit* for *Exeunt omnes*).

1.1.25 it in sense it sense; **1.1.141 his** is; **1.1.173 well-seeming** welseeing; **1.1.212 makes** make; **1.2.1SD a servingman** the Clowne; **1.2.38**

written here. written. Here; **1.2.46 One** On; **1.2.64–73** [prose in Q2]; **1.2.70 Rosaline and Livia** Rosaline, Liuia; **1.3.2–4** [prose in Q2]; **1.3.18–50** [prose in Q2]; **1.3.52–59** [prose in Q2]; **1.3. 61–64** [prose in Q2]; **1.3.69–70** [prose in Q2]; **1.3.77–78** [prose in Q2]; **1.3.101 make it** make; **1.4.21 SP Mercutio** Horatio; **1.4.29 quote** cote; **1.4.37 done** dum; **1.4.40 your** you; **1.4.43 light** lights; **1.4.51–93** [prose in Q2]; **1.4.55 atomi** ottamie; **1.4.64 maid** man; **1.4.72 on** one; **1.4.88 elf-locks** Elklocks; **1.5.93 ready** did readie; **1.5.139 this…this** tis…tis

2.Prologue.4 matched match; **2.1.10 one** on; **2.1.11 Pronounce** prouaunt; **2.1.11 "dove"** day; **2.1.13 heir** her; **2.1.39 open arse, and** open, or; **2.2.16 do** to; **2.2.41–42 nor any other part / Belonging to a man. Oh, be some other name!** o be some other name / Belonging to a man; **2.2.45 were** wene; **2.2.83 washed** washeth; **2.2.101 more coying** coying; **2.2.165 than mine** then; **2.2.170 nyas** Neece; **2.2.189SP Romeo** Iu.; **2.4.28 phantasms** phantacies; **2.4.33 "pardon me's"** pardons mees; **2.4.65 Switch…switch** Swits . . . swits; **2.4.193 dog's name** dog, name; **2.5.11 three** there; **2.5.56 And** An; **2.6.27 music's** music

3.1.65 injured iniuried; **3.1.88 o'** a; **3.1.96 o'** a; **3.1.103 o'** a; **3.1.119 Again** He gan; **3.1.121 fire-eyed** fier end; **3.1.163 agile** aged; **3.1.181SP Montague** Capu.; **3.2.1SP** [not in Q2]; **3.2.9 By** And by; **3.2.48 death-darting** death arting; **3.2.50 shut** shot; **3.2.52 of my** my; **3.2.61 one** on; **3.2.73SP** [not in Q2]; **3.2.74SP Juliet** Nur. [followed by l. 75 SP "Iu." in Q2]; **3.2.77 Dove-feathered** Rauenous douefeatherd; **3.2.80 damnèd** dimme; **3.3.19 banished** blanisht; **3.3.40–43 But Romeo may not; he is banishèd. / Flies may do this, but I from this must fly. / They are free men, but I am banishèd. / And sayest thou yet that exile is not death?** This may flyes do, when I from this must flie, / And sayest thou yet, that exile is not death? / But Romeo may not, he is banished. / Flies may do this, but I from this must flie: / They are freemen, but I am banished.; **3.3.52 Thou** Then; **3.3.61 madmen** mad man; **3.3.70SD knock [within]** Enter Nurse, and knocke; **3.3.73SD knock [within]** They knocke; **3.3.75SD knock [within]** Slud knocke; **3.3.77SD knock [within]** Knocke; **3.3.88 an** and; **3.3.110 denote** deuote; **3.3.117 lives** lies; **3.3.144 pout'st upon** puts vp; **3.3.168 disguised** disguise; **3.4.13 be** me; **3.4.20 O'... —O'** A . . . a; **3.4.23 We'll** Well,; **3.4.30 O'** a; **3.5.13 exhales** exhale; **3.5.19 the** the the; **3.5.36SD Enter Nurse** Enter Madame and Nurse; **3.5.53 SP Juliet** Ro. ; **3.5.81 him** [not in Q2]; **3.5.138 gives** give; **3.5.160 o'** a; **3.5.171SP Capulet** Father, [in text]; **3.5.172 SP Nurse** [not in Q2]; **3.5.180 limbed** liand

4.1.72 slay stay; **4.1.83 chapless** chaples; **4.1.85 tomb** [not in Q2]; **4.1.98 breath** breast; **4.1.100 To wanny** Too many; **4.1.110 In** Is; **4.1.110** [Q2 prints an extra line after l. 110, "Be borne to buriall in thy kindreds graue:", widely held to be an early version of ll. 112–113 and printed by mistake.]; **4.1.115 and** an; **4.1.116 waking** walking; **4.3.48 wake** walke; **4.4.70 long** loue; **4.4.80 behold** bedold; **4.4.94 cure** care; **4.4.128 by my** my my; **4.4.128SD Enter [Peter]** Enter Will Kemp; **4.4.147SP Peter** [after "with my wit" in Q2]

5.1.24 e'en in; **5.1.24 defy** denie; **5.1.76 pay** pray; **5.3.3 yew** young; **5.3.20 rite** right; **5.3.21SD Balthasar** Peter; **5.3.40SP Balthasar** Pet. [so through l. 44]; **5.3.68 commination** commiration; **5.3.71SP Page** [not in Q2]; [line arranged as SD]; **5.3.102–103 Shall I believe / That** I will beleeue, / Shall I beleeue that **5.3.107–108** [Between these lines Q2 prints an additional passage: "Depart againe, come lye thou in my arme, / Heer's to thy health, where ere thou tumblest in. / O true Appothecarie! / Thy drugs are quicke. Thus with a kisse I die."]; **5.3.137 yew** yong; **5.3.187 too** too too; **5.3.190 shrieked** shrike; **5.3.199 slaughtered** Slaughter; **5.3.209 early** earling; **5.3.299 raise** raie

Romeo and Juliet on the Early Stage
by Mario DiGangi

n our own time, *Romeo and Juliet* is revered above all for the un-
surpassed beauty of its poetry. Yet Shakespeare's most lyrical
tragedy also offers an exciting theatrical spectacle: a fervent
romance emerging from the violent energies of youthful im-
petuosity and civil strife. The Prologue's reference to the "two
hours' traffic of our stage" (line 12) suggests the rush of vigorous action that characterized the original performances of this intensely compact and passionate drama.

The large, open-air, public theaters in which the play was
originally performed were well suited to a fast-paced drama in which
busy scenes of public brawling and feasting alternate with tranquil
scenes of romantic intimacy. The first performances of *Romeo and
Juliet* probably took place at the Theatre, which was built in 1576 as the
first public playhouse in London. Like the later Globe, the Theatre
was a three-story "round" (multisided polygonal) structure encircling
a rectangular stage approximately 25 feet deep by 45 feet wide. The
playhouse could accommodate up to 2,500 playgoers, either seated in
the galleries surrounding the stage or standing in the yard to its front
and sides. Unlike modern theaters, Elizabethan theaters did not have
painted scenery, elaborate sets, or stage lighting. The expansive,
bare platform stage functioned like a blank canvas: it provided an

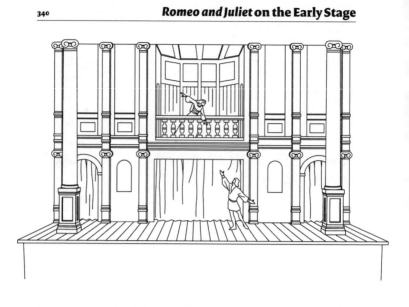

Fig 1. In the large London playhouses, the balcony above the stage could be used for staging, seating, or to house musicians.

Fig 2. English Renaissance drama made minimal use of sets or backdrops. In the absence of a set, the stage pillars could be incorporated into the action, standing in for trees and other architectural elements.

Fig 3. The discovery space, located in the middle of the backstage wall, could be used as a third entrance as well as a location for scenes requiring special staging, such as in a tomb or bedchamber.

Fig 4. A trapdoor led to the area below the stage, known as "Hell" (as contrasted with the painted ceiling, known as "Heaven" or the "heavens"). Ghosts or other supernatural figures could descend through the trap, and it could also serve as a grave.

unlocalized or neutral space that could accommodate rapid shifts of place and produce jarring contrasts of mood.

In the first act of *Romeo and Juliet*, sudden alterations of place and mood help to establish dramatic tension. The Prologue, a somber choric figure dressed in a black cloak and speaking in the measured rhythms of a formal sonnet, prepares us for a tragic story of enraged fathers and star-crossed lovers. When the action begins on the streets of Verona, however, we encounter neither fathers nor lovers but two clownish Capulet servants who boast about their military and sexual prowess, perhaps gesturing obscenely as they describe how valiantly they would "push" and "thrust" the Montagues. In the rapidly escalating melee that follows, the stage fills up with servants clashing swords and bucklers, young gentlemen flourishing rapiers, and concerned citizens brandishing clubs and spears. Cutting a ridiculous figure in his dressing gown, Old Capulet storms onto the scene demanding his antiquated long sword, only to be mocked by his wife's call for a crutch. Finally, Prince Escalus, wearing the rich attire of an Elizabethan nobleman and accompanied by a train of courtiers, arrives to restore order and to pronounce judgment. As the crowded and weapon-cluttered stage clears, the focus of the scene suddenly shifts to intimate conversations about Romeo's melancholy solitude and the unrequited love that is its cause.

Balancing this opening scene of public violence, the first act closes on an elaborate scene of domestic festivity. In Act One, scene four, the fluidity of locale on the Elizabethan stage allows for a seamless transition from an exterior space, the streets of Verona, to an interior space, the Capulet household. Costumed, masked, and accompanied by torchbearers (whose presence indicates that it is night), Romeo and his friends are making their way to the Capulet feast. As they walk around the perimeter of the stage, the arrival in center stage of servants with napkins and platters establishes the interior locale of the Capulet household. They play's astutely observed representation of the toil of various domestic serving-men and women, including the Nurse, would certainly have appealed to the many common laborers in the public theater's socially heterogeneous audience. Amidst the rushing of harried servants carrying trenchers, stools, and torches, and the dancing of elaborately dressed guests, Romeo and Juliet first meet, their brief dialogue carving out a space of intimate desire.

Shakespeare develops the lovers' intimacy in two scenes that exploit the visual and symbolic contrasts between the upper and lower areas of the playing space. At the back of the stage was the tiring ("attiring") house, a three-tiered structure that contained rooms for storing properties and changing into costumes. At ground level, the ornately painted façade of the tiring-house contained three modes of access to the stage: two side doors and a larger, central, curtained space. The tiring-house also had an upper level that could be used for window or balcony scenes. In 2.1, we are led to imagine that Romeo, under cover of darkness, has leapt the wall of the orchard beneath Juliet's window. As Juliet appears above with a candle, prompting Romeo's famous question, "But soft! What light through yonder window breaks?" (2.2.2), Romeo emerges from his hiding place, most likely behind one of the two large posts that supported the stage roof.

Although physically separated, Romeo and Juliet express their love through an intensely lyrical language that would have resounded through the large open space of the theater. The Elizabethan theater was primarily an aural performance space, and playgoers were attuned to the particularities of verbal style that contributed to the creation of dramatic character: Romeo's conventional Petrarchan laments over Rosaline; Mercutio's witty, bawdy puns and wildly imaginative tale of Queen Mab; Tybalt's petulant threats of revenge; and the Nurse's garrulous account of Juliet's past. Distinct styles of speech provided information about characters' social status, disposition, and mental state. Thus when Romeo rejects Rosaline for Juliet, his psychological transformation is revealed through his use of a more genuine language of desire, which in turn responds to

Juliet's own expressions of desire. Likewise, the trained boy actor who played Juliet would have used modulations of voice and gesture to emphasize the contrast between Juliet's modest compliance with her mother's recommendation of Paris in Act One and her newly awakened confidence in the balcony scene, as she expresses her determination to possess Romeo.

The play's second window scene takes place in Act Three, scene five, as the newly married couple enjoys a brief moment after their first night together. When Romeo uses the rope ladder to climb down from the window to the garden below, his descent from the upper to lower stage is accentuated by Juliet's premonition: "Methinks I see thee now: thou art so low / As one dead in the bottom of a tomb" (3.5.54–55). Romeo's drop from a high to a low space signals the decline of the lovers' fortunes and fore-shadows their deaths in the Capulet tomb.

The play's final scene at the Capulet tomb brings the tragic merging of love and death to a powerful conclusion. While Paris sweetens Juliet's tomb with flowers, perfume, and poetry, Romeo enters menacingly with pickaxe and crowbar, tools for violating that tomb. Shakespeare departs from his primary source, Arthur Brooke's *Tragical History of Romeus and Juliet* (1562), by having Romeo and Paris engage in a bloody duel: the Friar and the watch later remark upon the gore-splattered environs. The terror and excitement of this duel in what is supposed to be a dark graveyard might have been enhanced by having the combatants wield a torch in one hand and a rapier in the other.

On the Elizabethan stage, the tomb itself could have been represented in several different ways, each affecting the dramatic emphasis of the scene. A more realistic graveyard setting could have been achieved through the use of a freestanding verisimilar tomb prop; stage blood from Romeo's duel with Paris might have been visibly splattered on this large tomb. Alternatively, the symbolism of a tragic fall could have been emphasized by locating the tomb underneath the trapdoor in the center of the stage. When Romeo pried open the "tomb" door with the crowbar, stagehands could have thrust Juliet's coffin onto the main platform. Finally, the bed on which Juliet had taken the sleeping potion in Act Four, scene three, might have also doubled as the tomb. Juliet's bed was either a curtained piece of furniture visible on the stage or a simple platform concealed behind the curtains of the tiring-house's central space. Locating the tomb in the same visual space as the bed would have reinforced the play's verbal imagery, which continually links sex with death.

Elizabethan tragedies usually concluded with a funeral procession in which the dead bodies were carried offstage as if to burial. Such a procession is not literally necessary in the final scene of *Romeo and Juliet*, which takes place in a graveyard. However, the Prince's command, "Seal up the mouth of outrage for a while" (5.3.216), might be understood as a direction to conceal the bodies of the dead within the tomb, by closing either the tomb prop door, the trapdoor, or the central space curtains. Montague and Capulet finally reconcile by taking hands, and the Prince ritualistically concludes the play with a rhymed couplet that recalls the sonnet that had served as the play's Prologue. The restoration of social harmony could be represented by having Montague and Capulet exit together through the same door; such a reconciliation would appear even more emphatic had Montague and Capulet first entered the play aggressively storming toward each other from opposite stage doors. Nonetheless, the stark visual contrast between the bodies of the young that remain in the tomb and the surviving adults who walk away from this scene of death underscores the terrible price of the feud.

Significant Performances
by Mario DiGangi

1594/95–1599 *Romeo and Juliet* was probably performed first at the Theatre (1594/95–1597), then at the Curtain (1598–1599), and thereafter at the Globe.

1662 Upon the reopening of London's public theaters after the restoration of King Charles II, William Davenant's company mounted an adapted version of *Romeo and Juliet* in which an actress played Juliet, probably for the first time. Diarist Samuel Pepys, who attended the opening night performance, described the play as "the worst that ever I heard in my life, and the worst acted that ever I saw these people do." There is no way to know how many of his contemporaries shared Pepys' view, but the play continued to be popular, although in modified form: another production from this era modified the ending so that Romeo and Juliet survived.

1679 Thomas Otway rewrote *Romeo and Juliet* as *The Rise and Fall of Caius Marius*, a neoclassical political drama focused on civil war in ancient Rome, and glancing at current efforts by the English Whig party to prevent the Catholic Duke of York from succeeding to the throne. In Otway's version, Romeo becomes Young Marius, son of the senator Marius, and Juliet becomes Lavinia, daughter of a rival senator. While

Otway's play retained its popularity during the next sixty years, *Romeo and Juliet* itself went unperformed.

1744   Theophilus Cibber fashioned his own version of *Romeo and Juliet* by cobbling together scenes from several sources: Alexander Pope's edition of *Romeo and Juliet*, Otway's *Rise and Fall of Caius Marius*, and Shakespeare's comedy *The Two Gentlemen of Verona*. Cibber himself played Romeo to his fourteen-year-old daughter in the role of Juliet. Performed only a few times, Cibber's rather unimpressive version of the play nonetheless seems to have inspired David Garrick to mount his extremely influential production.

1748   David Garrick's immensely successful revival of *Romeo and Juliet* played over 450 times by 1800, and was the version of the play used for stage performances through the mid-nineteenth century. Garrick reduced scenes of social interaction to focus attention on the tragedy of the lovers. He also catered to eighteenth-century moral taste by raising Juliet's age to eighteen and by cutting bawdy dialogue; in 1750, he sought further to ennoble Romeo by eliminating altogether his infatuation for Rosaline. Building upon an innovation introduced by Otway, Garrick had Juliet awaken in the tomb before Romeo died from the poison; the lovers speak a passionate parting dialogue written by Garrick himself.

1815   In one of several unsuccessful early nineteenth-century productions of *Romeo and Juliet*, Edmund Kean played Romeo at Drury Lane. Nineteenth-century Shakespearean actors did not generally thrive as Romeo, in part because the character's youth and perceived effeminacy did not correspond to their proclivity for conveying the stern gravity of tragic warrior protagonists such as Macbeth and Othello.

1830–1869 Shakespeare's tragedy of doomed young lovers appealed to nineteenth-century European composers. Prominent musical settings of the story include Vincenzo Bellini's opera *I Capuleti e i Montecchi* (1830), Hector Berlioz's dramatic symphony *Roméo et Juliette* (1839), Charles Gounod's opera *Roméo et Juliette* (1867), and Pyotr Tchaikovsky's "Fantasy Overture" (1869).

1845 In a production that opened in London to great acclaim, the American actress Charlotte Cushman played Romeo to her sister's Juliet. Rejecting Garrick's standard adaptation of *Romeo and Juliet*, Cushman focused her version on Romeo, whose passion she was celebrated for expressing with great authenticity. During the Victorian period, other actresses played Romeo with varying degrees of success, including Ellen Tree at Covent Garden in 1829.

1882 Approaching *Romeo and Juliet* as a "dramatic poem," Henry Irving's production at the Lyceum Theatre emphasized the play's visual splendors. Irving used the technical resources of the Victorian theater to re-create an authentic Italian setting through elaborate three-dimensional sets, subtle lighting design, atmospheric music, rich costumes based on Renaissance paintings, and large, elaborately orchestrated crowd scenes.

1905 Reacting against lavish Victorian productions such as Irving's, William Poel's *Romeo and Juliet* at the Royalty Theatre attempted to re-create original Elizabethan performance conditions. Poel cast adolescent actors in the lead roles; set the action on a bare stage; and emphasized the group scenes that put the lovers' tragedy in a social context, such as the bustling activity of the Capulet household and the violent clashes on the streets of Verona. By demonstrating that *Romeo and Juliet* could have dramatic impact without the elaborate scenery of the Victorian tradition, Poel's groundbreaking production led the way for the more streamlined and raw treatments of the modern era.

1935 John Gielgud's *Romeo and Juliet* at London's New Theatre represents an important milestone in modern productions of the play for its powerful acting, fluid staging, and restoration of much of Shakespeare's original text. Gielgud and Lawrence Olivier alternated as Romeo and Mercutio: Gielgud's Romeo was lyrical and romantic; Olivier's passionate and earthy, reflecting a more contemporary approach to the character. The Elizabethan-style staging was facilitated by a simple, elegant set comprised of a central tower flanked by alcoves.

1936 Produced by MGM studios, this lavish Hollywood film directed by George Cukor starred a thirty-six-year-old Norma Shearer as Juliet and a forty-three-year-old Leslie Howard as Romeo. While the screenplay remained largely faithful to the text, the overly decorative scenery and staid, reverential acting by its middle-aged leads failed to capture a sense of the lovers' passion and vitality.

1947 Intent on making *Romeo and Juliet* modern and new, Peter Brook directed a poorly received production at Stratford that did away with lyricism and sentimentality. Brook emphasized crowd scenes and violent fighting, and his large, bare set meant to give the impression of an oppressively hot Italian summer: "For now, these hot days, is the mad blood stirring" served as the production's tagline. Brook went against tradition by casting young unknowns as Romeo and Juliet, and generated controversy by cutting directly from Juliet's death to the Prince's final speech (here delivered by a Chorus), omitting the reconciliation between Capulet and Montague.

1954 Shot in Verona and other Italian cities, Renato Castellani's gorgeously filmed *Romeo and Juliet* used striking images (such as a scene in which Romeo and Juliet pronounce their wedding vows through an iron grate) to convey the vulnerable young lovers' inability to escape the pressure of social and familial demands.

1957 A highly successful collaboration between Leonard Bernstein, Stephen Sondheim, Jerome Robbins, and Arthur Laurents, the Broadway musical "West Side Story" updated *Romeo and Juliet* as a social drama about prejudice and the longing for community in 1950s America. The Capulet-Montague feud is transformed to a gang war between the Jets (second-generation Americans) and the Sharks (newly immigrated Puerto Ricans) in New York City. Romeo becomes Tony, a Jet; Juliet becomes Maria, sister of Bernardo, a Shark. In 1961, "West Side Story" was adapted into a popular film starring Natalie Wood as Maria.

1960 Franco Zeffirelli, a young Italian opera director, staged a realistic *Romeo and Juliet* at the Old Vic Theatre that aimed to make Shakespeare's play immediate and accessible to a modern audience. Subordinating speech to action, especially the vivacious street life of Verona's youth, Zeffirelli cut about one-third of the text. The set resembled an Italian city, filled with the bustling activities of daily life; the costumes were unobtrusive; and the naturalistic acting of Judi Dench and John Stride conveyed the impetuous passion of the adolescent protagonists.

1968 Drawing on the energies of 1960s youth culture, Zeffirelli transformed his realistic stage production of *Romeo and Juliet* into an extremely successful and influential film starring unknown adolescent actors, seventeen-year-old Leonard Whiting as Romeo and fifteen-year-old Olivia Hussey as Juliet. In one of the film's most striking performances, John McEnery played a cynical, ostentatious Mercutio who was deeply attached to Romeo.

1973 Taking its inspiration from one of Friar Laurence's warnings—"These violent delights have violent ends"—Terry Hands's Royal Shakespeare Company production emphasized the cruelty of fate, the sadism of Veronese society, and the recklessness of the lovers' passion. A metallic set and studded leather costumes worn by the young men added to the grim atmosphere. To express his hostility to Romeo's heterosexual infatuation, a misogynistic, overtly homosexual Mercutio grotesquely dismembered a life-size female doll.

1986 Michael Bogdanov's cynical Royal Shakespeare Company production of *Romeo and Juliet* stressed the materialism and corruption responsible for the lovers' tragedy. The Prince was a Mafia boss in contemporary Verona, the Capulets social-climbing nouveau riche, and the Apothecary a drug dealer. One critic nicknamed the production the "Alfa-Romeo and Juliet" because Tybalt drove a red sports car onto the stage. Romeo committed suicide by injecting himself with drugs, and the play ended with a dramatic jump from Juliet's suicide to a busy press conference—photographers eagerly snapping pictures of the Prince and of the fathers' handshake—staged in front of the golden statues of the lovers.

1991 Some late twentieth-century productions of *Romeo and Juliet* have represented the feuding households through the lens of contemporary racial, national, or cultural differences. Using French-speaking Capulets and English-speaking Montagues, Canadian director Robert LaPage's *Roméo et Juliette* commented on the conflict between Anglophone and Francophone cultures within Canada.

1994 Using Shakespeare as a medium of intercultural dialogue, an Israeli and a Palestinian theater company jointly produced a version of *Romeo and Juliet* in Jerusalem. The Israeli actors played the Capulets, who spoke only Hebrew; the Palestinian actors played the Montagues, who spoke only Arabic. The production went forward despite tension among the actors and anonymous threats made to the Israeli director.

1996 Baz Luhrmann's fast-paced and inventive film *Romeo + Juliet* makes its attractive young protagonists (played by well-known film and television actors Leonardo DiCaprio and Claire Danes) victims of the violently materialistic, decadent, and media-saturated world of contemporary "Verona Beach," with its rival Capulet and Montague business empires.

1997 Joe Calarco's off-Broadway play *Shakespeare's R&J* centers on four male parochial school students who put on a performance of *Romeo and Juliet*. Through its innovative casting and staging, the play explores contemporary attitudes toward gender, homoeroticism, and homophobia, as when the boys playing Mercutio and Tybalt respond with hostility to the intimacy between the boys playing Romeo and Juliet.

1998 The premise of director John Madden's Oscar-winning Hollywood movie *Shakespeare in Love*, starring Joseph Fiennes as Shakespeare and Gwyneth Paltrow as his love interest Viola De Lesseps, is that a real-life romance with an aristocratic woman inspired Shakespeare to write *Romeo and Juliet*. Screenwriters Tom Stoppard and Marc Norman invent clever parallels between (supposed) events in Shakespeare's life and incidents in *Romeo and Juliet*: Romeo's guilt over the death of Mercutio, for instance, reflects Shakespeare's guilt over the death of rival playwright Christopher Marlowe, for which he mistakenly believes he is responsible.

2000 In an attempt to add a new supernatural dimension to *Romeo and Juliet*, Michael Boyd's Royal Shakespeare Company production had the spirits of the dead haunt the living. The ghosts of Tybalt, Mercutio, and Paris appeared above the stage to observe the ongoing action, and the production sentimentally projected a shared afterlife for the protagonists by having Romeo and Juliet rise from the tomb and walk off the stage together during the last scene.

2004 Aspects of Tim Carroll's Globe Theatre production attempted to re-create the play's appearance and sound on the Elizabethan stage. For instance, when Juliet took the sleeping potion and fell within the curtains of her bed, the bed remained fully visible at the back of the stage while the Capulet household made preparations for her wedding at the front of the stage. In the last scene, actors indicated the darkness of the graveyard by carrying lanterns and miming an inability to see clearly. Three of the Globe performances featured an approximation of Elizabethan pronunciation, which was derived from the spelling of words in the original published texts of the play.

Inspired by *Romeo and Juliet*

S ince its first performance some four hundred years ago, *Romeo and Juliet* has had a remarkably rich afterlife. The Shakespearean text itself remains one of the most commonly performed of the Bard's plays—second, perhaps, only to Hamlet. The basic story of *Romeo and Juliet*, however, has become so deeply embedded in our society's collective consciousness that one need not have read Shakespeare's play in order to recognize its central elements: the warring families, the passionate young lovers, the tragically fatal conclusion. Like Yorick's skull, Romeo's supplication at Juliet's balcony has become an iconic cultural image, recognizable even when completely removed from its original setting.

William Shakespeare was not the first to have dramatized the *Romeo and Juliet* story, nor was he the first writer to have set passionate love against tragically fatal violence: the classical myths of Tristan and Isolde, Hero and Leander, and Pyramus and Thisbe are clear forerunners to the *Romeo and Juliet* narrative in this respect. However, when he adapted Arthur Brooke's *Tragical History of Romeus and Juliet*—continuing an artistic daisy chain of revisions and adaptations that stretched back to a fifteenth-century Italian novella by Luigi da Porto—Shakespeare shaped what has become the archetypal love story for most Western cultures. Over the past several centuries, countless plays, operas, films and other artistic works have drawn inspiration from *Romeo and Juliet*.

Stage

The first theatrical adaptation of *Romeo and Juliet* to survive in print is 1679's *The History and Fall of Caius Marius*, by Restoration playwright Thomas Otway. From *Plutarch's Lives*, Otway derives the framing story of two rival Roman senators, Marius and Metellus, and their struggle for control of the senate. Otway adds a Shakespeare-inspired romantic plot to this historical framework by having young Marius, the senator's son, fall in love with Lavinia, the daughter of his father's political enemy. Several scenes from *Romeo and Juliet* have parallel scenes in *Caius Marius*, and over a third of Otway's lines are explicitly derivative of Shakespeare's text. In Otway's play, for example, Lavinia appears on her balcony and exclaims:

> "O Marius, Marius! Wherefore art thou Marius?
> Deny thy family, renounce thy name:
> Or if thou wilt not, be but sworn my love,
> And I'll no longer call Metellus parent."

In Otway's play, the larger issue of the families' political struggle overshadows the lovers' personal and social drama. Otway's production may have been ostensibly set in classical Rome, but the play is actually concerned with the political intrigues of Restoration England. In this way, *Caius Marius* anticipates many future adaptations of *Romeo and Juliet*, which often set Shakespeare's narrative in specific historical and cultural locations in order to comment on contemporary political issues.

Maxwell Anderson's 1935 verse drama *Winterset* sets its Shakespearean tale of star-crossed lovers against the political backdrop of the controversial Sacco-Vanzetti case, in which two Italian anarchists were executed in Massachusetts for alleged robbery and murder, despite slim evidence. In *Winterset*, a young man named

Mio attempts to clear his father's name when he is, as Mio believes, wrongfully executed. In his quest, Mio is drawn to Miriamne, a girl whose brother testified against Mio's father. *Winterset* is one of American literature's most significant verse dramas, and was awarded the New York Drama Critic's Circle Award for best play.

Arguably the most famous adaptation of *Romeo and Juliet* is the musical "West Side Story," which first appeared onstage in 1957 in a Broadway production directed and choreographed by legendary American choreographer Jerome Robbins. "West Side Story" (book by Arthur Laurents, music by Leonard Bernstein, lyrics by Stephen Sondheim) sets the *Romeo and Juliet* narrative amidst the mid-century youth gangs of New York City. Like many modern productions of *Romeo and Juliet*, the division between the lovers in "West Side Story" falls along ethnic lines, as the tension between Maria/Juliet's Puerto Rican family and Tony/Romeo's Anglo brotherhood effectively destroys any hope of a happy finale. However, as in Shakespeare's play, the terrible conclusion results in a wary, though ultimately hopeful rapprochement between the two warring clans. Along with Franco Zeffirelli's equally influential stage and film production of *Romeo and Juliet* (1960 and 1968, respectively), "West Side Story" was striking in its contemporary relevance, and went a long way toward cementing the now common understanding of Shakespeare's play as a story of youth culture in its most violent and romantic aspects, rather than a story about larger social and political forces. "West Side Story" was adapted for film in 1961 and won ten Academy Awards, including the Oscar for Best Picture.

In Ann-Marie Macdonald's playful *Goodnight Desdemona, Good Morning Juliet* (1988), a literature professor named Constance Ledbelly, while attempting to prove that Shakespeare's great tragedies *Othello* and *Romeo and Juliet* were originally comedies, manages to cross dimensions and fall into the plays themselves. In *Romeo and Juliet*'s Verona, Constance is taken for a boy (having suffered certain wardrobe malfunctions back in *Othello*'s Cyprus) and both Juliet and Romeo proceed to fall in love with her.

Shakespeare's R&J, Joe Calarco's 1997 adaptation, is a dynamic version of *Romeo and Juliet* for four male actors. In it, a group of boys at a strict Catholic boarding school discover a hidden copy of *Romeo and Juliet*, which has been banned by school authorities. Slightly giddied by their transgression, the boys start reading the play aloud. Though they begin lightheartedly, the boys are eventually drawn in by the play's emotional power. As their performance progresses, the boundaries between fiction and reality crumble away as the boys are completely overtaken by the characters they play. This private, secret performance of *Romeo and Juliet* allows the boys, among other things, to explore their sexual feelings toward one another—a version of the now-classic staple of sitcoms and youth literature in which two young students express their romantic feelings during a class performance of *Romeo and Juliet*. *Shakespeare's R&J* supports the reading of *Romeo and Juliet* as a play concerned with the power of pure, sincere passion: not only does Shakespeare's play depict such a situation, the text itself has the magical power to affect such feelings in its readers and viewers. Calarco's play, the dialogue for which is taken almost entirely from Shakespeare's text, was striking to many critics for its ability to make a stultifyingly familiar play seem freshly resonant.

In 2001, Gérard Presgurivc's musical *Roméo et Juliette—de la Haine à l'Amour* premiered in Paris. The production generated several pop singles that broke the top twenty charts, and went on to become the most successful French language musical in history. In translation, and with certain differences from production to production, the musical has thus far been performed in Belgium, Austria, the Netherlands, Hungary, Russia, and the UK.

Film

Romeo and Juliet has a long and varied history on film, its popularity in the cinema being commensurate with its popularity on stage. Numerous silent film adaptations exist from the early era of movies, many of them comic burlesques—films such as *Romeo in Pajamas*, *Romeo in the Stone Age*, and the Western-themed *Roping Her Romeo*. The comedian Fatty Arbuckle filmed *A Reckless Romeo* in 1917, and popular entertainer Will Rogers starred in *Doubling for Romeo* in 1921.

There have been several film productions of the text itself, the two most significant being Franco Zeffirelli's (1968) and Baz Luhrmann's (1996). Though stylistically quite different, both films follow the general trend of thinking in the late twentieth century and present the text as a story about youth culture and generational conflict. Both films can be seen as rising from their particular contemporary contexts: Zeffirelli's film is heavily influenced by the romantic, flower-power youth movement of the late sixties, just as Luhrmann's film steeps itself in the media-saturated, postmodern parlance of millennial teenagers.

Many film adaptations, both American and international, map the basic narrative onto specific ethnic and political divides: Czech Romeo and Jewish Juliet in the Nazi occupation–set *Romeo, Juliet, and Darkness* (Czechoslovakia, 1959); Italian Romeo and Chinese Juliet in *China Girl* (America, 1987); Israeli Romeo and Arab Juliet in *Torn Apart* (Israel, 1990); Hindu Romeo and Muslim Juliet in *Henna* (India, 1992); and Maori Romeo and Croatian Juliet in *Broken English* (New Zealand, 1996). Recently, the 2000 American action film *Romeo Must Die* featured martial arts star Jet Li as an Asian Romeo and hip-hop star Aaliyah as an African-American Juliet.

In a somewhat less dramatic vein, 1996's *Tromeo and Juliet*—a production from the avowedly B-movie house Troma Films, narrated by Lemmy Kilmister, of the British speed-metal band Motörhead—features soft-core pornography, slapstick violence, and a Romeo and Juliet who discover they are brother and sister but decide to get married anyway, eventually living happily ever after surrounded by their brood of deformed and inbred children. Along similarly parodic lines, a surprising number of pornographic films have adapted the Romeo and Juliet story, including *The Secret Sex Lives of Romeo and Juliet* (1968), *Shocking Shakespeare: Romeo and Juliet Get Juicy* (1999), and the gay romantic musical *Romeo and Julian*, winner of three awards from AVN (Adult Video News) in 1994.

The 1998 film *Shakespeare in Love* significantly reworks *Romeo and Juliet* by transposing the basic elements of the story onto the biography of William Shakespeare himself. In Tom Stoppard's heavily referential script, William Shakespeare is a promising yet besieged young playwright, stifled by the demands of the commercial theater and struggling to write a new comedy for his patrons titled *Romeo and Ethel, the Pirate's Daughter*. Will's life is transformed when Viola de Lesseps, a young woman who loves the theater but whose gender bars her from participating, disguises herself as a man and auditions for his latest play. As Will and Viola fall in love, Will springs out of his creative rut and, as Will's biographical story begins to parallel his fictional one, the gawky *Romeo and Ethel* blooms into the familiar romantic masterpiece *Romeo and Juliet*. Like Romeo and Juliet, Will and Viola are star crossed: after a climactic performance of *Romeo and Juliet* in which Will and Viola are unexpectedly called upon to play the title roles, Viola is ordered to return to her aristocratic fiancé and sail with him to America. Will is heartbroken, but he channels his pain into the writing of *Twelfth Night*, a melancholic comedy that features a sprightly, independent heroine named Viola. *Shakespeare in Love* reinforces the conception of William Shakespeare as the Western romantic poet par excellence, and locates his particular artistic genius not in his painstaking and careful application of his craft, but in his ability to spontaneously and organically respond to the power of true love.

Dance

Romeo and Juliet is the single Shakespeare play most often adapted for dance performances. Though Romeo and Juliet's dramatic passion and romantic lyricism has always attracted composers and choreographers, it wasn't until the twentieth century that the narrative became firmly established in the European dance repertory.

In 1926, Ballet Russes presented a Surrealist-influenced *Romeo and Juliet* with music by Christopher Lambert, choreography by Bronislava Nijinska, and design by the notable Surrealist artists Joan Miró and Max Ernst. Nikjinska set the production backstage at the Ballet Russes. Juliet was imagined as a rehearsing dancer and Romeo as an aviator; at the end of the ballet, the two flew off together in a plane. Miró and Ernst's fellow Surrealists were so enraged that their compatriots had involved themselves in such a commercial enterprise that they staged a riotous protest when the production arrived in Paris. The scandal helped propel the production to great box office success.

Most of the major *Romeo and Juliet* ballets in the twentieth century have used the 1930s score by Russian composer Sergei Prokofiev. Prokofiev's original score followed Shakespeare's text quite closely, though it did away with the tragic conclusion and substituted a happy reconciliation between the warring two families. Initially commissioned by the Kirov Ballet in 1934, Prokofiev's Kirov contract was cancelled when the company underwent a purge of its "avant-garde" artists. The Bolshoi Ballet, which had commissioned the work after the Kirov cancelled, deemed Prokofiev's score undanceable and refused to stage it. Eventually, a Yugoslavian company in Brno, Czechoslovakia mounted the first production in 1938, to considerable acclaim. Based on the success of the Czech production, the Prokofiev piece (now with the play's tragic ending reinstated) received its first Soviet production in Kirov in 1940. Choreographed by Léonide Lavrovsky, the production eventually became the standard against which Prokofiev *Romeo and Juliet*s were judged. It was finally staged at the Bolshoi in 1946.

Other important stagings of Prokofiev's work include John Cranko's 1959 production at La Scala in Milan, which emphasized the story's private, human drama; Kenneth MacMillan's 1960 production for the English Royal Ballet, which was heavily influenced by Zeffirelli's free-spirited stage version and starred ballet luminaries Rudolf Nureyev and Margot Fonteyn; and the French-Albanian choreographer Angelin Preljocaj's 1990 production for Lyon Opera Ballet, which presented a harshly Orwellian reading of the story that focused on the story's social and political dynamics. The Lavrovsky, Cranko, MacMillan, and Preljocaj productions are still being danced today.

In 2001 the Philadelphia-based dance company PureMovement, led by choreographer and artistic director Rennie Harris, presented a hip-hop production titled *Rome + Jewels* that went on to tour the United States and Europe. Inspired by *West Side Story*'s depiction of young, male street gang culture, *Rome +Jewels* tells the story of two gangs, the break-dancing Monster Q's and the hip-hop Caps, who battle each other in vicious dance sequences. Arguing that "rappers today are the only ones who come close to Shakespeare," Harris interweaves snippets of Shakespeare's text with free-form raps and American street slang. Jewels, the object of Rome's affection, never appears onstage; she remains an intangible idea, Harris has said, in order to keep the focus of the production on Rome's personal journey, as Rome comes to understand the ignorance, futility, and destructiveness he is surrounded by.

Music

Romeo and Juliet has continuously had a healthy presence in both opera houses and concert halls. Vincenzo Bellini's *bel canto* opera *I Capuleti e I Montecchi* (1830) pointedly bypasses Shakespeare's play, taking its source material from the earlier Italian versions instead. Bellini's opera focuses on the political dimensions of the story, depicting a factionalized Verona that resonated with the contemporary political realities of nineteenth-century Italy.

Hector Berlioz was inspired to write *Roméo et Juliette*, his 1839 dramatic symphony, after seeing his future wife Harriet Smithson play Juliet onstage in Paris. *Roméo et Juliette* follows the narrative arc of Garrick's adaptation, scoring certain portions of the text as vocal music. The characters of *Romeo and Juliet*, however, remain purely orchestral, as Berlioz believed instrumental music to be more expansive and capable of greater expressive power than vocal music.

Charles François Gounod's 1867 grand opera *Romeo et Juliet* adheres to Shakespeare's play more closely than either Bellini or Berlioz, though it follows popular seventeenth- and eighteenth-century theatrical conventions by adding a pre-death scene between the lovers in the tomb. Gounod's opera is lush, spectacular, and passionate, and remains the most popular operatic version of *Romeo and Juliet* today.

The great Russian composer Pyotr Ilyich Tchaikovsky's symphonic poem *Romeo and Juliet Fantasy-Overture* (composed 1869; first performed 1870) was one of his earliest successes. Tchaikovsky pares Shakespeare's narrative down to three essential motifs: the sober advice of Friar Laurence, the violent street brawls, and the tender love affair between Romeo and Juliet. Tchaikovsky's orchestral version emphasizes the psychological drama of the story, depicting the lovers' tender romance as brief respite from other, more tumultuous energies.

In the twentieth century, several pop songs have taken inspiration from *Romeo and Juliet*, including Donovan's "Under the Greenwood Tree," Tom Waits's "Romeo Is Bleeding," and Dire Straits's "Romeo and Juliet" (which was subsequently covered by the Indigo Girls). In 1993, Elvis Costello and the Brodsky Quartet released *The Juliet Letters*, a concept album inspired by a real-life Veronese professor who responded to letters written to the character of Juliet, which melded pop, chamber, and orchestral elements.

For Further Reading
by Mario DiGangi

Andrews, John F., ed. *Romeo and Juliet: Critical Essays*. New York: Garland, 1993. A useful compilation of representative and influential essays originally published between 1939 and 1989, divided into sections on the play's language and structure, on the play in performance, and on the play as a product of Elizabethan culture (particularly in terms of love, gender, sexuality, violence, religion, and authority).

Appelbaum, Robert. "'Standing to the Wall': The Pressures of Masculinity in *Romeo and Juliet*." *Shakespeare Quarterly* 48 (1997): 251–272. Appelbaum argues that in *Romeo and Juliet* there is no real escape from the "regime of masculinity"—the system of ideas about gender that incites men to define their manhood through acts of aggressive self-assertion—despite the seeming alternatives of civil peace (embodied in the Prince) and civil love (represented by Romeo and Juliet).

Boose, Lynda E. "The Father and the Bride in Shakespeare." *PMLA* 97 (1982): 325–47. Examining *Romeo and Juliet* as one of several Shakespeare plays focused on the father-daughter relationship, Boose argues that the father's possessive affection for his daughter is the "force that both defines and threatens the family," a force especially in view during the daughter's rite of passage into marriage.

Callaghan, Dympna. "The Ideology of Romanic Love: The Case of *Romeo and Juliet*." In *The Weyward Sisters: Shakespeare and Feminist Politics*, edited by Dympna Callaghan, Lorraine Helms, and Jyotsna Singh. Oxford: Blackwell, 1994. Examining the role played by *Romeo and Juliet* in the "cultural construction of desire," Callaghan argues that the play's vision of romantic love constitutes a dominant ideology that works to subordinate women within marriage.

Cook, Ann Jennalie. *Making a Match: Courtship in Shakespeare and His Society*. Princeton: Princeton University Press, 1991. Seeking to reconstruct the system of courtship in Shakespeare's society and to analyze how Shakespeare incorporates the experiences of courtship into his plays, Cook discusses many issues relevant to *Romeo and Juliet*, such as age at marriage, social status of partners, parental consent, go-betweens, and elopements.

Fitter, Chris. "'The quarrel is between our masters and us their men': *Romeo and Juliet*, Dearth, and the London Riots." *English Literary Renaissance* 30 (Spring 2000): 154–83. Setting *Romeo and Juliet* in the historical contexts of dearth and food riots in the mid-1590s, Fitter argues that the play's "populist sympathies" provide a critical view of the class privilege enjoyed by the wealthy (and well-fed) Capulets and Montagues.

Hunt, Maurice, ed. *Approaches to Teaching Shakespeare's Romeo and Juliet*. New York: MLA, 2000. Primarily intended to provide strategies and materials for teaching *Romeo and Juliet*, this volume contains brief essays that illuminate various aspects of the play of interest to the general reader, including genre, historical contexts, ideas about gender and sexuality, character, language, and dramatic technique.

Kastan, David Scott. "'A Rarity Most Beloved': Shakespeare and the Idea of Tragedy." In *A Companion to Shakespeare's Works, Volume 1: The Tragedies*, edited by Richard Dutton and Jean E. Howard. Malden, MA: Blackwell, 2003. For Shakespeare, argues Kastan, the deep logic of tragedy derives not from classical or medieval theories, but resides in the depiction of suffering which is "not only irreparable but is also neither compensated nor even effectively consoled"; although *Romeo and Juliet* finally gestures toward social harmony, the end of the feud fails to reassure or comfort us for what has been lost.

Khan, Coppélia. "Coming of Age: Marriage and Manhood in *Romeo and Juliet* and *The Taming of the Shrew*." In *Man's Estate: Masculine Identity in Shakespeare*. Berkeley: University of California Press, 1981. For Kahn, *Romeo and Juliet* is a story about "a pair of adolescents trying to grow up," which requires that they separate themselves from their parents to form new identities through heterosexual intimacy; the primary tragic force working against their development is the feud, "an extreme and peculiar expression of patriarchal society, which Shakespeare shows to be tragically self-destructive."

Laroque, François. "Tradition and Subversion in *Romeo and Juliet*." In *Shakespeare's Romeo and Juliet: Texts, Contexts, and Interpretation*, edited by Jay L. Halio. Newark: University of Delaware Press, 1995. Laroque argues that *Romeo and Juliet* depicts "a world upside down" in which the traditional rules and conventions of language, social order, and gender/sexual roles are temporarily suspended, thus subverting the ordinary opposition between life and death.

Levenson, Jill. "The Definition of Love: Shakespeare's Phrasing." *Shakespeare Studies* 15 (1982): 21–36. Demonstrating how the language of *Romeo and Juliet* "derives in large part from Petrarchan imagery and stylistic devices," Levenson argues that the play's verbal brilliance invigorates the sonnet tradition and makes its conventions work for a new dramatic genre, the love tragedy.

Liebler, Naomi Conn. "'There Is No World without Verona Walls': The City in *Romeo and Juliet*." In *A Companion to Shakespeare's Works, Volume 1: The Tragedies*, edited by Richard Dutton and Jean E. Howard. Malden, MA: Blackwell, 2003. Liebler argues that *Romeo and Juliet* indicts "the civic institutions and structures of authority" by shifting focus away from the protagonists and onto the city of Verona, a violent, plague-marked, and finally self-destructive "collective protagonist."

Mahood, M. M. "*Romeo and Juliet*." In *Shakespeare's Wordplay*. London: Methuen, 1957. Mahood argues that the dense wordplay and imagery in *Romeo and Juliet*, particularly its pervasive punning, contribute to the "tragic equilibrium" the play achieves between the strength and the fragility of Romeo's and Juliet's love.

Novy, Marianne. "Violence, Love, and Gender in *Romeo and Juliet* and *Troilus and Cressida*." In *Love's Argument: Gender Relations in Shakespeare*. Chapel Hill: University of North Carolina Press, 1984. Although the mutual love between Romeo and Juliet transcends the gender norms of Verona, in which "masculinity is identified with violence and femininity with weakness," the couple's "residual commitment" to gender ideals—evinced in Romeo's duel with Tybalt and Juliet's docile submission to the Friar's advice—leads to their deaths.

Peterson, Douglas. "*Romeo and Juliet* and the Art of Moral Navigation." In *Romeo and Juliet: Critical Essays*, edited by John F. Andrews. New York: Garland, 1993: 307–320. *Romeo and Juliet* is not an immature tragedy, Peterson contends, but a tragedy of moral choice; although Providence might have determined that the protagonists' love would settle the feud, Romeo and Juliet have free will in deciding how they will "manage their affections" once they have fallen in love: they may surrender to passion or temper it, as Friar Laurence suggests.

Porter, Joseph. *Shakespeare's Mercutio: His History and Drama*. Chapel Hill: University of North Carolina Press, 1988. Linking Mercutio to Mercury, the classical god associated with eloquence, travel, theft, and phallic sexuality, Porter demonstrates how Mercutio embodies such characteristics, which manifest especially clearly in his homoerotic relationship with Romeo.

Snow, Edward. "Language and Sexual Difference in *Romeo and Juliet*." In *Shakespeare's Rough Magic*, edited by Peter Erickson and Coppélia Kahn. Newark: University of Delaware Press, 1985. Although the matched speeches of Romeo and Juliet suggest the mutuality of their romantic bond, the gendered differences revealed by their "imaginative universes"—Romeo's characterized by visual imagery and emotional distancing; Juliet's by the integration of the senses—suggest the existence of "separate worlds of desire" within their shared experience.

Snyder, Susan. "Beyond Comedy: *Romeo and Juliet* and *Othello*." In *The Comic Matrix of Shakespeare's Tragedies*. Princeton: Princeton University Press, 1979. Discussing comedy and tragedy as "opposed ways of apprehending the real world," Synder considers the implications of the distinctive structure of *Romeo and Juliet*, which begins according to the pattern of comedy, and is transformed, following the death of Mercutio (who is "the incarnation of comic atmosphere"), into the pattern of tragedy.

Utterback, Raymond V. "The Death of Mercutio." *Shakespeare Quarterly* 24 (1973): 105–116. Utterback argues that when Mercutio blames his death on the feud instead of accepting responsibility for his provocation of Tybalt, he establishes a pattern of explaining tragic consequences—"a selective attention operating to emphasize the general and external causes of the events and to minimize the individual and personal responsibilities of the characters"—subsequently repeated at critical moments in the play.